RUNAWAY COMRADE

RUNAWAY COMRADE

BOB de la MOTTE

An autobiography with
Dave Hughes

Published by Quickfox Publishing
PO Box 12028 Mill Street 8010
Cape Town, South Africa
www.quickfox.co.za | info@quickfox.co.za

First edition 2014

RUNAWAY COMRADE
ISBN 978-1-502-82184-3

Copyright © 2014 Robert Aristide Lenferna de la Motte

Facebook: Runaway Comrade
Twitter: @RunawayComrade

All rights reserved. No part of this publication may be reproduced,
stored in a retrieval system, or transmitted, in any form or by any means,
without the prior written permission of the publisher.

Edited by Dave Hughes
Cover and book design by Vanessa Wilson
Typesetting and production by Quickfox Publishing

*The author intends to apply any net proceeds of the publication
of* Runaway Comrade *for the benefit of South Africa's leading black
ultramarathon runners from the 1974–90 era.*

Photo acknowledgements:
Front cover: JSE 50km ultramarathon August 1985 – jostling for gold medals after the
marathon mark and in hot pursuit of race leader Sam Ndala. Gibeon Moshaba in white cap
and Ben Cheou in black cap. Photograph by Danie Coetzer. *Back cover:* Silhouette of Thulani
Sibisi, arrested in November 1985 in Rosebank, Johannesburg, for not carrying his pass book
in a white residential area. He won the 56km Two Oceans ultramarathon in 1986.

To my parents, Coco and Frenchy

To Titus Mamabolo

To Vincent Gabashane Rakabaele

To Mark Plaatjes

To Hoseah Tjale

To Thulani Sibisi

To Johnny Halberstadt

The vast propaganda machine of the State creates a situation in which people do not know their own history.

DULLAH OMAR, first Minister of Justice in a democratic South Africa.

The runner is truly a man dissatisfied with the status quo. His object is to reach goals that are continually being reset. And he is only aware of where he is and who he is when he is challenged. Like the saint, he is everlastingly beset by doubt, and just as everlastingly asking to be tested.

DR GEORGE SHEEHAN, American cardiologist and running guru.

If you do not have that almost constant feeling of dissatisfaction with everything, recognising that no sooner is one pinnacle achieved, one goal realised, there will be another, success may well elude you.

PERCY CERRUTTY (1964), coach to the invincible Australian miler, Herb Elliot.

Life is not a problem to be solved but an adventure to be lived.

ANONYMOUS

I always loved running ... it was something you could do by yourself, and under your own power. You could go in any direction, fast or slow as you wanted, fighting the wind if you felt like it, seeking out new sights just on the strength of your feet and the courage of your lungs.

JESSE OWENS, black American winner of four track and field gold medals at the 1936 Berlin Olympics, snubbed by Hitler and never invited to the White House.

CONTENTS

Keywords 11

Foreword 13

Introduction 17

Preface 23

Drama at 45th Cutting – 1 June 1984 .... **29**

1. Sued for $1 billion 31

2. Comrades: Why the obsession? 39

3. Comrades flame-out 52

4. Growing up 59

Call back the past 1 .... **66**

5. Apartheid and sport 70

6. Soldier of apartheid 80

7. A kid at Wits University 91

Call back the past 2 .... **98**

8. Life on three continents 104

9. Comrades bronze, at last 112

10. The aftermath 121

Call back the past 3 ...... **134**

11. A silver lining 140

12. Snap, crackle, pop 149

13. There's gold in them thar heels 158

14. Pissing blood 169

15. Talking a good race 205

16. The fastest Comrades 212

Call back the past 4 ...... **228**

17. View from the moon 235

18. Runaway Bob 245

19. Unpacking in Perth 262

20. Striding out 270

21. Seismic shift 280

Call back the past 5 ...... **290**

22. Adding iron to my diet 297

23. Goodbye to work 313

24. Comrades crystal ball 325

Call back the past 6 ...... **332**

25. Boomerang Bob 342

Postscript: Boston Marathon, 21 April 2014 ...... **356**

Acknowledgements 359

Photo acknowledgements 362

Comrades route map 363

Keywords

Keywords based on the *Little Oxford Dictionary*

adventure *n.* unexpected or exciting experience; daring enterprise

anarchy *n.* absence of government, disorder, political and social confusion

apartheid *n.* policy of racial segregation in South Africa

capitalism *n.* economic system with ownership and control of capital in private hands

cheat *v.* trick, defraud; deal fraudulently; *n.* deception; swindler; unfair player

democracy *n.* government by people as whole, especially through elected representatives

greed *n.* insatiable desire for food or wealth

philanthropy *n.* love, kindness; practical benevolence towards humankind

sport *n.* amusement, diversion, pastime(s), game(s) especially of an outdoor or athletic kind

sportsman/woman *n.* person fond of sports; good fellow; person who is fair to opponents, cheerful in defeat

Illustration of time format used in text:

2:56.19 = 2 hours 56 minutes 19 seconds

38.07 = 38 minutes seven seconds

Currency:

$ = US and Australian dollar

R = South African rand

FOREWORD

The Comrades Marathon is a race of approximately 90km. Participating in it is an introduction to another way of being; it teaches humility and teamwork, respect and admiration for fellow competitors, courage in adversity, understanding and empathy. Above all, it creates a community of Comrades united in their joint and individual challenges. Completing the grueling event is a life-changing experience. Winning a gold medal (being a top 10 finisher) is the stuff of dreams. Being the runner-up is the preserve of a select few. Winning Comrades is the holy grail of long-distance running.

Bob de la Motte participated, won gold, and was runner-up three times. A mere 125 seconds, after five-and-a-half hours of grueling road running, was all that separated him from a Comrades Marathon victory in 1986.

When Bob asked me to write a foreword to Runaway Comrade, not only was I honoured to have the opportunity to contribute to his work, but his unexpected request evoked a multitude of images I have of this most unusual man – an astute, bold, decisive person with great foresight, always looking for new challenges. Our paths crossed in two important dimensions of Bob's career. Bob was a partner at KPMG and in 1985 assumed responsibility for the audit of Penrose Holdings, a financial printing company listed on The Johannesburg Stock Exchange. I was the Managing Director of Penrose and still deeply involved in the Comrades Marathon. Between the Penrose business and Comrades, Bob and I had much to discuss and share.

Bob's best chance of a Comrades win was in the 1986 down race. A fierce contest was anticipated. Two years previously Fordyce had beaten him by 3min. 41sec. in a record-breaking 5:27.18. As expected, the race developed into a three-man affair with De la Motte leading Hoseah Tjale and Fordyce after halfway. Former winner Tommy Malone and I were eager spectators. With 14km to go, Fordyce edged past Tjale and closed in on De la Motte, and in a most audacious act that was to become Bruce's "kiss of death" trademark, Fordyce and Bob shook hands with Bruce following up with a left arm bear hug, despite Bob's significant height advantage, as national television and press cameras zoomed in. This most extraordinary act at the most crucial point of this hotly contested event perhaps reflects the dominance that Fordyce exerted over his opponents. However Bob was no ordinary opponent, retorting: "Look Bruce, this race is not over yet, and whoever loses will have to buy lunch." Just being there at this climactic moment gave me time to reflect – I'd been there both as victor and vanquished. It's a runner's worst nightmare, but to his credit, Bob set the pace for another 8km before Bruce's final spurt up 45th Cutting gave him a 500m win and a record of 5.24.07 to Bob's 5.26.12 – also inside the record. A remarkable effort by both runners.

No other runner presented a greater challenge to the Comrades King in his nine-year reign than did Bob. Perhaps it was just as well for Bruce that Bob left South Africa in 1987. Or did Bob go because he could not face being beaten again? No, Bob left for deeper and more troubling reasons. The 1980s represented some of apartheid's darkest days.

True to his decisive, adventurous nature, he and his family emigrated to Perth. He graphically describes his resentment of the apartheid system, the unjust treatment of black South Africans and his personal experiences. Many South African families faced the same tough choices that Bob faced but were entrapped by economic and political oppression. They had no choice but to stay.

In 1963 I personally experienced the ridiculous situation of the first mixed trials held in Bloemfontein, South Africa. Two runners were to be selected to compete in an international marathon in Athens yet the trials had to be run as two separate races – one for black runners and one for white runners, staged one hour apart, over the identical course. The white race was classified as the SA championship – the black runners were relegated to their own Bantu championship. Politicisation of sport was an anathema to me.

Bob's adventurous spirit helped him settle into Australia professionally and recreationally. In his professional career he gained invaluable experience in investment banking and capital markets which brought him a measure of financial success, allowing him to retire at 55. In 2014 at the age of 60 he ran a 3:06 Boston Marathon and continues to pursue his adventurous lifestyle.

Runaway Comrade is a provocative, spirited and essential read. It's about running but more importantly it's about politics and its victims. It will touch all who read it. But be warned: it may leave you ashamed and angry, despite the thread of hope for equality that the Comrades Marathon so boldly offers.

Jackie Mekler – Comrades Marathon Green number 9

Five times winner
Ten gold medals

INTRODUCTION

I have an entry in one of my running diaries from January 1987. It reads: "Johnson Crane marathon; 2:47. Hard training run, Bob and Rob upped pace in the last two km. Did not go with them … thought they're crazy!"

You see, that was really what it was. A hard training run. Probably too hard for me. But Bob de la Motte, Comrades runner up and would-be king killer, was on a mission to finish every long run faster than he started it. We crazy marathon runners call it negative splits. Halfway at 21km in 84 minutes, then prance home in 82.

But here's the thing: I remember the day like yesterday. I remember Bob and the grey-haired fox, Dr Rob Dowdeswell, stepping it up and running away from me with no effort and my brain (and if I wanted to be really honest, my legs) told me to let them go. I can still see them in my mind's eye. Two runners clad in the all-white of our club, Rand Athletic, striding away to the finish in the Benoni stadium.

That's 27 years ago. I remember thinking maybe this is the year that Bob will dethrone Comrades King Bruce Fordyce.

I was in a strange position. Some of my journalist friends had warned me: "Don't get too close to these guys. You have a job to do and you have to be unbiased." I was a full-time reporter for the SABC sports news team and a freelance writer for the *SA Runner* magazine.

But these were my training partners. Tuesday night track with Fordyce. Wednesday night with the Sweat Shop crowd including Bob and Bruce: 22kms at sub-3min. 45sec. per km ending with an almighty surge up Jan Smuts Avenue hill. "Big Jan" as we use to call it, with a great measure of respect. Then hill repeats on the 405m long "Sweethoogte" (Sweat hill) on a Thursday with Bruce and a 16km run with Bob on the hills of Northcliff on a Saturday morning. Long group runs on a Sunday. We all understood the unspoken agenda: Bob's steady rise through South Africa's ranks of elite ultramarathoners in 1984 created speculation within the running cognoscenti that he was capable of winning the Comrades Marathon. Bob knew it. And Bruce knew it, too. Since 1981 Bruce had been unchallenged in the Comrades. Yet I really cannot ever recall any real or perceived tension between blonde Fordyce and tall Bob. Yes, there were camps, but it was never obvious and it never spilt over into anything else.

Our training runs revolved around a massive amount of social banter, continuous surges, little accelerations and a sprinkling of testosterone. That was what made us one of the most sought after training groups in South Africa. We had all comers there. From Mark Plaatjes with his 2:08 marathon to yours truly with a paltry 2:29. I was the third or fourth slowest standard marathon runner in the group. I had no business running with these guys … but, heck, they made me faster than I thought I could ever be.

It was the heyday of South African road running. We only had each other to compete against. I once ran 1:54 for the Springs Striders 32km race in my old hometown and could not crack the top 40. The winning time was sub-1:40, at altitude. Now you run sub-two hours and you're in the top 10. The standard was out of this world.

But there was another standard that a lot of us chose to ignore. Or did not do enough about. Or did nothing about. The living standards of our fellow runners. The black runners. We were still enveloped in the deeply entrenched racist days of old South Africa. The days when blacks and whites were not allowed to buy liquor at the same counter. Whites could vote. Blacks could not. The Rainbow Nation was a full 15 years away, and Nelson Mandela still had more than a dozen years to spend in a jail cell. For heaven's sake, the first black runners had only been allowed to run with whites a few years earlier. The playing fields, literally and figuratively, were not the same. These men, some of them the fastest on the planet, were racing against white men who ate better, slept better and did not have to win paltry prize money in world-class times to put a meal on their table. It was a part-time thing for most of us, with the exception of Bruce who made his incredibly marketable persona, fine intellect and superb athletic ability his meal ticket. He became the first full-time professional Comrades Marathon athlete, unashamedly so, despite Comrades not offering any prize money. No black runner could afford to do likewise.

The list of world-class black athletes was endless. Vincent Rakabaele, Gibeon Moshaba, Ben Cheou, Stephens Morake, Matthews Temane, Matthews Motshwarateu (the first man in the world to break 28 minutes for 10km on the road), Jan Tau and many more. These runners all needed to win weekly road races or at least finish in the top three to provide for their families. Yes, Temane and a few others were workers on South Africa's gold mines, but that did not mean that it was a free ticket to ride. Work still had to be done.

This is really who this book is for. For those forgotten ultramarathon men: men such as Hoseah Tjale and Thulani (Ephraim) Sibisi. These men were given names by their white employers that were easier to pronounce than their birth names. I only got to know what Ephraim's real name was in the mid-90s.

I look back though on those days with wonder and awe in my heart. I had an incredible blessing. They talk about a ringside seat. Well, I had one better. I was right in there. Running with these great runners and getting daily updates and feedback on who was hot and who was not. It gave me the opportunity to realise a lifetime ambition ... to anchor the Comrades Marathon broadcast live on television.

It was indeed as Bob has recorded it. On the 31 May, every year without fail, the whole of South Africa came to an abrupt halt. Everyone watched Comrades. I mean everyone. Shops would be closed. Some people stayed in bed all day, watching, riveted. In 1983 I worked as a reporter at the *Springs Advertiser* newspaper and even though we were on deadline, I took in a rickety black and white portable TV set on which the signal kept on doing what Fordyce did. Disappear. The whole office was spellbound.

RUNAWAY COMRADE

In 1984 Bob's 5:30 run, pushing Fordyce all the way to a new down record, was a display of magnificence and of athletic excellence. It was the start of his Comrades challenge.

It was often a tough internal debate: do I want Bruce to continue on his unprecedented winning streak or do I want the tall bean counter with his direct stare and penchant for honesty to win? They were both friends and training partners. Once you've run together as much as we did, you shared a brotherhood. An intimacy and level of mutual respect that very few men develop. It was a tightknit group. I never really made up my mind you know. Yet with this book, Bob is doing something that our group and, no doubt, many other running groups aspired to do: acknowledge the forgotten ones.

Bob has finally told us his nakedly honest story. He shares his extraordinary running experiences during the turbulent 1980s when South Africa was simmering on the brink of civil war. He explains his anguish at leaving South Africa and the challenges of the Chicken Run to Australia, his continued athletic performances, squeezed in between his demanding career and domestic priorities. He still managed world-class performances in Ironman and grueling cycling and mountain biking events. He also shares his joy at reconnecting with South Africa after the 1994 general election including his boyhood dream of summiting Mt. Kilimanjaro. His regular visits to a newly democratic South Africa over the past two decades afford him an objective observation of political cycles within South Africa and some inevitable crystal ball gazing about the future of the Comrades Marathon. Over the past 28 years only four Comrades winners have managed to run faster than his 5:26 duel with Fordyce in 1986. He tells his self-effacing story with candor, compassion and great wit.

As I wrote to Bob in an e-mail after reading his manuscript:

"Maybe I am just becoming an old fart, but I have just read your story and tears are actually streaming down my face. I can hardly see the key board. You see, my tears started off as laughter at our stupidity/drive/ commitment/sense of fun and chasing personal windmills up and down "Big Jan." Then my tears came for men such as Hoss, and Ephie and Israel

Morake. I cry for them and I cry for me ... that I did not have the sense to do more when I could have. Luckily in life, we do get second chances and as long as there is breath and a will ... one can try again. Right the ship, so to speak."

My favourite writer, running philosopher Dr George Sheehan, put it this way: "So, you see, it is not my future that determines my present, it is my present that determines the future."

Bob, you always were a champion, now more so than ever.

Arnold Geerdts – Comrades Marathon Green number 1120

Arnold Geerdts has seen the Comrades Marathon from a very unique perspective. He has anchored the marathon 12-hour live broadcast, seconded, commentated, written about the race, announced at the finish line and run it 11 times.

Preface

This story is important to me. I need to pinch myself occasionally because it feels like a dream, as though I have lived many lives and been touched by the lives of many.

I inherited a curiosity about the world. As a boy, my father would discuss science in the 1930s before the atom had been split, before Roger Bannister ran the mile in under four minutes, before Tenzing Norgay and Edmund Hillary summited Everest. However, he never spoke much about his experiences during WWII despite my inquisitiveness. The post-war economic recovery gave cause for much optimism but unbeknown to most South Africans, we would be severely disconnected from the rest of the world from the early 1960s as a consequence of the Nationalist government's pursuit of its apartheid policy. The consequences would be catastrophic, especially for black South Africans.

My father was a voracious reader and every Friday we collected our family stash of newspapers and subscriptions from the local Central News Agency: one of mine happened to be *Illustrated Sports History of the World*. It was the only way we had any chance of really appreciating what might have been happening in the rest of the world. The other option was to tune into BBC World Service on short wave radio.

At some point, I read an article about an Ethiopian marathon runner who mesmerized me, Abebe Bikila. As an absolute unknown, he became the first African to win an Olympic gold medal in the marathon, running barefoot on the cobbled streets of Rome in 1964. The leading European competitors were exasperated after the race; they could not hear him trailing them. His bare feet gave no hint of his foot strike, nor could they hear him breathing. He created Olympic history once again by winning the marathon at Mexico in 1968. At the time, I had no idea of the extent to which the spirit of Bikila and black South African marathon runners would enrich my life.

In my final year school exams I used Bikila as my topic for my English oral examination. I will never forget those lines about Bikila's silent footsteps devouring his opponents over Rome's cobbled streets. He struck me as a truly ethereal figure, epitomizing the spirit and gracefulness of Africans as I had got to know them in my childhood.

Black South Africans were less fortunate. They would have to wait until 1992 before returning to the Olympic Games at Barcelona and four years later, South Africa would celebrate a relatively unknown Josiah Thugwane winning the Olympic marathon at Atlanta. Apartheid had robbed Thugwane of his schooling and education; he was barely literate. Luckily, he could run.

My story covers some of the inhumane deeds that happened between Rome and Barcelona. It is a story I feel compelled to tell. The achievement of black runners cannot be isolated from the unimaginable social consequences of apartheid and the extent to which they were disadvantaged.

As a white South African male, I had to endure the ideological nightmare of military conscription and fumble my way through an undergraduate degree at Wits University in the 1970s while South Africa was close to melting point beneath a seemingly calm society. Well, that was if you were fooled by apartheid's propaganda mouthpiece – the South African Broadcasting Corporation or SABC – and draconian censorship in all facets of our lives. I despised it and I regarded the government of the day as criminals. So, too, did my father. He became actively involved in opposition politics, even opposing then Cabinet Minister Dr Piet Koornhof in a general election.

In the early 1970s, Wits University was a formidable force in distance running and especially the Comrades Marathon. One of its runners, Charles Coville, was instrumental in helping Vincent Gabashane Rakabaele and Michael Monaheng run the 1974 Comrades. Blacks were not allowed to compete. Both ran unofficially and runners and spectators alike gave them a rousing reception when they finished. This simple act helped stimulate the hopes of millions of black and white South Africans over the next 15 years as blacks, and women, were allowed to enter the Comrades from 1975. As a marathon runner, Rakabaele became a household name. At the time, no-one had any idea of the profound positive social impact the Comrades Marathon would have on South Africa. It remains so.

The Comrades would transcend South Africa's social, racial and gender challenges. While the Nationalist government was armed to the teeth fighting the spread of communism and godlessness in South Africa, the Comrades community was emancipating black South Africans and healing a nation severely fractured by apartheid. It cemented its position as the nation's foremost sporting event during the 1980s. Record entries. Record fields. Record performances. Record ratings. In a turbulent political decade when apartheid South Africa, in economic stagnation, was on the cusp of a civil war, the Comrades Marathon would provide the one day each year when citizens witnessed how South Africa could and should conduct itself.

At the end of the day black competitors had to return to township life and the indignity of apartheid but, for 11 glorious hours, everyone was equal and left the finish with dignity and the same sense of camaraderie, regardless of race, age or gender. It ameliorated racial tensions during a volatile time and inadvertently became a catalyst for social and political change. Most running clubs were integrated and South Africans were learning about one another.

My fortuitous Comrades Marathon experiences were beyond anything I could have imagined. My 1981 debut kept me on the road for more than nine hours and punished me brutally. I shared my pain, my fear and my will to finish with hundreds of other strangers. We were all Comrades novices yet our souls connected. Unbeknown to me, I had been exposed to the magic of Comrades that brings out the very best in a community. In retrospect it was one of the luckiest moments in my life.

My subsequent association with Comrades and South Africa's road running scene introduced another altogether unexpected dimension. My running improved out of sight and within two years I was training and racing with the best black and white South Africans. My Comrades time improved to 5:30 and then 5:26. I suddenly had an outside chance of winning and my exposure to Comrades at the pointy end also provided unimaginable experiences from near-celebrity media status to hyped-up rivalries to sports science. All totally unexpected.

Suddenly I was running some 4,500km annually, enmeshed with the likes of Mark Plaatjes, Thulani Sibisi, Kenny Jacobs, Hoseah Tjale, Titus Mamabolo, Matthews Motshwarateu, Gibeon Moshaba, Israel Morake, Petrus Kekana, Ernest Seleke, Zithulele Sinqe, Charles Vilakazi and many more. When the starter's pistol was fired at weekend road races, these great men were accorded a modicum of dignity within the heinous social sins of apartheid. From that moment we were all equal on the road and they ran for their lives. They ran with dignity. They ran with speed. They ran with grace. They ran for recognition. They ran to make a silent political statement. They ran because they wanted to prove that they were just as good as anyone else. They never had to remind anyone. They never had to say anything. Their results told the story.

My vehement disapproval of apartheid and the Nationalist government prompted me to seek a secure future for my three daughters in a free, democratic society. I emigrated, opting for the Chicken Run to Australia in 1987, totally devastated by the social and physical damage the government had inflicted on South Africa. And they showed no sign of letting up. My story will serve as a reminder of those dark days.

I first returned to South Africa after Nelson Mandela had been released from prison in 1990. Following the 1994 general election I have been a frequent visitor, marveling at the Rainbow Nation and observing the new democratic political wheel turn full circle.

In the intervening years, not only had I but also the South African running community, lost contact with those pioneering black marathon runners from the apartheid years. Some had died like Rakabaele whose burial in a pauper's grave in the foothills of Lesotho in 2003 was only announced to the public in 2009, through the forensic efforts of journalist Duane Heath. Some had simply vanished. Others had been murdered. During apartheid, they were despised by their oppressors yet subsequently appear to have been ignored by their liberators, despite running exultantly for black emancipation before liberation. No one seemed to care. As the years slowly passed I had a restlessness to track down the likes of Thulani Sibisi and Hoseah Tjale, fellow runners I had known intimately. This finally happened in 2013.

After 20 years of democracy, South Africa has healed many wounds of the past despite its self-indulgent government. The challenges ahead are great but, in my understanding, nowhere nearly as great as the challenges of 1987. South Africans have many great attributes including resilience and a capacity for change. These reserves will be tested once again in the years ahead.

I have written this book in honour of my black South African colleagues who were less fortunate than me. I have also written this book in honour of the Comrades and all of its participants over the years; years that have seen some remarkable changes in the South African landscape. I introduce you to some of the wonderful characters I was privileged to know, work with and run alongside. In doing so, I have relived my own personal triumphs, disappointments, challenges and achievements that have been intricately linked with the simple joys of running, my South African heritage and a hectic life lived on four continents. I also gaze into my crystal ball and speculate on the future of the Comrades

I hope that you enjoy this roller-coaster ride of a book as much as I enjoyed writing it.

Bob de la Motte
2014

Drama at 45ᵗʰ Cutting – 1 June 1984

Durban – South Africa

I'm where I want to be, at the front end of the greatest ultramarathon in the world, barely 7km from glory, and my blood is boiling. I'm angry at the world. I'm angry at myself. And I'm particularly pissed off with Little Boy Blue who has just popped up alongside me.

Little Boy Blue, topped and tailed with yellow: the flaxen hair and the blue vest and yellow shorts of Wits University. Uh-oh! Bruce Fordyce.

His appearance catches me flat footed. Only minutes earlier, spectators have told me he is 80 seconds behind as I pound over a roller-coaster section at Huntley's Hill. Isolated from my helpers I am livid at this inaccurate information from roadside.

I'm also furious at myself for not reconnoitring the exact route leading into Durban. It catches me by surprise. In Westville, the route deviates from the well-engineered freeway onto side roads that provide some of the steepest undulations of the 90km course. Short, but very sharp, and they hurt. Still, I'm looking forward to regaining momentum on the downhill after the entrance to Durban at 45ᵗʰ Cutting when I hear … "good running."

I glance to my left. There is no eye contact. He looks straight ahead. Where did he come from? His premature utterance was not what I had expected in the Comrades Marathon. My brain flashes, … "yep Bruce, save the platitudes, this race isn't over yet."

Yes, I'm hurting, but so are you. No need to try to psych me out with this "good running" stuff with the unspoken addendum … "but not good enough." There is still a tough climb up to Tollgate and the big drop down Berea Road. Plenty of time for you to crack the way you did on your last down run in 1982 when you could barely walk. Those demons are waiting for *you*.

If it was his intention to irk me, he had scored a bull's eye. The journalists write it up the next day as good sportsmanship but I didn't experience it that way. In all my years of competitive sport, handshakes and faint praise were reserved until the contest was over. His comment reinforces my will to beat him.

However, De la Motte determination is no match for the Fordyce Finish. I'm two paces behind, then five. He gradually pulls away from me and I can do absolutely nothing but stew over his comment. Making the finish and holding on to second place is a monumental slog. My arms are tingling and my eyes do not take in the full spectrum of colour. My universe is monochrome. I am spent. At 11.30am, I become the third fastest runner in Comrades history. It counts for nothing.

Less than 12 hours later I am in bed in my Johannesburg home, but I can't sleep. My veins are awash with adrenalin and anguish. Through the night, I replay in my mind the scenes of 45th Cutting and realise, in hindsight, squeezing out the first two words that popped into his brain was possibly all Fordyce was capable of. He was desperately close to losing the race to the last person he expected.

In the heat of the moment it was probably a Fordyce exclamation of extraordinary relief as much as an acknowledgement of what, to be honest, was my best effort yet in running shoes. What did I have the right to expect? A gracious speech? The offer of a tow? His supersonic second half of 2:37 reinforced the lesson I had been taught on 45th Cutting.

Just toughen up and run faster.

Little did I know that I and many others are to experience more of the supersonic Fordyce Finish the hard way in years to come when he reels us in, spits us out, and makes us eat his words. He remains the most formidable competitor I ever encounter.

1

Sued for $1 billion

Perth – Western Australia

I ignored the letter from London. I had more pressing things to do that September morning in 1994 as Director of Investment Banking for Hartleys Limited. I got the biggest jolt of my life when I eventually got around to my in-tray of snail mail. The sender was Herbert Smith, a firm of London solicitors, and when I interpreted the legal gobbledygook I discovered I was ensnared in a $1 billion claim lodged against Arthur Andersen by the liquidator of Alan Bond's company. Yeah, the guy famous around the world for winning the America's Cup in 1983 with the winged keel. *That* Alan Bond.

Holy shit! I grabbed a calculator. Hmmm … potentially a personal liability in the order of $21 million. A good way to ruin anyone's day. I was put on notice: "to refrain from disposing of any asset or incurring any debt or removing any assets from the Australian jurisdiction." That's legal speak for the liquidator warning all involved that he was intent on pursuing their personal assets. And I was going to be wiped out because I didn't trust my gut instinct back in May 1988.

I moved to Perth in Western Australia in 1987, expecting to be part of a merger that would land me back in the KPMG empire in which I had thrived as a chartered accountant in South Africa and Britain. Instead of merging with KPMG, the firm I joined did an about-turn and fell in step with Arthur Andersen. I was not a good fit with Andersen's aggressive American culture, and tendered my resignation on 18 May 1988.

It was not accepted. For 10 hours, the two senior partners in Perth tried to persuade me to change my mind. I received a 50% pay rise, without any negotiation on my part, and I was assured of admission into Andersen's Australian partnership on 1 September 1988, the annual date of all new admissions. What wasn't there to like? I sought the advice of a recruiting consultant about this unexpected turn of events because, despite the generous offers, I simply did not see my long-term future at Andersen.

The head-hunter's advice was to be pragmatic. Stay at Andersen, take the promotion to partnership status and sit tight for a year before you pursue other career options, by which time my CV would reflect two solid years' experience at Andersen including promotion to partner. I concurred and sat tight for a further 17 months, including a year as a partner, but it turned out to be a fateful decision.

When I was admitted to the Australian partnership, the firm was a blue-chip international organisation of 50,000 personnel in 160 offices across 47 countries. Revenue was more than $5 billion a year. The US represented about 50% of the business, both in terms of personnel and revenues, and had a bigger influence over the Australian operation than I would have liked. For example, my 1987 induction did not take place in Perth. I had to fly to Chicago.

I was in the Windy City when I first learned the company had decided to pursue the professional service work, including taxation, accounting and auditing, for two emerging Australian entrepreneurs who looked like they might make it on the global stage, Rupert Murdoch and Alan Bond.

Andersen's senior partners in Chicago and London decided, after much analysis and debate, to aggressively pursue these two accounts even though both were regarded as high risk because of excessively high levels of borrowings, high growth rates through acquisition, and relatively short track records. Nevertheless, the opinion of Andersen's leaders was that Murdoch, who had acquired 20th Century Fox Studios and was about to punt his entire empire by launching the first satellite free-to-air television news station – Sky – had the potential to become a global player in the media world, while Bond was a consummate dealmaker expected to emerge as beer baron to the globe.

After beginning his career as a sign writer, London-born Bond formed Bond Corporation in 1959 and made his fortune as a property developer. In 1974 he financed the first of his four challenges by the Royal Perth Yacht Club for the America's Cup. In 1977 he was named Australian of the Year and in 1983 his syndicate won the America's Cup in Newport, the first time in history that the US was relieved of the trophy. That audacious 4–3 victory elevated Bond's status globally and gained him access to international capital markets. Without exception, financial institutions were eager to do business with the man who had won the America's Cup.

In 1987 he paid $1 billion for the Channel Nine television network of Kerry Packer. The acquisition was financed by an $800 million loan from an Australian bank, and $200 million from Kerry Packer himself. Bond did not lay out a cent. In the same year he bought Vincent van Gogh's Irises painting for $54 million, the highest price yet for an artwork. It subsequently transpired the purchase was funded by a substantial loan from the auctioneer, Sotheby's, which Bond failed to repay.

By 1988 Bond Corporation controlled half of Australia's beer market with dominant market shares in Western Australia (Swan), Queensland (Castlemaine) and New South Wales (Tooheys). Bond Corporation also controlled G Heileman Brewing Company in La Crosse, Wisconsin, and had further ambitions in the global beer market.

The Murdoch News Corporation account was secured when Andersen acquired the equity in the relatively small firm of Australian chartered accountants who had the News Corporation audit. By contrast, Bond Corporation sought expressions of interest from a number of international accounting firms, and I was one of three members of the Perth team charged with the compilation of Andersen's initial submission.

Bond Corporation was headquartered in Perth and they insisted on the relevant professional competence being resident in the city. Bond did not want the account serviced by senior partners living in Sydney or overseas. We were up against the incumbents, Price Waterhouse, and other leading international firms.

Complicating the chase of the Bond Corporation account was the arrival of Black Monday. On 19 October 1987 the Dow Jones Industrial Average plummeted 508 points, losing 22.6% of its total value. The S&P 500 dropped 20.4%, falling from 282.7 to 225.1. This was the greatest loss Wall Street had ever suffered on a single day.

In five days, indices of market valuation in the US plunged 30%. The stock market crash precipitated the demise of a number of vulnerable businesses in Perth and exposed some extraordinary financial bail-outs between the Western Australian government and businesses run by people close – too close – to the seat of power. These controversial transactions were referred to as WA Inc., and State premier Brian Burke was subsequently sentenced to two years in prison. What happened in Western Australia was mirrored, albeit to a lesser degree, around the nation as highly leveraged companies toppled. The Australian banking system was going to be severely tested.

Against this backdrop, we submitted our Expression of Interest to Bond Corporation with the aim of making the shortlist and the chance to pitch for this multi-million dollar account. A few days before Christmas I received mixed news: Andersen had made the final cut on the Bond tender process, but my leave had been cancelled to do some urgent work on the project.

I was not a member of the team that eventually made the pitch in person, but Andersen won the account to the envy of all the other international firms. Andersen spent $300,000 pitching for the account that was predicted to yield professional fees of $4 million a year. It transpired that Andersen managed to earn $6 million in 1988 alone. At the time it looked like a good result.

I was assigned to the Swan Brewing account of Bond Corporation. It was a strong cash generator that was controversially up-streamed into Bond Corporation to finance other activities. The brewing assets were well managed by competent executives who had no say or influence over what happened higher up in the corporate echelons of Bond Corporation. These assets had been used as security for debt, sourced from the US bond market, running into hundreds of millions of dollars – and that was where the shenanigans began.

The lenders rightfully wanted the surplus cash to remain in the brewing business while Bond and his closest advisors wanted to get their hands on the cash to finance their plans. It was a game of cat and mouse, being played with hundreds of millions of dollars of other people's money. In my professional universe, it was like driving on the wrong side of the road. Within a year I realised the ethics of some of the clients I was working for would never align with my own values. I quit Andersen in October 1989 to pursue a career in investment banking.

Andersen did their best to keep track of Bond's deals, using external lawyers to check the financial records and getting assurances from the Bond directors that all records had been lodged. It turned out the declarations from the directors were about as honest as those of Lance Armstrong when he swore under oath he had never used performance-enhancing drugs.

As Armstrong found out, lies tend to get exposed. In Bond's case, it was Tiny Rowland who did the exposing. The British magnate reacted to a hostile bid for his company, Lonrho, by releasing a detailed financial analysis which contended that Bond Corporation was technically insolvent. This time the financial world looked past the America's Cup and reacted.

Bond was declared personally bankrupt in 1992 for $622 million, which was the second largest personal bankruptcy in Australian history. He was subsequently sentenced to seven years in prison for defrauding $1.2 billion from his own Bell Group, at the time Australia's biggest corporate fraud. Several of his Bond Corporation directors were also sentenced to time behind bars. Bond was paroled after four years but many small investors lost their entire savings.

I became entangled in this mess in September 1994 when the liquidator of Bond Corporation, which had morphed into Southern Equities, launched action no. 1474 of 1994 in the Supreme Court of South Australia, against Andersen, alleging negligence in the conduct of the 30 June 1988 audit of the then Bond Corporation. The claim was for $500 million plus interest of a similar amount. The audit report in question was dated 16 September 1988, just 15 days after my admission to the

Australian partnership. Despite the fact that I was not an international partner, I had been financially ensnared.

The former Australian Andersen partners, myself included, took legal advice and decided to defend the matter using Herbert Smith. In the words of then senior partner Mark Bryant: "Andersen are confident that the audit we did was done competently and professionally; to the extent that the accounts were wrong, they were wrong in ways that were created by the Bond executives themselves."

Thunderclouds were concurrently forming in the global universe of Arthur Andersen. The aggressive push to generate increased additional fees outside the traditional audit resulted in Andersen's implication in a number of accounting irregularities and corporate failures in the US, including Boston Market Corporation, Sunbeam Appliances, Waste Management, and ultimately the Enron scandal that led to the demise of Arthur Andersen in 2002.

Enron was the world's largest energy trader. It championed energy deregulation, rising in 2001 to be the seventh largest company in the US with assets of more than $100 billion. It was considered a cutting-edge aggressive entity, a Wall Street darling and a model of management innovation. In February 2001 *Fortune* magazine's ranking of America's most admired companies listed Enron as No. 1 for innovation, and No. 2 for quality of management.

Oops! In November 2001 Enron collapsed. Shares that had traded at $90.00 had fallen to 61 cents. Enron was undone by dodgy accounting, too much debt and an unwillingness to provide information to investors who began to doubt its financial reports. It, and chief executive Kenneth Lay, became symbols of greed, arrogance, deceit and everything that was wrong with corporate America.

Enron was an Andersen client and the auditing company had up to 150 staff on site at Enron's Houston headquarters. Although Enron's fees were just a small fraction of Andersen's worldwide revenues, it was the lifeblood of the Houston office and lead partner David Duncan.

The consequences of Enron's multi-billion dollar implosion were fatal for Andersen in the US and inevitably Andersen worldwide. It quickly became apparent that the 89-year-old firm of Arthur Andersen was not going to survive the fallout. On a country by country basis, member firms of Andersen sought mergers with the other big firms. The Big Five international accounting universe was about to become the Big Four.

The Bond claim against Andersen played out amid this upheaval. The highly complex matter was expected to take years to resolve but the global demise of Andersen accelerated matters. The Australian Andersen firm was poised to merge with Ernst & Young when the Bond Corporation liquidator reminded both entities he had a "substantive and proper interest" in the destiny of Arthur Andersen Australia. Translation from lawyer speak to plain English: Andersen would have to reach a settlement with him before they could merge. If they wished to continue practising as chartered accountants, they would have to act quickly.

The liquidator had indicated his access to Andersen's insurers would return a maximum of $100 million and the defendants were up for a predicted 40% of any Supreme Court judgment. I was facing utter financial ruin for no deed or recklessness on my part.

In business, this is called partnership.

I survived thanks to the exquisite timing of the liquidator. He struck when Andersen was most vulnerable, domestically and globally, and a deal was done. The deep pockets of Andersen Worldwide SC, headquartered in Geneva, were tapped to allow the Australian merger with Ernst & Young to proceed in May 2002 and, just like that, I was off the hook.

In business, this is called pragmatism.

The 14-year liquidation process of Bond Corporation ended in September 2007. The liquidators salvaged $220 million for creditors from a global asset search which spread across Australia, England, the US and Canada, and into the tax havens of Switzerland, the Bahamas and Cook Islands. Bond Corporation creditors received 15.7 cents in the dollar. The Bond liquidators were probably happier, earning fees of $8.3 million out of the process.

The Swan Brewery in Perth, which once enjoyed a 90% market share in Western Australia, was shut down on 31 March 2013. SAB Miller now owns the iconic Australian Fosters brand. At the time of Bond's foray into brewing, the SAB part of Miller was the isolated South African Breweries, with no international presence or capability. That all changed once Nelson

Mandela was released in 1990. SAB soared to become the second largest brewer in the world with labels like Miller, Peroni, Grolsch and Castle. Only Anheuser Busch is bigger.

In business, this is called good management.

Over the years, I would observe the similarities between business personalities like Alan Bond, Kenneth Lay, Conrad Black and Bernie Madoff, and sports stars like Lance Armstrong, Marion Jones and Barry Bonds.

Society enjoys nothing more than a winning story, a victory played hard either in the sporting arena or in the business world. But played within the rules. Sadly, there are also many adept cheats who get away with breaking the rules. Some are caught and exposed. Paul Barry subsequently published *Going for Broke*, or how Alan Bond got away with it. David Walsh subsequently published *Seven Deadly Sins*, his pursuit of Lance Armstrong.

In whatever sphere these people operate, it's called greed.

2

Comrades: Why the obsession?

I have been fortunate to earn five Comrades medals, ranging from a 9:02 bronze to a 5:26 gold. My nine-hour bronze medal debut was far more torturous than my 5:26 gold. Quite simply, the more hours spent on the Comrades course, the tougher it is. Regardless, it is brutally tough for everyone. It is metaphysical. It talks to your soul and connects with other souls. It torments you. It encourages you to accept the generosity of spirit of the amazing spectators. It teaches you to embrace life. It jolts you into realising you are capable of the extraordinary.

Every single participant leaves the event richer for the Comrades experience.

The running explosion of the late 1970s transformed the Comrades Marathon into South Africa's Royal Wedding. Before then it was more of a cherished annual tradition, but when the jogging craze flared into an endurance epidemic, the footrace between Durban and Pietermaritzburg of approximately 90km seized the fascination of a nation … and squeezed hard.

In 1975, 1,352 runners started the Comrades and the only cameras to be seen were around the necks of a handful of newspaper photographers and casual snappers along the route. By 1985, more than 9,000 crossed the start line and the race was televised live throughout the day. Runners were not the only ones to have to qualify to be on the route on race day; photographers had to produce the credentials of a major publication or network to get one of the sought-after spots on the media truck. With a million people now lining the route, it was the only way to access the action.

But what makes the Comrades Marathon the biggest annual sporting event in South Africa, and the greatest ultramarathon in the world, is not the mass of spectators or hours of on-air time it attracts. It is the sheer number of participants, more than 20,000 in 2000 and 18,000 in 2014; of which only a thousand represent the talented end of the spectrum, from the Olympic-standard marathoner to the moderately gifted runner. The other 95% are ordinary people who challenge themselves to do something extraordinary. This is the Comrades Marathon.

The annual trek by foot between KwaZulu-Natal's two main cities was dreamed up as a fundraiser for World War I veterans. Vic Clapham, a member of the Eighth South Africa Infantry Regiment which pursued Colonel Paul von Lettow-Vorbeck's askari army for more than 2,700km on foot through German East Africa, decided an event which demanded supreme endurance and a significant investment of courage would be a fitting way to remember the 10,000 British Commonwealth soldiers who died during the campaign, most from disease.

After returning from active duty at the end of 1918, Clapham, who had no athletic experience himself, canvassed support from the athletics hierarchy and the former soldiers' association, the League of Comrades of the Great War, to stage an annual foot race between Pietermaritzburg and Durban. The event was to be hosted on Empire Day, 24 May, to honour the fallen Comrades of the Great War. His suggestion was initially met with ridicule. Clapham's detractors suggested, not unreasonably, that the proposed race would be far too strenuous and might result in a fatality. On the contrary, pointed out Clapham, if infantrymen like himself, drafted straight into the armed forces from sedentary occupations, could get used to forced marches over great distances, trained athletes should be capable of completing the route from Pietermaritzburg to Durban. The Clapham logic of 1919 resonated and subsequently enabled tens of thousands of otherwise sedentary folk to earn a Comrades finisher's medal.

Thus it was that in 1921, 34 brave men of the 48 who had entered lined up in Pietermaritzburg at an altitude of 600m for the first Comrades

Marathon, to finish at sea level outside the Durban Town Hall 90km away. Except for a short tarred section outside the Town Hall, the race was contested over dirt roads.

The intrigue behind the inaugural Comrades revolved around whether it was possible for the runners to reach Durban before nightfall. Bill Rowan showed them. He breasted the tape after eight hours and 59 minutes and received a gold watch worth £25. His training had included 32km cross country runs at his Transvaal farm and daily skipping sessions. To lengthen his stride, he included some experimental sessions running behind a motorcycle holding onto two metal bars. Remarkably, he had forecast a winning time of nine hours.

Sixteen of the starters finished in less than 12 hours, each receiving a medal. A few others who arrived in Durban just before the 7pm cut-off were disqualified for cheating. As they entered Durban they accepted the offer of a lift from some passing drivers and felt it was the only way they would make the 12-hour limit. Perhaps, in a roundabout way, they inspired the bronze medal struck for a runner who plugged away resolutely through the dusk to miss the limit by 20 minutes. A *Natal Mercury* reporter wrote of the Comrades Marathon that year: "This can be regarded as one of the grandest accomplishments yet made in the annals of South African sport."

Those who completed the route indicated the inaugural Comrades was more akin to surviving a military expedition than the advertised "go as you please" jaunt through the misty Natal valleys to Durban along 54 miles and 1,120 yards of mostly rugged untarred roads. Yet the sheer craziness of the event struck a chord with both athletes and former soldiers still seeking adventure. Such was the interest that a second event was organised in 1922, this time finishing in Pietermaritzburg, thus starting the tradition of alternating directions. The rules confirmed a 12-hour cut-off with an earlier 6am start. Natal's three turf clubs, mindful of the soaring public interest in the race, donated a silver winner's floating trophy valued at £70.

Of the 114 entrants, 89 crossed the starting line. A Harding farmer, Arthur Newton, used a metronomic pace to cut through the field on the hills after Pinetown and, by Camperdown, had moved into the lead. Despite a struggle to get over Polly Shorts, he won the first up run in eight hours and 40 minutes, with Rowan, who had travelled from the Belgian Congo, in third place. Twenty-six runners managed to finish within the 12-hour cut-off. This Comrades Marathon idea appeared to have traction. Clapham was certainly on to something. Many of the participants were returned infantrymen and essentially a group of battle-hardened, tough survivors. Importantly, the public and print media had embraced the event.

The novelty factor inevitably waned after a couple of years-, and the number of starters dropped to 69 in 1923. One of them was an unofficial female entrant, Frances Hayward, unofficial because the race was closed to women. Hayward nevertheless showed she had what it took to finish, in 11:35. The Comrades officials huffed and puffed and chose to turn a blind eye. Not so those otherwise connected with the event; runners and spectators chipped in for a £100 silver tea service and rose bowl. The rigours of Comrades did not exactly leave Hayward supine: she changed from her running kit and went straight to the theatre that evening. Celebrating, too, was Newton, who chopped an impressive two hours from Rowan's time for the down run, by completing the course in 6:56.

The intrinsic fabric of the Comrades was woven during these embryonic years. Normality replaced novelty. The Comrades became an accepted race, with formal rules following the amateur protocol of the day and, with the growing sense of tradition, came the accompanying anticipation involving not only participants but helpers, spectators and journalists. The Comrades ethos accorded dignity and respect to each competitor for making the commitment in terms of preparation and will power, particularly those who had to struggle to make the cut-off time or overcome a particular disadvantage. Women, starting with Hayward, had to run unofficially until 1975 and they received particularly enthusiastic support, as did black runners, starting with Robert Mtshali's 9:30 run in 1935, and continuing to 1975 when Vincent Gabashane Rakabaele of Lesotho became the first official black finisher, clocking 6:27 in 20th place.

The previous year, Rakabaele ran unofficially to place 47th. According to Comrades historian Morris Alexander, the three loudest cheers of the day at the finish were reserved for winner Derek Preiss, Rakabaele, and the oldest finisher, Leige Boulle. That was how Comrades conducted itself. It still does.

Those who attempted Comrades in the 1920s were largely former servicemen from World War I. The camaraderie they had developed on the battlefields of East Africa and Flanders manifested itself in the comradeship of the road that sustained the race during its first tenuous decade. The average number of entries for the first 10 years was a modest 45 runners, yet the early organisers understood an 89km footrace was a feasible undertaking and, in 1928, reduced the cut-off time to 11 hours, increasing the challenge for those with discipline and fortitude.

The introduction of a team prize in 1931 encouraged an increase in participation. The Moths of the Gunga Din Shellhole provided an additional incentive of a race within Comrades other than the overall winner. The first four runners from each club competed for the Gunga Din Trophy – a steel helmet mounted on a wooden base – and it soon became the second most coveted trophy behind the winner.

Moths stood for Memorable Order of Tin Hats, a soldiers' charitable organisation who met at venues nicknamed shell holes. One of their founding aims was to ensure that their comrades who had fallen during the 1914–1918 conflict would never be forgotten. They recognised that the Gunga Din award would be a suitable way to perpetuate their memory.

Gunga Din is a poem by Rudyard Kipling, often recited in the trenches of WWI France, about an Indian water bearer who is initially treated with contempt by the narrator, a British soldier. Yet in battle, Gunga Din saves the soldier's life, only to be shot dead after dragging him to safety. The soldier regrets his earlier attitude and admits Din is the better man for sacrificing his life to save another.

> *Though I've belted you and flayed you,*
> *By the livin' Gawd that made you,*
> *You're a better man than I am, Gunga Din.*

Public donations fell during the Great Depression of the 1930s but, in keeping with the sentiment of an event that emphasised toughness, entries climbed and 57 men won finisher's medals in 1933. Robert Mtshali completed the 1935 Comrades in the creditable time of 9:30 finishing in 27th position. He did not receive a finisher's medal and was excluded from the results: he had just become the first black runner to complete Comrades unofficially. It would be another 40 years before blacks were allowed to compete officially. However, the onset of World War II threatened the viability of the race. More pressing matters were at hand for the fit and the resilient, and the Comrades was suspended for six years, stalling the number of finishers at 449.

The second great global conflict claimed the lives of two previous winners, Frank Sutton and Phil Masterton-Smith, both killed at Tobruk. Sutton had prevailed in the closest finish of the race when he pipped Noel Burree by two metres in 1931. When the living memorial to comradeship between servicemen resumed in 1946, many prospective entrants had yet to be demobbed, or were still recovering from the deprivations of being prisoners of war. Regardless, 22 starters climbed Berea Hill out of Durban and, seven hours later, 1935 winner Bill Cochrane led home a tiny complement of eight finishers. Cochrane's win was all the more remarkable because he had been captured in North Africa but his desire to compete in memory of those who had not made it home drove him to an extraordinary victory.

In 1948, another Comrades tradition was born when one of the starters, Max Trimborn, gave a loud imitation of a cock crow immediately before the gun was fired. That tradition has been sustained with a recorded version of Trimborn's lifelike crow played over the public address system at the starting line in the seconds before the race sets off. It was a rare innovation.

The somewhat moribund Comrades limped through to 1950 when Wally Hayward won his second Comrades in 6:46, 20 years after his first. The following year he bettered Newton's down record, clocking 6:14. He went on to become the first to better six hours, on the 1953 down run, and set world bests for 50 and 100 miles in the United Kingdom, in addition to winning the London to Brighton race in a record time. His feats injected new life into ultra-distance running in general, and the Comrades Marathon in particular. In 1950 Hayward led home 20 finishers. He went on to win the next three events to take his overall tally to five to emulate the great Newton and the 1930s dominator, Hardy Ballington and, at the end of his period of dominance, the entry numbers had soared to 95 in 1955.

Sadly, Hayward was not one of them. Officials had identified an inadvertent breach of the amateur rules during his visit to the UK, when he accepted a contribution to his travelling expenses, and suspended him indefinitely. Who knows how many wins he would have racked up had he been allowed to continue? The remarkable Hayward, who was decorated for bravery in North Africa during World War II, successfully returned to the Comrades as a competitor in 1988 and, at the age of 80, he finished the event for the final time the following year, barely beating the 11-hour cut-off.

Hayward's feats in the 1950s revived the Comrades and inspired elite athletes from universities to focus on the race. After all, had not a great man made the transition to distance glory from the track, on which he won a bronze medal in the six miles at the 1938 Empire Games in Sydney? Jackie Mekler, second in the marathon at the 1954 Empire Games in Vancouver – most famous for the Roger Bannister–John Landy duel over the mile – felt the 1958 Comrades would be a suitable outlet for the frustration of missing the Springbok team for the Cardiff Empire Games. He won and, two years later, became the first to better six hours for the up run, leading home 108 other finishers.

In 1962, the Road Runners Club of England sent four of their best distance runners including John Smith who won and missed Mekler's record by a mere 33 seconds. When Smith was watching the tail-enders struggling in hours later, he remarked to former winner Bill Cochrane that these competitors were generating as much applause as he had received.

"You are now witnessing the spirit of the Comrades," Cochrane replied.

With an increasing number of university students participating, an inter-varsity competition was introduced in 1968. The predominantly English-speaking students would mature into a powerful and influential group of Comrades ambassadors, enormously beneficial to the future of the event. When South Africa was expelled from the Olympic Games after the Rome event in 1960, the South African Broadcasting Corporation offered to provide radio coverage. This, in turn, encouraged more to attempt the event.

In 1965, blind runner Ian Jardine, 63, finished his 10th Comrades and earned his race number 26 in perpetuity. Blind runners have since become another part of the rich Comrades fabric. Those who piloted blind runners over the Comrades course formed a group known as Jardine Joggers and devoted their race day to assisting unsighted runners.

The second dramatic finish in the race's history unfolded in 1967 when leader Tommy Malone reached the finishing track at the Durban Light Infantry Grounds in Greyville 20m in front of Manie Kuhn. A fatigued Malone tried to sprint for the line but a spasm of cramp cut him down just three metres short of the line. He got to his knees and lunged for the finish as Kuhn swept past – and the judges gave it to Kuhn by centimetres. Had Malone crawled those last few metres, he would have won.

Mekler's vast talent earned him a fifth win in 1968, to match the feats of Hayward and Ballington, but arguably against stronger and deeper competition.

The decade closed with a record 586 finishers in 1969, all white males. The annual average number of finishers was 262, well up on the 41 of a decade earlier. As South Africa's sports isolation started to grip, so the Comrades Marathon fulfilled a need for a major event. If the 1960s provided a rich montage of human endurance sprinkled with vignettes of world-class athleticism and epic drama, the 1970s added more dynamic ingredients: blacks, women and television. Profound changes were made for the 1975 Golden Jubilee Comrades, with the 50th running opened to all who qualified, irrespective of sex or race. A year later, television cameras followed the race for a delayed telecast that pitched the race into pubs, clubs and homes around the nation. The Comrades was poised to become South Africa's pinnacle sporting event.

As its popularity rose, so did performances. The up and down records were bettered six times during the decade, and participation increased fivefold. Running clubs sprang up across the nation and the thousands of recruits had the same goal in mind: a Comrades medal. The new clubs inevitably included a few Comrades veterans and they would share their knowledge and encourage ordinary runners to give it a go. Television rode the wave of popularity: its live coverage of the 1983 race yielded impressive ratings, no doubt because the winner would be a South African. Comrades was promoted as the greatest ultramarathon in the world and was South Africa's equivalent of the championship series in US baseball, contested by two domestic teams but nevertheless hailed as the World Series.

The Comrades stimulated many other ultra events such as the 56km Two Oceans Marathon in Cape Town that claims to be the world's most beautiful marathon; the 56km Korkie event, a slow-poison uphill haul at altitude between Pretoria and Germiston (discontinued in 2009); and the 50km Johannesburg Stock Exchange Marathon between Johannesburg and Pretoria.

Dave Bagshaw opened the 1970s with a record 5:51 up win, the first of three triumphs. In 1975 Rakabaele was the first official black finisher and, a few hours later, Liz Cavanagh became the first official woman medallist. After a down record run of 5:39 by university student Dave Levick and two wins from Preiss, the next Comrades legend emerged at a relentless shuffle. Alan Robb of Germiston Callies Harriers used a clipped but rapid stride to win three in a row from 1976 to 1978, the last a fabulous 5:29 performance to become the first runner to better 5½ hours. The unassuming Robb beat runner-up Dave Wright by 20 minutes, or more than five kilometres, in one of the most commanding performances in race history.

The 1979 Comrades yielded more drama when cramp felled race leader Johnny Halberstadt. He was lying on his back when Piet Vorster and Dave Wright steamed by. Halberstadt got going again after eight minutes on the ground and caught Wright, but Vorster was over the horizon. And it was all replayed on television, still in its infancy in South Africa but becoming a major influence on the growth of the race. Sneaking into third place was a fast-finishing student from Wits University whose name was soon to become synonymous with Comrades, Bruce Fordyce.

The Comrades cemented its position as the nation's foremost sporting event during the 1980s. Record entries. Record fields. Record performances. Record ratings. In a turbulent political decade when apartheid South Africa, in economic stagnation, was on the cusp of a civil war, the

Comrades Marathon would provide one day each year when all citizens witnessed how South Africa could and should conduct itself. At the end of the day the black competitors had to return to township life and the indignity of apartheid but, for 11 glorious hours, everyone was treated the same and left the finish with dignity and the same sense of camaraderie, regardless of race, age or gender. It ameliorated racial tensions during a volatile time and inadvertently became a glue and catalyst for social and political change. Most running clubs were integrated and South Africans were learning much about one another.

A hallmark of the 1980s was the surge in standard of the women's performance. UCT student Isavel Roche-Kelly started the ball rolling in 1981 when she dominated the down race in 6:44, the second of her wins before she was killed in a road accident while cycling in Ireland. Cheryl Winn (nee Jorgensen) won in 7:04 in 1982, before a five-year duel sprang up between another student, Lindsay Weight, and Kiwi Helen Lucre.

Better was to come. Schoolteacher Frith van der Merwe was in a class of her own, setting an up record of 6:32 and a supersonic down record of 5:54 in 1989. In the same year she set records of 3:30 at the Two Oceans, and 3:04 at the JSE. At the time of writing, 25 years later, only her 6:32 up record has been eclipsed. The three other records remain intact.

Among the men it was a case of Fordyce. Fordyce. Fordyce. Fordyce. Fordyce. Fordyce. Fordyce. Fordyce. The flaxen-haired student from Wits University dedicated himself absolutely to the Comrades and won eight consecutive races from 1981 to 1988, setting new marks for the down run of 5:24, and the up run of 5:27. Articulate and professional, he saw off challenges from Halberstadt, Robb, Gordon Shaw, Hoseah Tjale, Nick Bester, Mark Page and myself to guarantee Comrades immortality. After skipping Comrades in 1989 to set a 100km world best of 6:25, he returned in 1990 and won for the ninth time. The Comrades community will forever debate whether he would have achieved 10 in a row had he not opted to run the lucrative 100km in 1989, when Sam Tshabalala finally became the first black winner, in 5:35.

By the end of the decade, the Comrades had achieved levels of participation and growth that founder Vic Clapham could never have contemplated in his wildest dreams. Apart from the unexpected stimulus derived from South Africa's sports isolation, the event had always been exceptionally well organised despite political and logistical challenges. The fortitude of the organising committees over the years, combined with excellent media coverage and fervent support of spectators, were major factors contributing to the consistent growth and success of Comrades. Runners were never let down or disappointed. They always received excellent value for money before walking away with their finishers' medals. It never failed. It never disappointed.

South Africa was set for major political reform in the 1990s. On 11 February 1990 a dignified Nelson Mandela was released from 27 years of imprisonment, and the shackles of apartheid were about to be discarded. As South Africa prepared for its first democratic election, it was gradually being readmitted into international sport. The Barcelona Olympics in 1992 would be South Africa's first Olympics since Rome in 1960. Rugby and cricket teams were once again competing internationally as was the predominantly black Bafana Bafana national football team. Sports lovers and participants were suddenly spoilt for choice. The Comrades Marathon was about to encounter some very stiff international competition from other events for participants, the sporting dollar, and public interest. It would also have to prepare for an international field of world-class ultramarathoners who would no doubt want to tackle the Comrades challenge.

Page, pipped by Fordyce in 1990, thought his day had come two years later when he had a decent lead at the bottom of Polly Shorts with less than an hour to go. Then he cramped. The leader stopped. The media truck stopped. The entire entourage at the head of the race stopped. Charl Mattheus and Jetman Msutu didn't stop and galloped past the stricken Page, who struggled on to finish third. The drama didn't stop there: Mattheus was stripped of his win six weeks later for testing positive for a stimulant, which he claimed was included in an anti-influenza medication, and Msutu was bumped up to first, while the luckless Page was second again.

The debate continued for years as to Mattheus's suspension. The obvious question is why a flu-ridden athlete would consider running the

Comrades, let alone how he could manage to beat the best in the world, but Mattheus proved he had the ability when he returned to claim the title in 1997, and passed the doping test.

By 1995, the 'go as you please' amateur Comrades Marathon had to face up to the introduction of prize money. For the first five years of the decade the winning times had not been within 10 minutes of Fordyce's up and down bests, but Russian Dmitri Grishine raised eyebrows in 1998 when he clocked 5:26.25 for the up run in 1998 on a course nearly 2km longer. Similarly, American Ann Trason chopped 20 minutes from Van der Merwe's up record with her 6:12.23 win in 1996, when President Mandela presented the winners with medals and trophies.

The foreign runners were making their mark, with 1993 winner German Charly Doll the first non-South African men's champion since Britain's Mick Orton in 1972.

Whereas race participation grew 164% in the 1980s, it plateaued during the 1990s with a modest growth of 9.8%. Everyone wanted to run the Millennium event, particularly with the cut-off extended to 12 hours. More than 20,000 left Durban for Pietermaritzburg for the 2000 race, but numbers subsequently stabilised at between 10,000 and 11,000 in the face of increasing competition from other endurance events such as mountain biking and Ironman.

Vladimir Kotov of Belarus, fourth in the 1980 Olympic Games marathon, made the 2000 race one to remember by lowering the up record to 5:25.33, at the age of 42. Kotov brought with him an amazing running pedigree, having won several major marathons in Europe, but if his feat raised eyebrows, those of Leonid Shvetsov dropped jaws. The Russian lowered the down best to 5:20.47 in 2007, and the up record to 5:24.47 a year later. He tested clean after both wins but was subsequently implicated in alleged EPO distribution and use. The sceptics' whispers were now a roar and many questioned the legitimacy of Shvetsov's performances. Testing for EPO at the Comrades was only introduced in 2002 when only two out of 26 urine samples were sent to Sydney for analysis.

Between them, Russian twins Elena and Olesya Nurgalieva won the women's Comrades Bowl every year from 2003 to 2013, with the exception of 2005. Elena, with eight victories, remains one win shy of matching

King Fordyce's record of nine. Elena holds the up record of 6:09, but even her best down run of 6:07 in 2012 does not approach Van der Merwe's astonishing run 25 years earlier. The 2014 winner Eleanor Greenwood beat the Russian twins though her time of 6:18 was still 24 minutes slower than Frith's supersonic record or, in distance terms, Greenwood won but still finished more than 6km behind Frith.

As recently as 2012, Ludwig Mamabolo of South Africa tested positive for a stimulant that showed up in both A and B samples. He retained his first place, and the substantial prize money, on a technicality relating to the handling of his test vials. Sadly, inadequate drug testing since the amateur era has damaged the reputation of the Comrades Marathon at the elite end, in much the same way the Tour de France has suffered a credibility crisis, and tainted the achievements of clean competitors.

Such cheating counts for little to the vast majority of Comrades runners. Sure, they have an interest in the front end of the race and winning times, but their focus is on getting themselves to the finish. Although in 2014, an analysis of negative splits by Comrades runner and Wits University statistician Mark Dowdeswell suggested that a number of runners in the middle to back of the field may be taking shortcuts. Nonetheless, Comrades is larger than any individual, including the winners and the cheats.

The Comrades Marathon serves as an annual pilgrimage and a rite of passage for tens of thousands of South Africans.

In the words of Blanche Moila: "Every South African should do the Comrades at least once in their lifetime – it is liberating."

3

Comrades flame-out

14 March 1976. A perfect autumn morning on the South African Highveld and I was jogging along with three others towards the 20km mark of the Vaal Marathon when a Volvo sedan pulled up alongside us. The middle-aged woman driver wound down the passenger window and in an excited voice asked: "Excuse me. Are you the race leaders?"

The four of us were momentarily dumbstruck. The only "real" runner amongst us, Dave Gurney, politely replied that unfortunately we were not the race leaders. He was impeccably polite, spoke with the clarity of a radio announcer and offered his usual characteristic smile beneath longish red locks and through his generously freckled face. The Volvo driver was encouraged to reciprocate his kindness and continued: "If you are not the race leaders, where are the other runners?"

Our gregariously polite spokesman replied: "Well, I'm confident that if you continue driving along this road for a few kilometres, you will find them."

To which she bemusedly smiled at us, even more generously than Dave had smiled at her, and drove off to find the race leaders of the 1976 Vaal Marathon.

Only then did we become aware that no competitors were visible ahead of us despite the absence of any geological features that might have obstructed our line of sight to the horizon. We were hardly camouflaged in the flat *mielie* (corn) fields and when we glanced behind there were but a pair of stragglers who looked like the walking wounded.

With less than half the 42.2km marathon distance covered, we were in a spot of bother. Apart from the effervescent Gurney, marathon runner and perpetual Wits University student, the rest of us were about to discover the painful lesson of misplaced ambition together with the terrifying debut marathon experience of hitting the wall.

How on earth had I ended up in this predicament? I was no different to any other bullet-proof 22-year-old. I had got married in January and returned from a honeymoon in Reunion and Mauritius in mid-February to start my second year of Articles of Clerkship with KPMG in Johannesburg, the firm I had joined after graduating from Wits University at the end of 1974.

I had been assigned to the audit of Unisec Ltd, an investment company listed on the Johannesburg Stock Exchange, with a highly talented and entrepreneurial CEO, Peter Thomas. Unlike KPMG's old blue chip mining house clients, such as Anglo American, Unisec was more new wave and demanding. So the internal word was that the audit required a very smart audit partner.

The audit partner was a youthful Stuart Morris, while his audit senior was Brian Mallinson. Within KPMG and the wider Johannesburg business community, these guys represented a highly respected professional team. I had the good fortune to be assigned to this audit as the most junior member of staff.

Unisec's Johannesburg head office, in the architecturally contemporary Standard Bank tower, was only a couple of blocks from KPMG and I was instructed by my audit senior and audit partner to head over and ask the Unisec receptionist to show me to the audit room. Mallinson duly gave me the key to the filing cabinet containing all the KPMG confidential audit files. I was told to take a look at the previous year's files and the audit programme to develop an understanding of the Unisec business and our looming audit assignment.

When Morris and Mallinson arrived, they zeroed in on a sheet of paper taped to the filing cabinet. Both recorded a couple of numbers on the sheet and then spoke about their "training progress". I politely enquired what it was they were logging and what they were training for.

"The Comrades Marathon," Morris casually replied.

I was gobsmacked. "What? The Comrades Marathon! *You* guys?"

The sheer disbelief and candour of my response must have loomed as a very serious career-limiting blunder. I drew my breath and tried not to laugh. Almost as though rehearsed in unison, Morris and Mallinson chorused: "Yes, we are training for the Comrades and you are welcome to join us."

I had painted myself into a serious corner.

It was to be a moment I would initially regret but subsequently treasure for the rest of my life. I had been a pretty handy 800m runner at school; I was 22 years old and indestructable so of course I accepted the invitation.

Confidence and ignorance are wonderful bedfellows at times. The Comrades Marathon was usually run on 31 May, a public holiday for Republic Day, although it was not specifically linked with the political significance of the day. The marathon was an event I had been in awe of since my early teens when the populace tuned in to the live radio broadcast of the race. Because the Nationalist government viewed television as a potential threat to both its apartheid strategy and the Afrikaans language, test broadcasts only began in selected cities in 1975, with nationwide service the following year. Before then, the Comrades Marathon legend had grown through storytellers, participants and live radio commentary.

Only a year or two earlier, while a full-time student at Wits University, I had got to meet real Comrades runners; my first encounter with this apparently extraordinary breed of superhumans. Through university contemporaries Denis Sacks and Weston Dickson, both active Wits University athletes, I had met some contemporary Comrades runners like Trev Parry, Dave Wright, Robbie Gardner, Pete Gordon, John Bush and Dave Hodgskiss. They had all finished in the top 50 positions in the Comrades, so Wits had a very proud tradition and great strength in ultramarathon running.

Yet here I was, disbelieving my good fortune: through my KPMG employment, I now had an opportunity to participate in the legendary Comrades Marathon.

My initial disbelief in Morris and Mallinson was unfounded. Morris had phenomenal sporting prowess. He was one of the leading tennis players at the Old Johannians Club, in addition to being one of the toughest squash players around Johannesburg corporate circles. He was also a very competent golfer; in short, a born natural ball player with great skill and tenacity.

Mallinson added yet another overwhelming dimension. He had attended school at Queens College in the Eastern Cape of South Africa and represented Border at provincial cricket. One of his school mates and fellow cricketers was the late Tony Greig who went on to captain England. Mallinson was still a first-grade club cricketer and hockey player, and also cunningly smart on the squash court.

When I asked them about their running experience I was assured they knew what they were doing. Morris had also been a Springbok or King's Scout and so knew how to cope with thirst (little stones under the tongue) and how to combine a walking–with-jogging effort, with the resulting benefit of being able to keep going for hour after hour. As for training, between all our commitments, including KPMG and my tertiary nocturnal obligations at Wits, it transpired that late Sunday afternoons would be ideal for our Comrades training. In reality it was the only slot we had available.

Then Morris and Mallinson added the first real sense of immediacy about our Comrades odyssey. Apparently, the CMA had, for the very first time, introduced a standard marathon as a pre-requisite to entering the Comrades Marathon. A year earlier, the Comrades organisers had restricted the overall number of entries, without any pre-qualification requirements, to 1,500 in a bid to avoid growing traffic congestion. A total of 1,241 runners, or 82.7% of entered runners, completed the race that year, including the first black and female entrants after the CMA decided to open the event to runners other than white males under the age of 65.

The South African dialect around immediacy uses three different levels: now, just now and now-now.

For those unfamiliar with this vernacular, *now* has a Bob Marley Caribbean vagueness to it; *just now* means *yes, when it suits*; whereas *now-now* assumes nuclear missile urgency. The Comrades *now-now* was about to be launched when Morris and Mallinson advised that the last possible qualifying marathon available to us was the Vaal Marathon on 14 March, four weeks hence.

Morris volunteered to host our first training run from his home in Sandringham on Sunday 21 February. He shared his jogging-with-walking theory from his scouting years as we circled the Glendower golf course, returning to his home after about an hour to bemused wives anticipating the typical African sunset *braai,* or barbeque.

We were pretty confident, finding time for two more Sunday afternoon training sessions and a dinner party for our Comrades team at the De la Motte home on 13 March. Our spirits could not have been more buoyant and we were reminded of that early the next morning when Morris called past in his azure Renault T16, with Mallinson in the passenger seat, to collect my wife, Vern, and me. We had asked Vern to assist with the seconding throughout the marathon so she would drive the Renault and transport our food and drinks. Aid stations were not a feature of road running at the time. Distance markers were unheard of.

We paid our entry fees and lined up alongside 440 other entrants. I was wearing my Dunlop Volley tennis shoes with thick tennis socks and a beach singlet. Morris wore his favourite squash shoes, and Mallinson his hockey shoes and shorts. Just before the start, I recognised a runner in Wits kit, Dave Gurney. Not only was he properly attired for running, he sported those amazing Tiger (Asics) Cubs that cost about two Rand at the time. The soles were half the thickness of contemporary *Havaianas* and only good runners wore them. Gurney had already completed four Comrades Marathons at an average time of 10 hours. We were in luck as we would be piloted home by a highly experienced Comrades runner who, instantly, had become an absolute legend in our eyes.

Gurney was one of the most sociable and likeable characters on Wits campus. Although he was many years my senior, he had never quite managed to graduate. His academic record was exemplary, but he always seemed to change faculties and start a new degree when he was about 85% though his current degree. So he knew almost everyone on campus, academic staff included, plus a lot about many different subjects. He was clearly indulged by his parents, as there did not appear to be any urgency about Gurney joining the workforce as long as he was making academic progress.

The Wits Cross Country and Marathon Club was one of his many active memberships, from Archery to the Zoological Society, and that morning he added us to his list of projects. Once he got wind of our objective, he took us under his wing and assured us that he had the experience to judge marathon pace such that we could finish within the five-hour cut-off using our energy optimally.

Our foursome had mysteriously infused the Volvo driver with enough doubt to stop and ask us whether we were the race leaders. I confidently believed that we must have looked good. Unfortunately, we were not feeling too great.

Beyond the 25km mark there was an out and back loop where we suddenly saw the front-runners coming back at us. Up to this point, Vern was meeting us about every 3km to provide us with drinks and she enquired of one of the returning runners how far the turnaround point was.

Told it was just a couple of kilometres further on, she parked in a shady spot to wait for us. As it happened, the couple of kilometres turned out to be five. And five more back to the car. In a state of rising dehydration, we experienced the marathon phenomenon of hitting the wall at 32km and staggered out of the loop at 35km begging for a drink. We were a spent force.

Actually we were no force at all. We stopped for a rest and some overdue refreshments. Tragically, our enthusiasm had deserted us. Being the youngest, I was the first to volunteer to run on. The marathon significance was not lost on me. Surely my life would be so much more meaningful and that much richer if I could complete just one marathon?

Eventually I limped home in 4:25.51 in 392nd position. Mallinson was the first runner to miss the five-hour cut off in 433rd position. Gurney timed it brilliantly, finishing in 4:51.31 in 428th position, with only another four runners behind him making the five-hour limit. Morris didn't make it home, encountering a problem related to major surgery he had undergone years earlier.

Vern drove us home in stunned silence. We were soundly beaten in physical terms and left to assess our own personal scars as we headed north back to Johannesburg.

The following morning my feet were so swollen and so sore I could barely fasten the laces of my office shoes. When Mallinson and Morris arrived at the audit, no one mentioned the Comrades Marathon and no further training stats were logged. We tacitly agreed the Comrades was best left to those with the ability to go the distance.

So wounded was I by this failure that years would pass before I again contemplated making the journey between Durban and Pietermaritzburg on foot.

4

Growing up

The South African Irish regiment needed volunteers. Any volunteers. They were going to war against the Italian occupiers of East Africa and did not have a full complement of infantrymen.

Which comes to explain how the SA Irish ended up with the distinctly un-Gaelic Aristide Charly Robert Lenferna de la Motte. My father was born in Mauritius in March 1918 and received a classical education both at home and at the Royal College in Curepipe. This explains his knowledge of Shakespeare and Rousseau, ancient Greek history, and a family that played the violin, flute, clarinet and piano. He was also fully bilingual, benefiting from the British education system, and yet indelibly French. A healthy mind occupied a healthy body; he was also school champion over the half-mile and mile.

In 1939 my father sailed out of Port Louis, aged 21, heading for France via South Africa. Economic prospects on Mauritius were not as rosy as they were 149 years earlier when his great-grandfather arrived at the island on the vessel *Le Dauphne*, to help transform Mauritius into the seat of government of all French possessions east of the Cape of Good Hope. By the time my father departed, the family wealth of earlier generations had been dissipated and the island's utter reliance on the sugar crop was a concern.

His father had died but his mother Eva remained on Mauritius with three children when my father set sail for greener pastures. Shortly after his arrival in South Africa, war broke out in Europe. My father hated the thought of large parts of the world being subjected to a jack-booted dictatorship and willingly volunteered. He was assigned to the South African Irish Regiment, incorporated into the Fifth South African Brigade and the British Eighth Army. His enlistment photographs confirm that he was the only soldier in the regiment who knew how to wear a beret. He resembled a colonial Clark Gable with jet-black hair and a black, pencilled moustache, and instantly acquired the nickname of *Frenchy*.

The regiment sailed from Durban in July 1940 and disembarked in Kilindini, Kenya, to sweep the Italians out of Southern Abyssinia by February 1941. My father and his comrades were then moved to Egypt in May 1941 to prepare for the invasion of Libya and the relief of Tobruk.

Unfortunately for the South African Irish, German General Erwin Rommel had other ideas. In November, shortly after the Allies marched westwards into Libya, Rommel's Panzer tanks countered by spearing east into Egypt. The armoured assault took the SA Irish and other regiments by surprise and the Fifth Brigade suffered a smashing defeat at Sidi Rezegh on 23 November.

The SA Irish were at the forefront of the fighting and were decimated. Only 140 men of all ranks survived to try to make their way back to British lines; the others were killed or captured. My father was one of the lucky ones and I recall the story he told me about being trapped behind the German line. Technically they were all prisoners of war but, come nightfall, his group had not been rounded up by the Afrika Korps, so they headed south into the desert and lay low until the following dawn. My father managed to slip Rommel's noose and eventually reconnected with the decimated South African Brigade, together with the New Zealand forces at Mersa Matruh.

My father was lucky. Most of his fellow troopers were rounded up as POWs and shipped across the Mediterranean, bound for prison camps in Italy. En route their ship was torpedoed by an unwitting British submarine and so many more drowned.

In February 1942 the SA Irish ceased to exist as an independent infantry regiment and the remnants were drafted into the South African Artillery. They went straight into action again at El Alamein where the

Eighth Army stood grimly between Rommel and the Suez Canal. On the night of 23 October 1942 they were part of the massive artillery barrage directed at Rommel. After 10 days and nights of ferocious pounding by the Allies under the command of General Bernard Montgomery, they smashed the German line at El Alamein and then drove Rommel from Cyrenaica and Tripolitania by early February 1943. By May 1943 the campaign was over and the Allies dominated the Mediterranean. The battles of El Alamein and Stalingrad subsequently proved to be the watershed of the war against Germany.

My father never spoke much about the war. He earned his sergeant's stripes and received four war medals and the Eighth Army Clasp. His younger brother, Philippe, was a major in the British Army in Malaysia while his youngest brother, Serge, served with the British Navy.

My mother's father was also well acquainted with the rumble of artillery. He volunteered for service during World War I and fought in France at the Battle of Delville Wood. In the early hours of 14 July 1916 the First South African Brigade that attacked Longueval and Delville Wood numbered 121 officers and 3,032 other ranks. Six days later, Colonel Edward Thackery marched out with two wounded officers and 140 other ranks. The shock and injuries my *oupa* (grandfather) suffered during the First World War disqualified him from active service during the Second World War.

He served the gold mining industry in South Africa for more than 50 years after joining the Rose Deep Gold Mine in 1908. In 1960, the golden jubilee of the Union of South Africa, the Chamber of Mines presented him with a gold medallion for his long service and contribution to the industry, particularly in occupational health and safety in the deep mine shafts, where he served as a member of the proto teams that rescued miners trapped underground.

My oupa and ouma spoke English at home and they were keen supporters of General Jan Smuts. Smuts was a Cambridge-educated, moderate visionary who, over time, transformed from Boer War guerrilla leader to become an ally of Britain in World War II.

He declined to associate himself with the Afrikaner nationalism movement after the war that propelled DF Malan and his fellow pro-

Nazi colleagues to victory in South Africa's 1948 general election. My grandparents referred to the Nats as being *verkramp*, or insular and narrow-minded. Malan's election win also facilitated the foundation of the Broederbond, an Afrikaans self-help organisation, which became a sinister force in South Africa when secrecy was combined with power. It aimed at ensuring Afrikaner dominance in all walks of South African life and subsequently succeeded.

When my French Mauritian father started courting the beautiful young Yvonne Liebenberg in the year following his return from war service, he connected easily enough with his future wife's family. There was a considerable intellectual alignment and both my father and his prospective father-in-law had experienced and survived the horrors of war. Yet both were fundamentally gentle individuals and non-aggressors, notwithstanding their love of sport and physical endeavours.

My mother, who attended Johannesburg's first Afrikaans high school, Helpmekaar, fell for the good-looking Mauritian and they married in May 1950. I emerged into the world on 28 February 1954, the second of five children.

I grew up in a house adjacent to the Rose Deep gold mine, north of the railway line between Johannesburg and Germiston. We lived on the corner of Richdale and Sunflower Roads; the former a dirt track that provided unlimited opportunity to do rear-wheel skids on bikes or play in the puddles left by summer thunderstorms, the latter a sealed road easily marked for use as cricket pitch, tennis court, hop-scotch or model aircraft runway.

My dad taught me to fly a model aircraft with a fuel engine, which rotated around us on a control line, as well as how to collect stamps, play chess, appreciate foods like garlic, stuffed aubergines and olive oil, and drink tea, eggnog and wine.

My schooling started by accident at the age of five. My mom was doing most of the administrative work for my father's business, Les Parfums Incorporated (Pty) Ltd – representing Carven, Weil, Jean Patou and Nina Ricci among others – as he became more and more involved in South African politics with the official opposition at the time, the United Party. In addition, she had her hands full keeping an eye on my two-year-old sister Michele, and winning the ladies singles tennis championship three years in a row at our local tennis club. Midway through 1959 she asked the nuns at St Joseph's Dominican Convent in Fishers Hill, where my elder sister Yvonne was a student, if I could attend Grade 1 to prepare for the regular intake the following January.

When the 1960 school year started, the nuns decided to let me continue into Grade 2. It transpired that I was coping with the schooling and had a similar physique to the other Grade 2 kids, so I ended up a year ahead of schedule in my education. I was the youngest in my year five class when I transferred to Christian Brothers College, Boksburg, in 1963. Getting there was more complicated. Instead of a quick car trip, I had to take a bus to Germiston Station, catch a train to Boksburg East, and walk along East Street to the grounds of CBC on Konig Road, all at the age of nine.

The following year was my first exposure to the 'Christian' Brothers. Our class teacher was Brother Doyle who was very odd and very old. Brother Doyle loved to use the cane. We were obliged to lie horizontally on his desk and pull our shorts or trousers tight across our buttocks to ensure the maximum effect of his caning, for minor spelling mistakes or arithmetical errors or scuffed shoes, or whatever his whim might have been. We used to talk about his oddness amongst ourselves, although as far as I am aware no boy was ever sexually abused. My mother asked me this very question in all seriousness 30 years later.

School sports at CBC provided me with my first introduction to the world of track and field. This experience was the equivalent of the Olympic Games in my little world. The college had four factions or houses and I belonged to Albion. We ran in white shorts and white singlets with a badge of the rose of England stitched onto the front of our singlets. School sports involved a field sports day followed by the real track championships on cinders under the floodlights of Prince George's Park in Boksburg.

After two years at CBC, I was old enough to compete in two field events and two track events in the under-12 category being the entire offering available to my age group. I won the high jump, placed second in both the long jump and 220-yard sprint, and managed a fourth place in the 100-yard sprint. Although I was never destined to win a sprint title with my slow twitch muscle fibre, my endurance ability surfaced with a strong showing in the junior cross country championships against much older boys.

In the mid-1960s, my father contested his first political election in challenging a Nationalist, Herman Immelman, in the Germiston Council elections. Unsurprisingly in such a conservative, predominantly Afrikaner working-class electorate, he lost to Meneer (Mr) Immelman. I cannot help but grimace mentally when one of the grandest athletics venues in Africa was built in Germiston a decade later and named after this die-hard disciple of apartheid. I doubt Herman Immelman had ever run a lap of any athletics track and it was irrelevant to him and his National Party cronies that Germiston Callies Harriers stalwarts Fred Morrison and Mavis Hutchinson were among those who assisted my father contest many elections in opposition to the Nats. Pleasingly, the ANC government renamed the stadium the Germiston Stadium and it is currently the training home of the South African football team Bafana Bafana, who would never have been permitted to use the facilities under the rule of the apartheid government.

Puberty arrived along with a beautiful new teacher, Miss Cohen. What a happy coincidence. Instantly, we all became inordinately clumsy, dropping pencils and erasers so that we could crawl around on the floor and try to peek up her dress. She had obviously dealt with testosterone-charged youths before because she coolly kept her legs forever crossed. She also declined to cane us and, for a year, every boy in the class was in love with her.

While my passion for Miss Cohen remained undiminished, I cannot say the same for attending CBC. I was developing a jaundiced view about Catholicism, celibacy and mandatory weekly mass attendance, and I wished to attend my local co-ed high school along with most of the other teenagers in the neighbourhood.

In 1968, I transferred to Dawnview High for my final three years of schooling. I threw myself into sport and took on a weekend job to help the cash flow. With five children now in our household and my father still devoting most of his energies to challenging the despised Nationalist government, there was no pocket money allowance in our household. If you wanted pocket money for anything above schooling and sporting activities, you had to work for it. And so I spent many weekends pulling soft-serve ice creams at the local Dairy Den owned by our neighbour, Tony Liberatore.

Academically I cruised along, comfortably positioned in the university stream and doing enough to stay out of trouble. Where I excelled was in the 800m on the track. I was unbeaten over two laps in my final two years at school and, in my matric year, won the inter-high 800m against eight other white schools. I wasn't ready to step up to the one mile, though. A Dawnview runner who had gone to study and compete in the US on an athletics scholarship held the school record of 4.45. The general consensus was that he had been a good guy, albeit a little unorthodox. So it was that Johnny Halberstadt went on to clock a sub-four-minute mile and achieve great things in many walks of life. His subsequent athletic performances confirmed his status as South Africa's most versatile runner, ever.

I finished the year as a school prefect, achieving colours in athletics, hockey and tennis, and won the Track Champion of the Year. I decided I wanted to go to university to study commerce with the ultimate goal of becoming a chartered accountant, but would first have to deal with the great conundrum for male school leavers of the time, compulsory military service. Serving the racist government of the day in uniform was a prospect which repulsed me. I was 16 years old, emotionally immature, bereft of life experience and a recently lapsed Catholic. So what did I do?

I grew my hair.

Call back the past 1

Super-patriots or traitors? While my father was in North Africa fighting the Germans on behalf of his new country, thousands of Afrikaners were dynamiting post offices and sabotaging electricity and telegraph lines in South Africa on behalf of the Nazis.

As Hitler imposed National Socialism on Germany, a broad section of Afrikanerdom, from the intellectuals to the working classes, was promoting a similar ideology called Christian Nationalism.

Dutch Reformed Church minister turned politician Daniel Francois Malan was the driving force behind the creation of Christian Nationalism. When Barry Herzog and Jan Smuts formed a political alliance under the banner of the United Party in 1934, Malan and 19 other hardline Afrikaner Nationalists defected to form the Purified National Party.

In 1937 Malan's Purified National Party, the South African Fascists, and the Blackshirts agreed to form an opposition coalition which, two years later, campaigned unsuccessfully to oppose South Africa's entry into World War II on the side of Great Britain.

Malan allied himself closely with a populist Afrikaner movement called the *Ossewabrandwag* (Oxwagon sentinels) which at its peak, in 1939, had an estimated 300,000 members. The *Ossewabrandwag*, or OB, had close ties to the Nationalists. For example, Paul Sauer and Frans Erasmus were OB generals and the anti-Semitic Eric Louw was a firebrand OB mouthpiece. All were to become cabinet members after Malan rose to power in 1948, while CR Swart, a member of the OB Supreme Council, later became South Africa's State President.

The OB's leadership radicalised the organisation after the outbreak of war and formed an elite cadre called the *Stormjaers* which set about undermining the South African war effort while tens of thousands of troops, including my father, were risking their lives for democracy and freedom.

OB policy had an ominous Nazi whiff to it. Afrikaans would be the only official language. Anti-Communism and anti-Semitism were important principles of policy. The emphasis was racial purity and members were exhorted to "think with your blood."

Malan's Nationalists and the OB worked closely to oppose the country's involvement in the war. When South African boxer-turned-Nazi secret agent Robey Leibbrandt was captured and sentenced to death, Malan's Nationalists agitated until the sentence was commuted to life imprisonment. Leibbrandt, who once fought heavyweight champion Max Schmeling in Hamburg, was a fanatical Nazi who, after being landed in Namaqualand in 1941, met the OB leaders but failed to impress them with his call for all-out rebellion against the Smuts government.

The OB general for Port Elizabeth was not so reticent. He welcomed the Nazis as allies in the fight to rid South Africa of what he perceived as English dominance. He was such a thorn in the government's side that Smuts ordered his arrest under emergency regulations in September 1942. Future Prime Minister and President Balthazar Johannes Vorster went on hunger strike after two months and was transferred to Koffiefontein internment camp in the western Orange Free State. Another internee was Hendrik van den Bergh, who went on to head the notorious Bureau of State Security (BOSS) during apartheid's most repressive years.

These were men who supported, whether overtly or tacitly, the very enemy which was doing its utmost to kill my father and his comrades in their fight against fascism and oppression. Yet, three years after my father was demobbed, Daniel Malan's Nationalists won power from Smuts' United Party by five seats.

The Nationalists immediately imposed on South Africa the system of apartheid. Segregation was effectively already in place; Malan's government institutionalised it in law. Inhabitants of South Africa were classified into four racial groups: white, native, coloured and Asian. The government immediately began disenfranchising those who were not classified as whites. Residential areas were divided along racial lines, sometimes by forced removal; sex and marriage between different races was prohibited; and public transport, facilities, health, education, courts and prisons, all public services, sports buildings and organisations, and beaches were segregated.

My father was livid at the ascent to power of those who he considered traitors during the war and for the neo-Nazi Christian Nationalism they imposed on South Africa. He determined to fight them, but legally, as an opposition politician.

Others were to fight them in any way they could. The African National Congress, founded in 1912 as the South African Native National Congress, had fallen into obscurity in the 1930s, but the growing power of Malan's Nationalist Party convinced young black intellectuals like Nelson Mandela, Walter Sisulu and Oliver Tambo to form the ANC Youth League in 1943 to mobilise the population against racial discrimination. Following Malan's 1948 election victory and the imposition of apartheid, the ANC Youth League took charge of the organisation and the following year announced a programme of action advocating boycotts, strikes and civil disobedience.

In 1952, Mandela travelled the country to promote the Defiance Campaign against unjust laws, aiming to start mass civil disobedience first with volunteers and then the ANC's 100,000 members. The press referred to him as the Black Pimpernel because of the disguises he used to elude the security police. He was eventually arrested, given a suspended six-month sentence and prohibited from attending gatherings.

After the Sharpville massacre in 1960, when police killed 69 and wounded 180 unarmed black protesters, Mandela convinced the ANC to form a military wing, *Umkhonto we Sizwe* or Spear of the Nation, which launched a campaign of sabotage against the government. As head of the new paramilitary organisation, Mandela was smuggled out of South Africa in 1962 for eight weeks of training in Addis Ababa, Ethiopia. He was arrested shortly after returning and received a five-year hard-labour sentence for his actions. Two years later, the Nationalist government decided to deal with him for once and for all and sentenced him to life for treason and sabotage in the infamous Rivonia Trial.

5

Apartheid and sport

On a Wednesday night in November 1985, Thulani Sibisi was waiting for his girlfriend to pick him up after an end-of-year dinner for Rand Athletic Club (RAC) committee members at a venue in the plush residential suburb of Rosebank in Johannesburg. He never got to climb into her car.

Instead, he was arrested by plainclothes policemen for allegedly breaching pass laws. Since 1952, blacks were required to carry an internal passport, known as a passbook or *dompas*, which set out conditions for blacks to remain in white areas. No Rosebank resident had complained or called the police. The cops simply spotted him and nabbed him.

Sibisi was one of RAC's foremost runners and served on the club's executive committee. He also acted as the club's liaison officer, on behalf of its black runners, to help white committee members better understand their needs. He was a highly respected individual and sportsman, yet was detained and taken to the Norwood police station, where he was held overnight and allegedly assaulted by the police.

He was released the next morning after pass law infringement charges were withdrawn. When I heard the news I was livid. The incident represented everything I detested about the Nationalists' abuse of human dignity. I phoned Mark Etheridge, sports writer with *The Star* newspaper in Johannesburg, to tip him off so that the public would learn of Sibisi's arrest and treatment.

Four months earlier, when Sibisi had finished second to me in the 50km JSE Marathon, the Nationalist government published a colour photograph of us embracing at the finish, on the front of one of their propaganda publications, *SA Digest*. Supposedly, this was to show racial harmony in South Africa, with blacks happily living under apartheid.

Only days before Sibisi's arrest, I had attended a Sportswriters' Awards Dinner where the guest speaker was the Australian Wallabies rugby coach Alan Jones. A speechwriter for former Australian Prime Minister Malcolm Fraser, Jones had diversified into radio, and he had just started hosting Sydney's most popular breakfast show on station 2UE. He was one of the few international sports personalities prepared to visit South Africa during apartheid's darkest days to encourage political reform. Not that the Nationalist government would listen. Repression, not reform, was its agenda.

Etheridge's story quoted Sibisi, RAC secretary Vreni Welch, champion runner Mark Plaatjes and me. White liberals were predictably outraged over what had happened in the 'old money' suburb, but blacks had more to be concerned about than this example of petty apartheid. On 21 November 1985 in the black township of Mamelodi near Pretoria, police had fired on a crowd, killing 13 people and injuring 80.

Plaatjes raised the added complication of the pressure he faced from the anti-apartheid South African Council On Sport, which accused him of being a puppet of the white regime by participating in white-controlled and managed races. He would rebuff their Uncle Tom claims by arguing that running was free of racial prejudice, but Sibisi's arrest undermined his stance and hastened his departure to the US.

Not that he was entirely welcome there. The marriage of convenience between politics and hypocrisy is a worldwide phenomenon, not restricted to 1980s South Africa. In early April 1985, Plaatjes had slipped out of South Africa with the intention of running in one of the world's oldest and most famous marathons, the Boston Marathon. None of us were aware of Mark's clandestine trip because any advance publicity would have derailed his prospects of starting, even in the land of the free and the home of the brave.

Home of the lawyer, too. When Englishman Geoff Smith learned he would have to defend his title against Plaatjes, he hired counsel to present an argument against the South African champion's participation. Smith's case revolved around the global sports boycott of South Africa and the potential knock-on effect this could have on his own career. He was concerned that if he and others competed against Plaatjes, they might themselves face suspension.

That this measure was aimed at preventing rebel team tours of South Africa and not individuals – British golfers, boxers and tennis players were happily competing against South Africans throughout this period – was of no concern to Smith. Despite the monumental difficulties Plaatjes faced in trying to build a first-class career as a second-class citizen, Smith had him scratched from the start list and went on to defend his title in 2:14.05. Three weeks later, Plaatjes won the South African national title at Port Elizabeth in a record 2:08.58.

One day, I hope Smith's grandchildren will ask him to explain how he and others prevented this victim of apartheid from running the Boston Marathon in 1985. Speculation at the time was that a major sponsorship deal with a shoe company was up for renewal and a second Boston win would have a material impact on the negotiations. Commerce ahead of compassion?

The unrelenting battering from posturing liberals and racist conservatives finally caused Plaatjes to flee the country of his birth. He travelled to Chicago in January 1988, applied for asylum and was in limbo for nearly five years before gaining citizenship. Within a few months of this milestone he qualified to represent his new country at the 1993 world championships in Stuttgart. He had waited 12 years to run in a major championship and was not about to waste the opportunity.

Sixth after 28km, he scythed through the field to capture second place with 8km to go, still 90 seconds adrift of leader Lucketz Swartbooi of Namibia. He had assumed the grey cloud of his long struggle to compete internationally would hold a silver lining but Swartbooi slowed dramatically and Plaatjes overtook him in the final kilometre to become the first American to win the title, clocking 2:13.57. No longer would he have to sneak into events or fight for starts. When he ran his next marathon, in South Korea the following March, he was paid $100,000 to show up and treated like a celebrity.

Sadly, Plaatjes represented generations of runners who received a double dose of punishment: discriminated against inside South Africa because their skin was not white; disqualified from competing outside South Africa because of their nationality. They were trapped in a lose-lose situation.

In April 1968 Paul Nash equalled the 100m world record of 10 seconds at Krugersdorp, the first of four occasions he achieved the feat. In May he won the national title at Potchefstroom in 10.2 seconds from an all-white field. A week later, Joseph Leserwane won an all-black race on a slow earth track at the nearby Libanon mine in 10.3 seconds. South Africa's sprint prospects were looking good in both the individual dash and the one-lap relay at the upcoming Mexico City Olympics. The country also had a potential world beater in Humphrey Khosi, who had clocked an exceptional 1:47.9 for the 800m at altitude. Both Leserwane and Khosi worked on gold mines, while Nash was a product of the elite Michaelhouse School in Natal.

Unfortunately, the trio's involvement with the Games was limited to reading about the competition in a newspaper. South Africa had been expelled from the Olympic movement. Nash and Leserwane had to deal with the frustration of never racing Mexico City gold medallist Jim Hynes (9.95 seconds) and Khosi's season-best indicated he would have made the final of the 800m, eventually won by Australian Ralph Doubell in 1:44.3.

Interestingly enough, black American athletes Tommie Smith and John Carlos used the 200m medal ceremony to stage their famous silent protest against racial discrimination. They stood with their heads bowed and a black-gloved fist raised in a black power salute as the American national anthem played during the ceremony for Smith's victory. Within hours, the International Olympic Committee condemned their actions. They were expelled from the Olympic Village and sent back to the US.

"It is very discouraging to be in a team with white athletes," explained Smith. "On the track you are Tommie Smith, the fastest man in the world, but once you are in the dressing room you are nothing more than a dirty

Negro." He suggested black Americans in future refuse to be "utilised as performing animals in the Games."

Runner-up, Peter Norman of Australia supported them by wearing a human rights badge on his tracksuit. Indeed, it was Norman who suggested the US duo share the pair of gloves brought to the stadium by Smith for their clenched-fist salute, which is why the famous photograph shows the winner raising his right hand, bronze medallist Carlos his left. Australian Olympic authorities reprimanded Norman and shunned him; he was not picked for the 1972 Munich Olympics despite running five qualifying times, and 32 years later was not invited to the 2000 Sydney Games by the Australian Olympic Committee.

South Africa's Olympic involvement had a 32-year hiatus between Rome in 1960 and Barcelona in 1992 because of apartheid. Growing up without television kept us ignorant, as the Nationalists had hoped. We had no idea of the extraordinary debut of the superhuman Ethiopian, Abebe Bikila, in Rome. Running barefoot, he won the marathon over the cobblestones in a record 2:15.16. He was the first black African athlete to win an Olympic medal and, at Tokyo four years later, he would become the first person to win the Olympic marathon twice, just six weeks after having his appendix removed. His prowess was not something we were encouraged to know about.

We never saw black runners. In fact, we never saw black kids anywhere near our schools and had no idea where they lived and whether they attended school. School attendance was compulsory for all whites, whereas blacks were either relegated to the city-fringe townships, which provided a pool of labour, or to a rural existence in demarcated homelands with limited prospects of any formal education. The Nationalist government had planned it that way. When Bikila, this time wearing shoes and socks, decimated the field in Tokyo in a world-best 2:12.14, Nelson Mandela was starting his term of imprisonment on Robben Island. In the absence of television, I would not have recognised either man.

There was more political turmoil in sport in 1968, following England's selection of Basil D'Oliveira in its cricket team to tour South Africa. Born in Cape Town, D'Oliveira had Portuguese-Indian heritage and was classified as a 'coloured'. He was therefore barred from domestic first-class cricket and moved to England in 1960, eventually gaining selection for the Test team and being named as one of the five Wisden cricketers of the year for 1967.

Prime Minister BJ Vorster – the leading example of those graduates-made-good of the wartime Koffiefontein internment camp who my father so despised – made it clear the Marylebone Cricket Club which controlled English cricket would not be permitted to enter the country with a player whose skin was not lily-white. He raged: "We are not prepared to receive a team thrust upon us by people whose interests are not in the game but to gain certain political objectives which they do not even attempt to hide. The MCC team is not the team of the MCC but of the anti-apartheid movement."

The tour was called off and the incident culminated in a ban on all international sporting ties with South Africa that would last until the early 1990s. But there would be even more to follow as cultural bans, trade embargoes and travel restrictions were applied to South Africa. It was the work of the evil communists, we were assured by the Nationalist government and its very effective propaganda media machine, the South African Broadcasting Corporation.

In 1974, South African track and field officials of the white-controlled South African Amateur Athletics Union made the first move towards the racial integration of the sport. For the first time, two national championships were held; one for whites and the other an open meet in which anyone, irrespective of race or nationality, was welcome. In the latter championship, a titanic 5,000m contest emerged between whites-only champion Ewald Bonzet and Titus Mamabolo, with the latter victorious in 14.09. Bonzet emerged from the confrontation with no credit at all: he struggled to deal with losing to a black man and was disqualified for trying to block Mamabolo from overtaking him three times during a vigorous final lap.

Mamabolo thus earned his place in South African history by becoming the first black athlete to win a South African athletics title. Richard Mayer, in *Three Men named Matthews,* wrote: "With black athletes given their first opportunity to compete against their white countrymen at an open South African championships, the battle for track supremacy between

Bonzet and Mamabolo unavoidably echoed the stirrings of the struggle for the eradication of apartheid from sport and, more broadly, for black political emancipation."

International sport was non-existent. Apart from Olympic sports, South Africa had been booted from cricket, football and Davis Cup tennis. The Afrikaners favoured rugby union and managed to sneak a few rebel tours into South Africa in the 1970s. They managed a few outward tours too, although at huge disruption to the hosts. Those in individual sports like tennis, golf, boxing, motor racing and surfing avoided the boycott and participated in the major events but, in the absence of television, South Africans had to pay at the turnstiles for their fill of the mass-appeal sports: the Currie Cup competitions in cricket and rugby union, and the two main football competitions, segregated on racial lines.

Although my interest in local athletics was passive because of my professional career priorities, I read in early 1977 that the International Amateur Athletics Federation had precluded international athletes from competing in South Africa. The Comrades Marathon, whose victory roll in the 1960s and 1970s had included Englishmen Bernard Gomersall and Mick Orton, would remain a closed domestic affair until 1993, after sports sanctions had been lifted.

Durban Athletics Club opened its membership to athletes of all races in 1977, a breakthrough that paved the way for all athletes to compete. A Durban newspaper editorial reported: "It was a sad couple of years ago that a great marathon dedicated to comradeship was nearly torpedoed by the bitter efforts of some to keep it an all-white affair."

The local running scene offered a glimmer of hope on a very bleak socio-political horizon for blacks. The 1977 Comrades field included 65 non-white athletes including Vincent Rakabaele, a 1976 Comrades gold medallist, plus 20 so-called coloured athletes the Nationalists could not neatly categorise into an apartheid box. Alan Robb won the uphill race in 5:47 and Rakabaele finished fourth for his second gold medal, in 6:03. The Comrades Marathon was destined to exemplify the power of sport over politics as runners of all colours and backgrounds entered an event that would very soon receive saturation media coverage. The Comrades

Marathon united all South Africans on that one very special day of the year.

The television coverage of Comrades had grown from an amateurish 15-minute documentary in 1976 to live coverage by 1983, but South Africans still had very little idea of the scope and spectacle of the Olympic Games. The LA Olympics were irrelevant to South Africans other than the most fervent of sports fanatics because of the sanctions that denied the country a team, and the corresponding television black-out. The only footage to reach our screens comprised brief clips classified as world news. So, apart from a quick snippet of the contest between Zola Budd and Mary Decker, track and field viewing was restricted to those few who had relatives in Great Britain prepared to tape the Games on VHS video cassettes and post them for later viewing. This is how a handful of the hard-core running community learned that Rakabaele had represented Lesotho in the marathon, finishing a disappointing 61st.

Sports scientists were more interested in another aspect of the 1984 Games, the advances in the then-legal practice of blood doping and its widespread application by the host nation. Literature describes blood doping as the practice of boosting the number of red cells in the bloodstream, carrying oxygen from the lungs to the muscles, in order to enhance an athlete's aerobic capacity and endurance. Blood dopers would have between 450ml and 1.8 litres of blood withdrawn several weeks before competition. The blood is immediately centrifuged separating the plasma and corpuscular elements, or red blood cells. The plasma elements are immediately re-infused to in the doper while the red blood cells are re-infused in the days before the endurance event, boosting the red blood cell count.

Sporting literature suggests blood doping probably started in the 1970s but was not outlawed until 1986. The first suspected case of blood doping related to Lasse Viren, the Flying Finn, who won very little apart from his 5,000–10,000m doubles at the 1972 Munich and 1976 Montreal Olympics. After Moscow in 1980, compatriot Kaarlo Maaninka admitted to being transfused with one litre of blood before winning medals in the 5,000m and 10,000m events.

US cyclist Pat McDonough admitted to blood doping at the 1984 Olympics. It was subsequently revealed a third of the US cycling team received blood transfusions before the Games, at which they won nine medals, their first cycling medal success since 1912. The process clearly worked for endurance athletes.

Although the IOC banned blood doping in 1986, no test existed for it and seasoned dopers continued to rewrite the record books for many years. Cycling was notorious for using blood doping. Bjarne Riis, the 1996 Tour de France winner, admitted to using the technique that boosted his haematocrit count (the volume percentage of red blood cells in the blood) as high as 64%. Normal adults have a haematocrit of 40% to 45% of blood volume and the International Cycling Union set a limit of 50% for its super-fit superstars. In his tell-all book, *The Secret Race*, former professional cyclist Tyler Hamilton confirmed blood doping provided him with an instant boost of 3% in power – and it was undetectable if done correctly. By inference, blood doping could equate to an improvement of up to 10 minutes over the Comrades distance and, until very recently, would have been virtually undetectable. In 1985, my haematocrit count was 46% when I was living and training at altitude in Johannesburg. Living at sea level in Perth, my haematocrit count ranged between 38% and 42% during my actively competitive years.

Because of South Africa's topography, comprising a high interior plateau at an altitude of about 1,800m where the majority of the population lives, the accepted practice was live and train high, race low. This was thought to provide competitors from the inland Transvaal and Free State an advantage in that they built up a higher red-cell concentration at altitude, like well-acclimatised mountaineers. It was popularly considered to be legal blood doping to make them near unbeatable.

Competitors from the coastal cities did not necessarily agree. Zithulele Sinqe was born in Mthatha in the Eastern Cape, beneath the mountain range that separates the lowlands from the dry, often chilly inland plateau, and lived near the port of East London. No excess red cells to be found in his blood vessels. He clocked a scorching 62.17 in his debut half marathon in East London in 1982 and lowered that to 60.11 in an epic duel with Matthews Temane in 1987. Temane got the judge's nod but both were credited with the same time, a significant improvement on Mike Musyoki's world best of 60.43.

Sinqe, killed in a car accident in 2011, was an astonishing talent who would have been a world beater had he been able to compete against the best, rather than read about them in *SA Runner* magazine. He ran a personal best 2:08.04 marathon to win the national championship in 1986, a feat for which he was named South African Sportsman of the Year.

Sinqe collected his award from State President PW Botha, which earned him flak from fellow Xhosas in the Eastern Cape, who said he should not have shaken the hand of the Nationalist hard-liner and warmonger. His wonderfully wry retort was:

"Why not? I am one of the first black men that PW Botha has had to shake hands with."

6

Soldier of apartheid

During my matric year, South African Defence Force (SADF) personnel visited all white schools to screen boys like me who were on the verge of being conscripted for nine months of military service, followed by annual army camps. The SADF was an extension of the Nationalist government and as such, provided additional firepower to maintain their policy of apartheid or separate development. The military assisted in suppressing black South Africans and their aspirations both within South Africa's borders and in neighbouring countries. To serve in such a military was, in my personal universe, a totally abhorrent and a dismal prospect.

When I was interviewed by the SADF, I thought I would make the most of my conscription and requested I be drafted into the parachute battalion. I believed I would at least keep really fit during nine months of mindless soldiering, learn to parachute and enjoy some extreme adventure. I had no interest in rifle shooting or pursuing any sort of warfare. Yet when my friends received their military call-up papers, I was ignored. I called the SADF to establish my destiny and was bluntly told I would not be called up for military service that year because I was too young; I had to turn 18 in the year of conscription.

I was advised to start full-time university studies and would be conscripted after a year into the Commando unit, to serve my conscription in annual instalments. The army would provide basic training for six weeks during the summer university holidays at the end of my first academic year, followed by annual army camps of 30 days for a minimum of 13 years. Thirteen years of that! To a 16-year-old, it felt like sitting on death row.

I had no intention of surrendering my good health and freedom to the Nationalist government for more than a decade, as a pretext for confronting the communist threat posed by Soviet and Cuban expansion in Africa – and coincidentally suppressing the aspirations of black South Africans. I decided to invest in a suitable professional qualification that would enable me to exit South Africa and live and work internationally.

After my first year of university, the time came for the enforced conversion from student to soldier. In January 1972 I was conscripted into the Danie Theron Combat School outside Kimberley in the Cape Province. My SADF identity number was 70314026K; this counted for more than my first name or surname so I learned it by heart pretty quickly. One positive aspect about the part-time commando regiment being assembled was that we were all full-time university students; the lowest common denominator was a respectable tertiary level.

Foolishly, most of the English-speaking university students, myself included, reported for duty with shoulder-length hair in defiance of military requirements. Most of the Afrikaans-speaking conscripts arrived with fresh crew cuts and polished shoes. On arrival in Kimberley, we were marched from the station to the military barbers who salivated at the opportunity of shaving our heads, commencing with a hot cross bun – St George's cross – across the crown. We exited from the barbers with bald, white skulls shining like polished light bulbs. Within a couple of days in the sun on the parade ground we would look like true *rooineks*, or red-necks, the Boer reference to the sun-burnt British soldiers who wore pith helmets on campaign in South Africa. The term is usually used as an insult, although not half as insulting as *soutpiel* or salt cock. This was a reference to ambivalent Englishmen living the life of Riley in South Africa without any commitment to the country. The Afrikaners regarded a *soutpiel* as having one foot in England and the other in South Africa, with his *piel* (or penis) dangling in the salty Atlantic Ocean beneath.

We were marched to the quartermaster's store and kitted out with military attire, .303 rifles and bedding. Groaning under the weight of a stuffed 30kg duffel bag, we were marched off to our platoon tent and allocated a bed and a steel trunk or *kas*. The order was given to change into our military kit, make our beds, and then fall in to platoon formation on the parade ground within 10 minutes. Very few of us knew how to make our own domestic beds, let alone a military bed squared off at the edges with turned down sheets and blankets all in perfect alignment for the length of our dormitory tent. As for the uniform, we instantly turned to the Afrikaans guys who knew in advance exactly what kit we needed to wear and how it was to be worn. We were already getting along much better since we had our haircuts and all looked the same.

It took our platoon leader and other permanent force soldiers a few days to knock the shit out of us and hammer us into subservience, just as they told us they would. We spent a couple of days being marched around the parade ground and being sent on random runs around distant trees on the horizon. The physical stuff was no hardship as far as I was concerned. Sleep deprivation was more difficult to deal with, as was the resentment of being there against my will and taking orders from these ignorant dolts.

On the first Sunday of our training we had to fall in for church parade. How we envied the Jewish guys in our tent, excused from church, whilst sniggering at the Christian torture we were about to endure. This also triggered a mindset to survive within the SADF; that of always trying to find a way out.

Come sermon time, we were all seated on the African dirt in the bush. After thanking God prodigiously for selecting us as the chosen ones, the Afrikaans preacher's sermon shifted to the evils of the devil, the Soviet invasion of Africa, communism and more particularly, swearing. Yes, he told us, this *fok* (fuck) word had no place in our Christian vocabulary and daily lives because every time we used this *fok* word we were acting as an agent of the devil and too many *foks* would make you an agent of the communists. At this point most of the English-speaking conscripts started looking at one another in disbelief, with laughter desperately restrained in our lungs. Before the sermon, none of us had heard that *fok* word so many times within the space of a few minutes, not even on our liberal university campuses. This was the standard of the moral leadership of the

South African military. These guys weren't just from Mars; they were from beyond the known universe.

After another week or two of mindless parade ground bashing, we were marched to the shooting range with our .303 rifles; relics from WWII. I guess the SADF had made one smart decision in not equipping our part-time Commando unit with weapons that were beyond our soldiering ability. The visit to the rifle range was, on face value, quite straightforward. Any prospective soldier in any army in history had to earn a minimum score at the rifle range to earn the status of rifleman. Throughout history a foot soldier with a rifle, or spear, or bow and arrow, is the lowest entry point for an army. Quite understandably a foot soldier ought to be able to fire a weapon at the enemy with a reasonable degree of accuracy. The timetable suggested our platoon would visit the rifle range in the morning and by lunchtime we would all have shot the required points to progress to our next level of training.

The Afrikaans recruits, including many who grew up on farms, never missed a target and qualified as riflemen in no time at all. On the other hand, we English-speaking conscripts were a different breed. Not only was there a dearth of marksmanship in our group, there was also an element of passive resistance, like consciously missing the entire target board. We fired round after round of ammunition at the stationary yet elusive targets, much to the chagrin of our instructors and platoon leaders. They simply could not believe that we could miss such an easy target every time. Passive resistance is empowering, and the last soldier to qualify as a rifleman in our platoon managed to stretch it out to the third day on the rifle range.

We also delighted in all that wasted ammunition, almost as much as the reassurance that they would not be taking us back to the rifle range because, in strict military terms, we were no good at all. South Africa would have been ill equipped if it had relied upon us as its first line of defence. We loved it. The SADF despised us.

A couple of weeks into our training we received another anti-communist pep talk from another SADF strategist. My father always told me that these full-time soldiers and officers who earned a living propping up the Nationalist government's apartheid regime would be unemployed in a free and open economy. Even the uncomplicated task of delivering the mail to suburban post boxes was an occupation reserved for whites at over-inflated wages.

The functionary's introductory remarks were poignant in that none of us really knew much about communism because all left-wing literature had been banned in South Africa, and we were also precluded from travelling to Eastern-bloc countries. We did not know what Nelson Mandela looked like. He was a prisoner sitting out his time on Robben Island. Every single image of him and all his writings and speeches were also banned. In reality it was virtually impossible to learn anything about communism in South Africa unless you went underground. So we had no option other than to listen to this SADF expert who assured us he knew all about communism. We waited with bated breath.

His talk went along identical lines to the fok sermon. He described how terrible it would be to live under a communist regime. As individuals we would have no rights, would be denied the right to own property, vote, freedom of religion, worship, education, and selection of vocation. Even worse, you would be told where to live and what work to do. In short, our civil liberties would disappear. He was super-confident that we could all see the pitfalls of communism and unite in our fight to combat the advancement of this evil society throughout Africa, just like in many other parts of the world. A few of the Afrikaans conscripts nodded heads in agreement and sighed their disbelief at such an evil threat.

When questions were invited at the end of his prep talk, I politely suggested that the awful life of a communist he had just described to us, devoid of all civil liberties, sounded identical to the way black South Africans were forced to live. What were the differences? His blood pressure rose in tandem with his predictable response.

"Hey, so you think you are bleddy smart, soldier. What's your name?"

I became a marked man and this realisation provided me with more than a gentle nudge to prioritise academic studies at Wits to secure those CA credentials, earning an exit ticket out of this nightmare. The alternative was to continue dealing with these SADF morons for more than a decade. As a white South African boy, I would have to deal with the consequences of being a conscriptee.

A few days later on the parade ground, there was an appeal for all those enrolled to attend the Christian College of Theology at Potchefstroom University to line up. By this time, I had become street smart and willing to test the system at any opportunity so I lined up with the Dutch Reformed ministers or *predikants* of the future. Being unsure of what it was we were lining up for, I had already prepared my excuse if there was no upside in this queue for me, along the lines of: "Sorry officer, I thought it was a call for students studying commerce; I don't understand Afrikaans too well."

When it was my turn to be questioned by the supervising officer, all he asked was my name and home destination. He wrote out a train ticket to Johannesburg and said it would depart that evening. It transpired the theology students were starting their university course two weeks earlier than Wits and I scored an express exit from my basic military training. My parents could not believe it when I called them from Johannesburg station early the next morning for a lift home. They initially worried that I had gone AWOL.

My second year at university was interrupted by my return to the SADF for my next conscription stint in the commando unit. My call-up papers arrived and I was destined to spend the 1972 midwinter university break as a private – the lowest of the low. I reported for duty and was trucked out to Johannesburg's main airport, Jan Smuts, now OR Tambo International. We were a totally disengaged company of English-speaking university students, predominantly anti-conscription, and our task was to guard and protect South Africa's most significant international and commercial airport. What a joke! Very few of us could even fire a rifle effectively and we had no training in anti-aircraft artillery (if Russia or Cuba attacked by air) and absolutely no training in covert operations if a guerrilla unit chose to sabotage the airport's infrastructure.

Even worse, we were sleeping in tents on the eastern side of the runway alongside the Atlas Aircraft factory. Anyone who has lived on the Highveld will attest to the bitterly cold winter nights at 1,694m above sea level. It dropped below freezing on our first night in the tents. The water in the fire buckets outside our tents froze solid and few of us slept very much at all. Our teeth were chattering.

The next morning, when we were in company formation on the parade ground waiting for the mindless instructions for the day, the commanding officer declared they needed volunteers for the kitchen. Very quickly a few of us filled the quota. We foresaw the prospect of a warm kitchen and no guns. We marched off the parade ground to be briefed in the kitchen about our new roles as kitchen hands, and were required to collect all our army kit from the tents and move into brick and mortar accommodation alongside the kitchen, where the officers and non-commissioned officers slept. We had hit jackpot, even if none of us could cook.

There were so many perks to this job we all took to it instantly. We were excused from all further military training and uniform inspections. No more guard duty in the middle of the night, no more marching around the parade ground and no more shooting practice at any rifle range. We merely had to get up a little earlier than the troops and keep everyone fed, army style. Nothing elaborate, just bland, tasteless food and warm drinks slopped up to the troops in a canteen tray called a *varkpan* or pig's tray. Our duties rotated from preparing the oatmeal porridge, boiling the urns of tea and coffee, manually peeling bags of potatoes with grossly oversized butchers' knives, mopping up the mess after the troops had finished and then doing the usual kitchen clean up. We were never in trouble for poor performance; the military cook who gave us our instructions had less culinary talent than his newly recruited kitchen hands.

Fortunately Russia, China and Cuba declined to attack Johannesburg airport during our military stint and we returned to our studies albeit in the sobering knowledge the SADF had increased conscription from nine months to one year, as well as 19 days of service annually for another five years. In retrospect, this increase in the size and manpower of the civilian army might explain why the SADF temporarily lost interest in the part-time Commando unit that had ensnared full-time university students like me. I didn't know it at the time but I would be spared a few call-ups for annual camps over the next few years.

With military service lurking in the background, I tried to keep track of what was happening in Southern Africa in a political sense. By the middle of 1974, control of northern Namibia was handed over to the SADF from the South African Police; and in 1975 the SADF invaded

Angola. To keep up with increased security and military demands, annual military camps for members of the Citizen Force were extended up to three months. This might have explained why, as an involuntary member of the Commando Force, I did not receive any military call-up in 1975 or 1976, the year the lid blew off the apartheid pressure cooker with the Soweto uprising.

With the townships in a state of revolution and concerns about border insurgents, the SADF eventually resorted to calling up commando soldiers like me for another military camp in January 1977. Desperate times call for desperate measures. I grudgingly reported for duty at the Drill Hall in Johannesburg to find out where I would be posted. Because it was summer, the thought of sleeping in tents at Johannesburg's international airport was far more appealing than our mid-winter ordeal a few years earlier. After a couple of hours, we were loaded into British Leyland Bedford trucks and escorted by higher ranks in Landrovers to the Modderfontein dynamite factory, about 30km north east of Johannesburg. This plant was clearly of strategic interest to the Nationalists and the economy. It manufactured all the dynamite for the mining of gold, South Africa's single biggest export. Denying the country the use of these explosives would be highly attractive to black activists aiming to sabotage South Africa's strategic infrastructure.

The only flaw in the strategic thinking of the government in sending troops to Modderfontein related to the competence of the troops themselves. By this stage, most of the university students I had met during my basic military training in Kimberley in January 1972 had either graduated or were about to graduate. Most had completed tertiary study and the collective enthusiasm for our military duty was inversely related to our years at university. It was at an all-time low. By late afternoon of our first day at camp, we had sorted out our tents, uniforms and other logistical issues before we had to fall into company formation and take our next set of orders.

I remember thinking it was not a bad location to be camping on the African Highveld in summer, as long as the dynamite factory did not explode. Apart from the factory, we were in rural surroundings, reasonably well wooded with abundant bird life. There were peacocks in every direction, reminding us of the extraordinary beauty of this country.

I thought of these same hills and the battles fought over them at the turn of the century between the Boers and the British Army. All that had changed was the enemy. No longer the British Army, it was now the evil Russians converting South Africa's black population to communism. As I stood to attention and shouldered arms with my antiquated .303 rifle, I focused on the absolute necessity of passing my final qualifying exam, or FQE, in a couple of months in order to exit South Africa on a one-way ticket at the end of 1977. I had a plan. I was determined. I wanted to take charge of my own destiny.

A sergeant knocked us into platoon and company formation until we were meticulously assembled to his satisfaction, at which point he invited the major to address us. He was articulate, he was a surgeon and he had come into the commando force in the same manner as we had. The chief difference was that he was older and his surgical skills were considered to be of such strategic value to the SADF that he was promoted to rank of major without any real military training. This was unusual, given that he was also Jewish.

Things were already looking better but there was more in store. He said he needed to train some medical corpsmen who could attend to the wounded and help with their evacuation. According to him, he would have to teach us everything he had learned in medical school in just two weeks. This camp would serve as a core part of this training and he was looking for volunteers. My swift assessment was that virtually anything would be better than being marched around the bush during the day by the sergeant, combined with endless push-ups, and then having to guard the dynamite factory during the night. I reckoned a lesson in first aid would also be handy, so I stepped forward. My military prowess would be broadened from the kitchen to the field hospital. My only challenge would be dealing with blood. I had never coped terribly well with blood, including my own, and would feel faint at the sight of a syringe or a bleeding wound. Luckily, the major did not ask us this question nor submit us to a squeamishness test.

The next couple of days followed a pattern. We sat on the ground, under the shade of a mature eucalyptus tree, while the major taught us anatomy using sheets of butchers' paper clipped to a large easel. Quite clearly, the major was politically and philosophically aligned with us even though he daren't say so out loud. He was a conscript and had to serve his time, just like us. He was happy to share his medical knowledge and he never once gave us a hard time or tried to abuse his rank.

On the first Sunday of our three-week camp the major suggested four of us accompany him to the Johannesburg General Hospital that afternoon. He was scheduled for a session of surgery and wished to take us through the emergency and intensive care wards to give us a feel of what patients suffering from traumatic injury looked like.

After arrival at the Jo'burg Gen, we dutifully followed him and breezed through every single security point until we reached the intensive care, or IC, ward. He identified three patients who had all been injured within the past 24 hours and proceeded to explain their likely prospects of survival. It was grim, including the sight of a 12-year-old boy who had slipped off a cliff alongside a rock pool and had absolutely no visible sign of injury. He was, however, brain dead and on life support. He looked as though he was sleeping peacefully except that our major told us "he's dead."

After the IC ward we were required to scrub down meticulously before being gowned up, with caps, masks and gloves. The major advised that we would be observing abdominal surgery to repair a ruptured spleen. The patient had suffered the rupture the previous evening when, while drunk, he fell from a first-floor apartment balcony in Hillbrow. In addition, he had fractured his skull, smashed some teeth and broken his elbow. His elbow had been operated on earlier in the day. I had no idea of what a spleen was until our major explained it was like a delicate little plastic bag of liquid inside the abdomen and it had ruptured on impact because it was not as robust as our skin or other organs.

The major requested we move in a little closer to watch the procedure. It all happened so quickly. He took a scalpel and sliced the patient in a long vertical incision starting beneath the rib cage. The bleeding started, aptly managed by the nurses, then they opened up the abdomen by inserting stainless steel abdominal retractors on either side of the incision and pulling the abdominal wall open. The major asked us to assist by holding these stainless steel retractors at the appropriate pressure to keep the abdominal wall open. I declined the offer as I took one final look at the patient's innards plus his bleeding abdomen, all coupled with the most awful stench. I was about to faint. I retreated a few steps to regain my composure and distract my brain.

When the major had repaired the spleen with intricate sutures, he left the patient in the capable hands of other medical experts to complete the surgical tidy up. He bluntly said the procedure we had observed was tame. Battlefield conditions would be far more challenging. I did not sleep that night. I had never before witnessed death, or been so close to blood and guts. I could still smell the awful abdominal stench. My lungs were filled with the hideous odour.

I had no intention of ever being on a battlefield for the Nationalist government.

7

A kid at Wits University

Too young for the army and way too young for university. At 16, I felt like the baby of the giant University of the Witwatersrand campus on the fringe of the Johannesburg business district. Witwatersrand translates from Afrikaans to White Water Ridge and the university indeed sprawled across both slopes of the ridge that divides Johannesburg into the posh, leafy northern suburbs and working class southern suburbs. The ridge runs east and west, following the rich gold seams along the East Rand and the West Rand. I grew up in an East Rand neighbourhood, next to a gold mine, and I had a lot of adjusting to do in a hurry.

Wits chose me as much as I chose it. Along with the University of Cape Town, it had the reputation of being the most liberal university in the country, which also turned out the best chartered accountants. It was also my hometown university and, as the biggest in South Africa, had plenty of places available for those wishing to study commerce. I enrolled and in February 1971 I strolled onto campus in a navy tee shirt and a pair of faded denim jeans, naively believing I had disguised my youth under a cascade of long, hippie-style hair.

A few immediate challenges confronted me: trying to look as cool and as mature as possible; adapting to the total freedom of the laissez-faire campus; earning enough pocket money to fund the life of a full-time student; and learning to take an afternoon nap. The challenge of slotting into a peer group reinforced just how much of a boy I was in the midst of these worldly young men and women, at least two years my senior and generally in their early 20s. Most of the men had completed their conscription stint and had some European travel under their belts. They were predominantly from the affluent northern suburbs and were suitably funded by their parents. They had drivers' licences and their own cars, whereas I was restricted to buses and trains, and had a couple of part-time jobs. They could legally drink beer at the local student hangout, the Devonshire Tavern, and discuss the hot musicians of the time like The Who, The Doors, Neil Young, Jimi Hendrix, Janis Joplin, Deep Purple, Uriah Heap and Bob Dylan. I sort of knew Simon and Garfunkel, Cat Stevens, and the Mamas and Papas.

Politics was the only topic of discussion where I could hold my own because of my father's involvement as an opposition politician. I was well informed from what I heard at home, and took no coaxing to support the call of the Students' Representative Council at Wits to protest for democratic rights for all South Africans, irrespective of colour. Such affiliation instantly earned me and others of a similar mindset the tags of communist and *betoger* (protester) amongst the conservative elements of white South Africa.

The National Union of South African Students (NUSAS) was a representative organisation of university students on English-speaking campuses actively opposed to the government. The South African government made it illegal for NUSAS to obtain financial support from overseas, many of its leaders had been banned or detained, and a number had gone into exile. All students on English-speaking campuses automatically belonged to NUSAS and the organisation was guaranteed a modest income from its constituent universities. While not an ideal economic model, it was the only means for NUSAS to sustain itself in opposition to the Nationalist government.

What made the Afrikaner government particularly antagonistic towards Wits was the fact that Nelson Mandela studied law at the university between 1943 and 1948, the year the Nationalists won power. A combination of increasing involvement in politics and the opposition struggle, and the difficulty of studying without the benefit of electricity in the poorest area of the Alexandra township, nicknamed Dark City, caused Mandela to leave the university without completing his law degree. However, he subsequently managed to complete his articles and remaining academic requirements and established his own legal practice in 1952 opposite the Johannesburg magistrates' courts.

In contrast, my academic universe seemed to be a breeze. Lecture attendance was optional and there was neither a grade given in any subject nor any other form of point scoring ahead of the end-of-year examination. It was all or nothing at the end of the year: a single examination determined if you passed or failed, regardless of whether you had attended a single lecture.

Our Economics 101 lecture was big, about 300 students in one of the largest lecture theatres. The demand for the course was high because it was offered as a first-year credit by a wide variety of faculties like arts, architecture, building science, law and commerce. The first challenge during one of these lectures was when I had to sit near the back and realised I could not read the board. My poor eyesight would resurface when I eventually took my driver's licence a year later.

Meanwhile my hair was growing longer and my jeans were growing shabbier. They weren't the only thing in my life requiring repair; it became clear my academic progress also needed some patching. I found the mathematics and statistics courses pretty easy but I was floundering with an intellectually challenging economics course.

The end of my first year delivered a couple of rude academic shocks and with one more birthday behind me, my day to be inducted into the army had arrived. My ego and false optimism were deflated but these setbacks also sharpened my resolve and I matured faster. My second academic year was considerably easier. Socially I was still a wonderfully ignorant virgin, focusing more on my looming 18th birthday and to ending the stigma of being too young to hold a driver's licence.

The examiner who took me out for the test drive climbed from the passenger's seat of my father's Valiant and, with a penetrating glare, pointed out: "Hey, mister, I think you have been driving for quite a long time because you don't drive like a learner." I remained silent. The final hurdle was the eye test, which is where the examiner finally got his man.

When I could not read any letter below the third line I surrendered and was told to get my eyes checked.

My glasses arrived along with my licence. Of course, I opted for those round, metal-rimmed John Lennon spectacles, in the hope someone might mistake me for an intellectual. The added bonus was being able to read everything on the blackboard for the first time. I didn't even have to restrict myself to the front row. I don't know if it was the glasses or the transition from boy to young man but I nailed my exams at the end of the year.

I was back to the full-freight five subjects in third year which, combined with part-time jobs in a bottle store, clothing store and betting agency, combined to cramp my available time, and my style. I could not afford my own car and had to plead with my mother for the occasional use of her VW Beetle. This is the main reason why I never got involved in the strong road running scene on campus. The Wits club was churning out regular winners on the weekend racing circuit, but I was too busy selling beer or checking betting tickets to manage anything more than an occasional jog when I felt under pressure.

I was also spending more and more time developing my interest in computing. These were exciting times in data processing. The university had invested in a computer centre and students could view the IBMs from behind a glass panel while white-coated operators did their thing. I learned to write the COBOL programming language and found the whole thing stimulating, plus terribly cool. Across the Atlantic, a young man called Steve Jobs had decided that physics and literature were not for him, and dropped out of college to attend calligraphy classes.

A couple of weeks before our exams, while we were waiting for a law lecture to start, one of the guys revealed he had discovered the most amazing holiday offer on earth. He told us about a Portuguese liner, the *Principe Perfeito*, which was to cruise the Indian Ocean for the summer. To fill the boat on the first two-week cruise before the peak school holiday season, the company was offering a berth in a communal bunk-bed cabin for an astonishingly paltry R140, meals included.

The Portuguese owners wanted to use this as a shake-down voyage to check out their logistics on Mauritius, Seychelles and Mozambique

Island, and had mistakenly presumed that the South African university and school holidays coincided. Ha! Word spread like wildfire across the nation's campuses and the boat was booked out within 48 hours. My buddies and I had tickets, of course. We had abandoned the lecture and fled for the nearest travel agent before the news got out of a two-week Indian Ocean cruise at half the price of a one-way air fare to London. The poor captain of the Principe Perfeito had no idea of what lay ahead.

I sailed through my exams and was in the best of moods when my mate Weston Dickson and I boarded the 19,000 ton vessel in Durban. Sure, our cut-price cabin was below the water line, next to the engine room, but who cared? The strategy was to live on the pool deck, next to the bar. The booze was duty free, far cheaper than that I peddled in my part-time job, so we students no longer had to swig beer but got stuck into the spirits. The only thing that distracted hundreds of booze-fuelled young male university students from commandeering the ship was the presence on board of hundreds of booze-fuelled young female students.

We had a fun time on that old liner that had long since lost any trace of the splendour that might have been present on her maiden voyage in 1961. The Seychelles promotes itself as a modern-day Garden of Eden, and the 50-rupee note on which palm tree leaves intertwine to clearly spell out the word SEX – albeit right next to Queen Elizabeth's prim head – did nothing to dispel the image. Yet it was all reasonably tame, just young people having fun. About the worst thing that happened was the loss of half of the ship's glassware because of a habit that developed of sinking a drink and tossing the glass over your left shoulder into the sea. The captain was angry but he didn't have much room to manoeuvre; every day we watched the ship's garbage being tossed over the stern into the propeller churn. That was the extent of 1970s recycling.

We made the most of the stopovers at Mahé in the Seychelles, Port Louis on Mauritius, and Mozambique Island, the former penal colony referred to in James Michener's novel *The Drifters*. When we disembarked in Durban, many of us toted duty free Asahi Pentax SLR cameras acquired on Mauritius, with souvenir turbans on our heads. The following weekend, Durban's *Sunday Tribune* newspaper published a full-page article headlined "Students turned cruise into sex orgy," with the sub-head "Shocks at sea for elderly tourists."

It transpired about 50 retirees had booked before the cut-rate deal that snared 500 students was advertised. "It was sex and drink all the way, and it began even before the ship had sailed," thundered the report. "Members of the group said the goings-on reached their peak at the ship's fancy dress party when:

- A young man in scanty bathing trunks sported five ping-pong balls, suspended beneath his crotch, and a label "The Magnificent Seven". He won the first prize for originality.
- A young couple came as Adam and Eve, naked except for cabbage leaves.
- Another young man, dressed as a petrol pump, made 'suggestive gestures' with a nozzle and tube from a petrol bowser."

One of the full fee-paying complement tut-tutted: "Wherever I looked there were young people mauling and slobbering over each other. They openly caressed one another. I heard a girl remark that there would probably be some souvenirs of the voyage in nine months' time."

I started my final year of university in 1974 feeling pretty good about life and my future. I elected to take three majors out of the four units necessary to complete my degree because I was enjoying the intellectual challenge and no longer seeking the path of least resistance. My betting agency job was adequate to cover all my needs, even though it meant missing an entire day of lectures every Wednesday. Most weekends involved some 21st birthday celebration and I started dating Vern Lloyd. I met her on a blind date, arranged by my sister Yvonne, and we got on well because we shared similar political values and sporting interests. Vern was very easy on the eye which also played a role in stimulating my interest. She was my first serious girlfriend and I spent as much time as I could with her and her family. Her mother, Brenda, was a feisty critic of the Nationalist government and an active member of the Black Sash protest organisation.

My final semester signalled not only the need to focus on my exams, but also to secure articles of clerkship with a firm of chartered accountants. This was necessary to complete the required three years of practical experience which, in tandem with the final academic requirements and the much-feared FQE, would result in a CA qualification. In 1974, professional standards prevented accounting firms from advertising their names anywhere outside a telephone directory listing, in larger than standard-size print. On-campus recruiting was unknown and we had no idea of the size, status and reputation of any of the firms. I did what everyone else did: opened the white pages and started dialling. The A section yielded two hits of firms I had vaguely heard of but knew nothing about: Alex Aiken & Carter (now KPMG) and Arthur Andersen. I called both and secured interviews. Although I reckoned I still looked pretty sharp in the pin-striped suit I had bought for my matriculation high school dance in 1970, I was not ready to conform to the world of short back and sides. I rebelled and kept my long hair.

Within days of my talk to Alex Aiken & Carter, I got a letter offering articles of clerkship if I graduated, at the encouraging salary of R350 a month. The exams went well, but I understood I was only halfway to my ultimate goal – and the second half of the course would be much harder. I had matured considerably and the boy had become a man, with goals and ambitions.

At the age of 20, I was mapping out a three-year progression from university graduate to chartered accountant while a 19-year-old teenager at Woodmead School, outside Johannesburg, had just completed his matric year and opted to study for a Bachelor of Arts degree at Wits with English, history, philosophy, and classical life and thought as his first-year subjects. Fordyce was the name on the university enrolment form. Bruce Fordyce.

Call back the past 2

The strong arm of the law introduced itself to me when I was 11 years old. My CBC classmate, David Sunney, committed the offence of giving me a lift on the crossbar of his bicycle from the school to Boksburg East Station. A traffic officer, resplendent in white helmet, aviator sunglasses and knee-high black leather boots, on a gleaming black and chrome BMW 500cc motorbike, cut us off into the kerb. He admonished us for our irresponsibility and reckless disregard of the traffic rules, and warned us we would pay the consequences.

He pulled out his ticket pad, recorded our details and issued each of us with a traffic infringement ticket. I walked to the station and missed my train, which gave me plenty of time to contemplate the horrible fate which awaited me. Once home, I hid the ticket under my pillow but broke the news to my parents when they came to say goodnight.

They did not make a fuss about it but I nevertheless had to front up to the Boksburg traffic department the following Saturday morning and write out all the traffic rules for a couple of hours in silence. I did not like those law enforcement guys. They were bullies and one of my friends later remarked I should be grateful I was white because I had gotten off so easily. What if I had been black?

It took me some years to figure out the significance of the question. As I grew older, I became aware of apartheid. I noticed that commonplace items like bus seats had either a 'whites only' or a 'non-whites only' sign stencilled on them. Similarly labelled were the entrances to facilities like post offices, train stations, liquor stores and government buildings. As a university student, I worked behind the non-whites counter of a bottle store, where the biggest-selling item was sorghum or maize beer brewed by the government specifically for the black drinking market. It was cheaper than the malt-based beers or lagers, but still very profitable.

I also noticed certain big buyers, the front-runners who stocked the *shebeens* or illegal retail outlets in black townships. The government had outlawed the sale and distribution of alcohol in black townships, outside of the government beer halls which sold sorghum beer. Blacks knew both the venues and sorghum products were controlled by the Nationalist government they despised. The front-runners would arrive with trucks and stock them up with caseloads of lager beer and spirits. By law, we were required to record in a register the names and addresses of all black customers who bought more than six litres of alcohol. Government inspectors could ask to check the register at any time. Meanwhile, white customers next door could buy as much alcohol as they desired without having to provide any details.

Shebeens became the social venues of black townships in the same way that pubs and bars have served the communities of Western Europe and North America for centuries. They operated illegally and sold both commercial liquor and home brew. They became a crucial meeting place for activists during the apartheid era. The music of many great black musicians like Hugh Masekela and Miriam Makeba played to the souls of shebeen patrons with their rich jazz and powerfully anti-apartheid lyrics. Needless to say, shebeens were often raided and shut down by the police, resulting in the confiscation of liquor and the arrest of patrons and operators alike.

There was a law in place enforcing job reservation and the protection of white workers. The Group Areas Act prevented blacks from living in white areas, let alone owning property. The Immorality Act made it illegal to engage in sex across the colour bar in order to preserve the pure breeding stock of whites. Any white South African caught having sex with a black, coloured or Asian (mostly of Indian descent) person was liable to be sentenced to jail. In 1968, when my teenage hormones were on the boil at Dawnview High, a 24-year-old white railway clerk, John O'Brien, and a 25-year-old black woman, Nellie Tlaitlai, were each sentenced to six months' imprisonment under this law.

The South African government which propagated these laws was a God-fearing collection of Calvinists who worshipped under the auspices of the Dutch Reformed Church. These church pulpits were beacons for broadcasting state propaganda and reinforcing Afrikaner nationalism. So conservative were the Nationalists that when I was a teenager, in one week the censors banned the movies *Bonnie and Clyde*, *In the Heat of the Night* and *Guess Who's Coming to Dinner* for fear they would erode the moral standing of the people. The Nationalists feared their God so much that it was illegal to dance on a Sunday, the day of worship. Yet many Afrikaner farmers would work their black labourers to the bone on Sundays and some would occasionally have sex with them.

Education was also segregated. Blacks attended school in the townships or homelands and received an inferior education, designed to prepare them only for semi-skilled or manual labour. The Nationalist government had enacted the Extension of University Education Act in 1959, separating universities according to race. White universities were prevented from admitting any black or coloured student who might apply to study for a course or degree available at a black or coloured university, like Fort Hare or the University of the Western Cape. Because commerce was offered at other universities to black students, I saw no black students in my lectures at Wits University.

Medicine was another matter, though. There was no medical school at any black university, although the University of Natal in Durban had a blacks-only medical faculty. This enabled Professor Phillip Tobias, renowned anatomical scientist and later dean of the Wits Medical School, to embark upon a programme of reverse discrimination. He argued that black students had been so heavily disadvantaged during their frugal schooling that they could never match white students competing for entry into medical school on a raw score basis. He allocated 20 of the 100 available first year places to the top 20 black applicants, regardless of the scores of the white applicants who might otherwise have been ranked 81st to 100th. He pushed the rules even further by allowing the same black students two years to achieve all the first-year academic credits. It was a radical position to take but one that was supported by the Wits Council and the student body. Wits University was putting to shame the Australian government that, in the early 1970s, still upheld a white migrant policy and did not include indigenous Aborigines in the census, let alone the ballot. This glaring hypocrisy did not prevent Australia from joining the call for a sports boycott of South Africa.

Former Pretoria Boys High School pupil Peter Hain moved to London in 1966 after his parents were declared banned persons and briefly jailed. Such repression was, over the years, to prove a self-inflicted wound by the Nationalists. For decades, Hain was a thorn in the side of the white South African Nationalist. He spearheaded the sports boycott campaign preaching the slogan: "No normal sport in an abnormal society". I remember collection tins in the Wits student canteen to help fund the Hain-led 'Stop the Tours' campaign against Springbok rugby tours of England and Australia. Hain subsequently served in the cabinets of British Prime Ministers Tony Blair and Gordon Brown and was the Leader of the House of Commons from 2003 to 2005.

Student politics started hotting up in 1972. The National Union of South African Students had consistently campaigned against apartheid and, on 22 May, NUSAS launched its Free Education campaign. Mass student meetings, peaceful demonstrations and the distribution of information took place on all NUSAS-affiliated campuses. Police arrested scores of students for protesting illegally, but they were mostly acquitted by judges who still believed in the right to freedom of speech. The Nationalist government responded with ominous statements which signalled their future tactics in dealing with the contrary views of the English-speaking universities.

The Minister of Labour, Marais Viljoen, referred to Wits and UCT students as terrorists and insisted that all student protests, peaceful or otherwise, be stopped. Minister of Indian Affairs, Owen Horwood and Deputy Police Minister, Jimmy Kruger warned that police would not hesitate to act against students, despite the recent acquittals. The government would only uphold the law as long as it corresponded with its own views. Our peaceful poster protests along Jan Smuts Avenue, the campus perimeter, would soon be baton-charged by police after they had ordered us to disperse. Their bombastic, strong-armed assaults on passive

RUNAWAY COMRADE

students aroused the ire of even those who had previously elected not to participate.

Many of our student leaders were detained under draconian legislation that enabled the government to hold them in prison for up to 180 days without being charged, and without access to family or legal assistance. Right-wing terrorism against Wits and UCT students mounted during the year. Death threats were received by various student leaders, and also by Mr Justice Watermeyer, who had granted an interdict restraining the police from intervening in meetings at UCT. The house of UCT student council leader Geoff Budlender was torched in a bomb attack. The government repeatedly banned student newspapers at Wits and UCT, with Horwood claiming in the Senate that an edition of the *Wits Student* newspaper lampooning the Prime Minister was part of a communist conspiracy to subvert the campuses.

As my university crackled and hissed against the oppression, the Nationalists abandoned any pretence of restraint and declared they would retain control at any cost. They formed the Schlebusch Commission to investigate anti-apartheid Christian organisations, an intimidating interrogation of all religious leaders who openly deplored apartheid. Only the Nationalists believed they could be both Christians and racial supremacists at the same time.

In January 1973 black workers in Natal went on strike. By early February all of Durban's major industrial complexes were faced with a wave of rolling strikes as factories downed tools, involving 30,000 workers, and including Durban's 16,000 municipal workers. The demands were not unreasonable: better wages and improved working conditions. Although black trade unions were still illegal, the widespread media coverage of the shockingly low wages caused an outcry, domestically and abroad. For the first time, the government recognised the strategic significance of black workers withholding their labour. They countered with minor concessions, including the right to strike (albeit with severely restrictive conditions) and the right to attend Industrial Council meetings (but not to vote) that would subsequently pave the way for the formidable consolidation of African labour under the leadership of Cyril Ramaphosa in the 1980s.

A number of white university academics and students, mostly from the University of Natal, who actively assisted black workers in striking and arguing the case for a minimum wage above the poverty datum line, were subsequently banned by the government. They included Rick Turner, Neville Curtis, Halton Cheadle, David Hemson, Paula Ensor and David Davies. That was just the start of the descent into darkness involving the security police and English-speaking student leaders who refused to be silenced.

In 1974 Curtis fled to Australia on board a ship from Durban harbour to avoid being charged for breaking his banning orders, and the inevitable detention and torture which would follow. On the morning of 8 January 1978 Turner was assassinated in his own home in front of his two young daughters. No one was ever charged with his murder. Six years later it was Curtis' sister's turn. Jeanette Schoon and her six-year-old daughter Katryn were killed by a letter bomb addressed to her husband Marius, an anti-apartheid activist, while living in Angola. At least we know who was responsible for this atrocity: a police major and spy called Craig Williamson admitted this and other heinous acts when applying for amnesty to the Truth and Reconciliation Commission in 2000.

Williamson had completed his schooling at one of South Africa's most prestigious schools, St John's College in Johannesburg. He attended Wits at the same time as me, wore his hair long and actively participated in student politics as a pseudo-revolutionary. During our Wits years there were constant whispers that Williamson was an undercover agent of the Nationalist government. We never trusted him.

8

Life on three continents

Being inducted into the workforce at the bottom of the corporate food chain is a sobering experience. We new graduates thought we knew a lot. In reality, we were clueless. It was essential you received good instruction and mentoring from the start and I was fortunate to be allocated to my first audit team that was managed by Stuart Morris, with Brian Mallinson as my immediate superior. They helped me a lot and, unlike some of my university colleagues, I was not biding my time to finish my articles before clearing out.

Every working day paid homage to obligatory time sheets, recording no less than seven and a half hours of client chargeable time, before I travelled to Wits University for an evening lecture. I'd get home at 8pm to scoff down a meal before hitting the books. I also had Saturday morning lectures and, if I was sufficiently motivated to get my assignments done in the afternoon, the reward was a free Sunday with which to pursue Vern or play the odd game of squash or tennis.

I must have been doing the right things with Vern because we married on 31 January 1976. We both detested the prospect of further military service for the benefit of the Nationalists and yearned for adventure, agreeing that we would travel and live abroad as soon as I had finished my three years of articles and gained my CA. All that stood between me and the status of chartered accountant was three university units and the dreaded FQE.

I got an eye-opener into the life of a black person when the Johannesburg office of KPMG hired its first black articled clerk, Fort Hare graduate Josias Tsanwani. The previous year, the South African Institute of Chartered Accountants had acknowledged that it did not have a single black member amongst its professional ranks and was lagging behind other professions such as law and medicine. It also recognised the potential of the CA qualification to blacks as a pathway towards economic prosperity under apartheid, through education and financial self-sufficiency. KPMG played a pivotal role in this initiative and I was to spend the next two years working on most of my audit assignments with Tsanwani, under the guidance and supervision of Allister Rogan, Morris and Mallinson.

Tsanwani was a real pioneer. I lived in an affluent white suburb with all necessary infrastructures to support a high standard of living. He lived in Tembisa, then a black informal township 30km from central Johannesburg, with no electricity, sanitation, running water or tarred roads. We drove cars. He caught buses and trains. We could study for our remaining academic credits at Wits University on the fringe of Johannesburg's business centre. He was forbidden to study the same courses at a white university and had to do so by correspondence. At work it was more of the same. Whites in clerical or administrative roles were not used to having to explain any discrepancies in their work to a better qualified black man. They felt humiliated at having to do so. At one company, Tsanwani was told not to use the white toilets. When he was served tea in one of the porcelain cups normally reserved for white workers, they almost stopped taking refreshment for fear of catching some disease. Yet he reacted with a smile and the forgiveness of a saint.

Tsanwani had worked in New York as an exchange student the previous year and amused us with his travel tales and experiences, like that of being mugged. We could not imagine anyone as street smart as him, living in dangerous black townships in South Africa, getting mugged in New York. Most mornings he would catch his blacks-only bus to a nominated location where I would pick him up and continue our journey to the offices or factory premises of our clients. He never tried to spook or discomfit us, but he was living in the township community and had a better understanding of black issues and the level of discontentment than any white South African.

By the end of 1976, I had passed my remaining university courses and satisfied all the prerequisites to sit the FQE in mid-1977. In the weeks leading up to the FQE I enjoyed a recreational jog every evening after a day of studying. It was the best outlet imaginable, running along tree-lined avenues, listening to those wonderful African bird calls. The FQE comprised three four-hour written exams and, when I sat them, I realised they were way harder than anything Wits University had thrown our way.

Two months later, the business section of the *Sunday Times* newspaper published an article, which read:

Blight on the 1977 CA crop

This year has been a tough one for most of us, but for fledgling accountants it's been the worst since 1962. Of the 896 students who wrote their final examinations to qualify as chartered accountants, only 307 (or 34%) passed. A spokesman for the education committee of the Public Accountants and Auditors Board says that this is the second worst pass rate in the history of the examination of the country.

The education committee spokesman says the examination papers this year were not particularly difficult and were marked objectively, and emphasises that the poor pass rate does not suggest university teaching standards are not up to scratch. Indeed, the feeling among leading accountants in Johannesburg is that the Year of 77 was one of doubtful vintage.

Fortunately I was one of those lucky 307 students who managed to pass. KPMG achieved a 46% success rate. I had attained my CA credentials for the next stage of my career. Internationally it was far more valuable than my South African passport although I was under no illusion that my financial aptitude and professional competence, combined with lots of hard work, would determine my destiny in the world of commerce.

I had already more than doubled my starting salary of R350 per month and word had it that some of the audit managers were earning R1,000 a month. This was the equivalent of three return airfares to London every month. My schoolboy dream of 1970 had materialised. I had earned my ticket to participate in the world of business as a CA. But my greatest reward was the luxury of having time. For the first time in a decade I was not required to study at night and over weekends.

As a 23-year-old CA, I felt like a king when I booked a restaurant dinner for my parents and my in-laws. We celebrated over a feast of peri-peri prawns, washed down with a good South African white wine. Both sets of parents had helped Vern and I to reach this point and it was wonderful to be able to reciprocate out of my own earnings for the first time. It was a bittersweet celebration for them, though. They knew we would leave South Africa within months.

In January 1978 Vern and I arrived in London. We each had one suitcase plus a sports bag with our tennis and squash racquets. More significantly, Vern was six months pregnant. We had been warned that British immigration might question us on arrival, suspecting we were conspiring to have our baby born in the UK, which is exactly what we were planning to do. Fortunately we sailed through immigration at Heathrow, whereas many other travellers of Indian or African origin were detained and questioned. We caught a black cab into central London for our first few nights because the underground had not yet been extended to Heathrow.

The financial capital of the world came as a shock. Compared to mid-summer Johannesburg, London was wet, cold and grey. Very grey. So grey it was almost black. There was not a speck of colour or light to be seen besides that of shop fronts and billboards. By the time we got to our modest bed and breakfast it was dark, yet barely 4 pm. I had experienced my first nightfall in England in a real sense. The night literally fell on you. No golden glow of the African sun engaged in the colourful sunset duel with a far more subtle night sky. Welcome to the winter world of London, central heating and television. The city looked grim and bleak.

Yet London soon provided a wonderful awakening to our personal torment over South Africa. Debate on BBC television was vigorous and unrestricted. It revealed a democratic spirit and a freedom of speech I had never before experienced. London exuded a freedom of expression – from any religious organisation or culture to punk rockers to the Communist Party. A Sunday afternoon at Speakers' Corner in Hyde Park would have it all to hear and see. The South African government would have been apoplectic had it witnessed this rich debate across political, cultural and religious beliefs, peacefully conducted within a civilised and well-behaved democracy, where every citizen was entitled to an opinion.

After finding rented accommodation in Wimbledon, I settled into the London work scene. I was trained to work numbers, financial mathematics and complex accounting issues; my peers were mostly PPE (politics, philosophy, economics) graduates of posh public schools and Oxbridge universities. On entering articles of clerkship, they simply sat a bridging exam that eliminated any need for a highly specialised commerce degree. During my time in London, I would discover that the level of my technical training as a CA from the South African system was as good as any, but my general education was extremely narrow.

A few weeks after my arrival, the office hosted a cocktail party for all new joiners. We were from all corners of the old British Empire and had to some extent been exposed to British education, customs and rituals. Regardless of whether you were from Bombay, Sri Lanka, Christchurch, Sydney, Johannesburg, Lahore, Auckland or Toronto there was a common thread. The staff partner lamented: "Unfortunately you people from the colonies have not done justice to the English language and should always remain conscious of your pronunciation, diction and vocabulary because all too often it is very difficult to understand what you are saying." Later that evening, between rationed sips of our French claret, I suggested to the partner that I had found it difficult to understand the cockney cab drivers and newspaper sellers from the East End. On the other hand, I had no difficulty at all comprehending my colleagues from around the world. Perhaps there were more challenging linguistic issues in London than in the colonies? The partner looked at me in astonishment. In his class-conscious world he would never regard Cockneys as his own people, in the same manner that so many white South Africans considered blacks to be only fit for servant duties.

My working day in London started with a one-kilometre walk from our apartment at 101 Ridgway, alongside the Wimbledon Common and down the hill to Wimbledon station, wrapped in a Burberry trench coat, briefcase in left hand and umbrella used like a hiking pole in the right hand.

The British Rail express connection to Waterloo comprised carriages that appeared to be of World War II vintage, with manually operated doors.

At Waterloo we disembarked in an orderly sort of way but at a pretty smart pace and disappeared into the catacombs of the Underground. Most of my fellow passengers headed for the non-stop service, affectionately known as the Drain, to Bank or the City. Returning to street level from the depths of the Drain, I would walk up Princes Street to our offices at 70 Finsbury Pavement. On a good day, my morning commute would take 75 minutes.

Living through the Winter of Discontent of 1978–79 was another trying experience. James Callaghan's Labour government was attempting to keep the lid on public sector pay rises because inflation had hit 26.9% in 1975, resulting in widespread strikes by local authority trade unions. A wide swathe of workers, from refuse collectors to gravediggers, withdrew their labour and even hospital entrances were blockaded. With nowhere to dump rubbish, councils resorted to using parks. Westminster City Council used Leicester Square in the heart of the West End for piles of rubbish, attracting rats, which in turn attracted widespread media coverage. The weather turned icy in the early months of 1979 and blizzards added to the nation's misery.

Vern gave birth to Nicole, our first daughter, in London in April 1978. This life-changing event, combined with a tight domestic cash flow, determined the extent of our leisure and recreational pursuits. Given the dreadful English weather, squash became my main physical outlet. In summer, Vern and I played tennis on the grass courts of the Wimbledon Club on the opposite side of Church Road from the All England Club where the famous championships are held. During the tournament, we would stroll into the grounds after work with Nicole in her pram and meander around the outside courts.

After 18 months of professional experience in London we had reached decision time. We could no longer deny that we were outdoor creatures, and needed to seek further professional and life experience elsewhere. The shortlist was Canada, Australia, and the US. We had an interview lined up at the Australian High Commission when I was offered a job in Fort Lauderdale in Florida. The climate was a plus and the client base looked interesting, with the NASA space programme at Cape Canaveral, combined with manufacturing, publishing and real estate development in the Palm Beach precinct.

We settled in quickly after our arrival in Florida at the end of 1979. I was again quietly delighted that my CA from Wits held me in good stead. My training and education more closely resembled that of the American CPA than the British CA. The trend in the US was to specialise in very narrow fields of expertise, without the base of broader education. Americans saw this as a career maker, but I viewed it as a serious limitation because I felt I was far too young to pursue one narrow aspect of business without experiencing what the others might offer.

That being said, the single greatest lesson I learned from my American experience was to make a significant investment in planning any assignment. Typically, 15% of total assignment time and costs would be invested in comprehensive planning, detailing all the critical risks, including industry issues, peer group benchmarking and management competence, before deciding how to approach the assignment. In effect, one had to complete the job intellectually, with validly documented justification, before launching into the actual work.

Another invaluable benefit of living in America was the opportunity to correct my short-sightedness through inexpensive contact lenses. Goodbye, glasses. This was a quantum leap for me in terms of quality of life.

Even though I was putting in 60 hours a week at work, this did not prevent Vern and I from access to Ernest Hemmingway's hideout, Key West, or a holiday on sparsely inhabited Little Exuma in the Bahamian archipelago. Tennis could be played any day or night of the year and I competed in my first 10km road race, the 1980 Fort Lauderdale Heart Run in 41.48 in 248th position out of 4,000 runners, predominantly male and many running bare chested. I recall Ken Misner of Tallahassee won the race in a time of 31.36.

In April 1980 the Freedom Flotilla ferried 125,000 Cuban refugees to Miami, just south of Fort Lauderdale. These new migrants immediately sought employment in the hospitality industry in a very Hispanic Miami and displaced thousands of African-Americans from the workforce on the grounds that they could not speak Spanish. Tempers were at boiling point as black Americans pointed out that Spanish fluency had not been a pre-requisite when they were conscripted to fight in Vietnam.

The tinderbox was ignited when five white Miami cops, who had beaten black citizen Arthur McDuffie to death after a traffic violation, were acquitted in 1980. The initial protest turned into a riot; three were killed and 23 critically injured. Two days later, Miami imposed an 8pm to 6am curfew with a temporary ban on the sale of firearms and liquor. About 3,500 National Guardsmen were sent to Miami to restore order. The influx of Cubans had further fuelled the racial flames and tensions. I had to pinch myself to remember that I was living in the US and not South Africa. This was all happening a few miles south of where I lived and I empathised totally with the local African-Americans. They were being screwed.

This accelerated the soul searching that Vern and I were doing. After a year in the US we were financially comfortable, with the treasured prospect of American residency and citizenship awaiting us. Sadly, the conservative Republicans were, in a number of philosophical respects, very similar to South African Nationalists. With blatant discrimination evident, we were, frankly, not jumping out of our skins to become American citizens.

Meanwhile, many political and business figures from around the world had raised the volume and frequency of appeals for Nelson Mandela's release. Negotiations were taking place to move him from Robben Island. South Africa's stretched military resources and the threatened withdrawal of essential foreign capital and trade investment had convinced the Nationalists to listen to world opinion and open dialogue. A narrow window of opportunity had been prised open. Like so many South Africans around the world, we thought the government had seen the light and would work towards a sensible political agenda to emancipate the country.

Despite all of the problems wracking our homeland, we were acutely aware that we missed many aspects of South Africa, family included, and our marriage had been strained by the continual moves. We made the decision to return to Johannesburg and try and make a difference.

We were optimistic, excited even, but still naïve.

9

Comrades bronze, at last

I returned to South Africa at the end of August 1980 profoundly wiser than I had been when I left three years earlier. I had gained professional experience in London and the US. Consequently, I could not wait to impart my newfound knowledge. At a personal level I had also been exposed to the power of democracy in the UK and the US. Accepting there was so much about my native South Africa that I had ignored during my youth, I resolved to make the best out of every opportunity and to assist with a peaceful transition to democracy.

Oh, and I also decided to revive my dream of one day running the Comrades Marathon.

Within 48 hours of landing in Johannesburg, I entered and completed the Golden Reef Marathon on 1 September 1980. All the jogging I had done since my struggles at the Vaal Marathon four years previously must have banked some miles in my legs. I finished in 3:24, in 289th position, notwithstanding that every single step beyond the 28km mark was painful. My brother JP kept me going during the last 14km through his vociferous seconding efforts.

Johnny Halberstadt won the race in a record 2:20.07, followed by an 18-year-old Wits student, Mark Plaatjes, in 2:24.10. There were two black runners in the top 10. Of the 703 runners who completed the route in less than five hours, 120 managed to record what to me was a mythical sub-three-hour time. Sonja Laxton won the women's race in an all-Africa record of 2:46.33. But it was the achievements of black runners that gave me some indication of the emerging depth of quality and increased participation of black runners in the South African road running scene, especially since the sport had only been opened to them in 1975.

When I got to know my KPMG colleagues in the Johannesburg office, I learned that among them, Godfrey Franz, Greg McCue and Claire Taylor had all run the 1978 Comrades Marathon. All three were in the process of completing their CAs yet had still managed to participate in the Comrades. Franz achieved an excellent 6:55, McCue also managed to achieve a silver medal, and Taylor a bronze medal in 10:40. Franz seemed to be a reasonably serious runner, while McCue and Taylor had not even run at school. The appeal of running to this group was that it did not require as much time as other sports and could be squeezed into a professional career. They also waxed lyrically about the amazing crowd support during the closing stages of the Comrades when it was most needed. Franz and McCue ran with the Wits University running club, while Taylor ran with Rocky Road Runners, a new social running club. In addition to these three runners, another young CA at KPMG, Jeff Malin, was making his mark over the standard distance. He subsequently finished seventh in the Golden Reef Marathon and 14th in the 50km JSE Marathon.

I further discovered that in 1979, after completing her CA and some earnest training, Taylor had won the South African women's marathon title in East London in a South African and an all-Africa record of 2:57. Franz once again ran Comrades but finished with a disappointing time of 7:39 after aiming for 6:40. The cold weather had hampered him but not a Wits University running mate of his, Bruce Fordyce, who Franz declared to be a "new star." Franz had trained with Fordyce since university and was delighted when he finished third in 5:51, a mere 45 seconds behind the runner-up, Johnny Halberstadt, and less than six minutes behind winner Piet Vorster. The running feats of these four young KPMG professionals inspired me no end. I, too, could see my way clear to maintaining a high level of work and still putting in the roadwork needed to complete the Comrades.

On the political front, events in South Africa still perturbed me, notwithstanding the fact we had voluntarily elected to return with our eyes wide open. In 1980, the Nationalists continued to pursue anyone they deemed to be a political agitator. More than 16,000 people were convicted on politically related charges and 768 people were detained. The only positive political development was the formation of The Council of Unions of South Africa (CUSA) to represent black workers.

The unpredictability of my workload was causing chaos with my twice-weekly squash fixtures and I had to default on squash more often than not. My lack of a physical outlet was a frustration so when I caught up with my friend from student days, Weston Dickson, he filled me in on the social road running scene. He confirmed that many new running clubs had been formed with the objective of participating in weekend training runs or races that served as a training build-up for the Comrades. He mentioned that several runners from Wits had formed a highly sociable running club called Varsity Kudus, chaired and organised by another CA, the larger than life Dave 'Smooch' Hodgskiss. Dickson also reminded me that one of the greatest benefits of jogging in the early morning, well before work, was that you managed to exercise before starting the professional day.

I finally plucked up the courage to call Hodgskiss in February 1981. I enquired about joining Varsity Kudus with the hope of running the 1981 Comrades Marathon on 1 June. He responded: "Well, I need to ask you three very important questions. One, are you fat? Two, can you spit straight? And three, can you fart loudly?"

I was briefly speechless, then replied: "I'm not fat and I seldom spit. I don't believe I have ever farted loudly. Blame my parents."

"Hmm," deliberated Hodgskiss. "Luckily you pass the most important test if you want to run the Comrades in 14 weeks' time. Don't worry about the spitting and farting, it will all be pretty natural after a few Coke stops on our long runs."

He invited me to join them for a group run from Professor Walker's home in Parkwood the next day, to meet some fellow Kudus runners and amble an easy 20km jog as part of the Comrades build-up. Unfortunately, I could not make it – Vern was on the brink of giving birth to our second child.

The 14-week Comrades Marathon countdown, as explained to me by Hodgskiss, rekindled memories of my disastrous Vaal Marathon experience. Hodgskiss thought that the 56km Korkie ultramarathon, five weeks away, would be a suitable qualifying run for Comrades. Although I had managed to finish the Golden Reef Marathon in 3:24 six months earlier, my subsequent training had been very sparse. There was another very solemn reality. The qualifying marathon suggested by Hodgskiss was not a standard marathon of 42.2km. It was an uphill 56km slog that Hodgskiss said I had to run to get a feel for Comrades. He should know as he had already completed the Comrades 10 times, including three top 50 finishes and nine silver medals. Naturally, I believed everything he told me.

The first week of March was highly productive by any measure. I managed to sneak in an early morning jog every morning before putting in a solid day at the office. Vern went into labour in the Sandton Clinic on Saturday morning, giving birth to Simone, our second daughter, early in the afternoon. On Sunday, I managed an 11km jog before visiting Vern and Simone at the clinic. Vern and Simone were discharged five days later so I took some leave to help settle the new family member. It was a 10-day break from the office that did me the world of good. In addition to assisting with the babies and domestic chores, I used the opportunity to run for six mornings in a row without the distraction of staffing issues and critical client deadlines.

On Sunday 22 March I ran the Olympia Half Marathon in Bedford-view, my first half marathon. I remember bumping into one of the more seasoned runners at the start and asking him what he had eaten for breakfast. I felt as though my own bowl of muesli, orange juice and yoghurt was still sitting heavily and uncomfortably in my gut. He looked at me in disbelief, saying: "Are you serious? Surely you don't eat before you run or race?"

I asked him what I was supposed to do and he told me to drink a cup of coffee or energy supplement, but not eat. That was my first piece of serious running advice and it has never let me down.

I did not own a running watch because at my novice level of running, I was not much concerned about minutes and seconds. Charles Vilakazi won the race over a tough undulating course at an altitude of 1,609m, in an astonishing time of 66.23, taking it from Plaatjes, two minutes back. Given my lack of training, I was pleased with my 75th place in 82.00, only 80 seconds behind women's winner Sonja Laxton.

I felt less impressed with myself when I met Ian Laxton who mentioned that he and Hugh Patterson had jogged a 75-minute finish as a medium-effort training run. I had run flat out. I realised I had a lot of work ahead of me but I was confident I could improve. My training log for that week exceeded 80km for the first time ever, principally because of the luxury of the annual leave I had enjoyed following Simone's birth.

On Monday morning it was back to the grindstone. Two baby daughters with several nocturnal interruptions, a pre-dawn jog around Emmarentia Dam from my house in Linden, shower, breakfast, followed by a 45-minute drive into Johannesburg CBD, and then home by 7pm with work files to be reviewed after dinner. I managed to jog Monday through to Thursday and was then advised by Hodgskiss to rest until the Korkie on the Sunday. I had absolutely no idea of what to expect other than to get a taste of what Comrades would be like.

It was a long, tough morning for me. Race organiser Germiston Callies Harriers boasted that if you could finish Korkie, Comrades would be easy. The running cognoscenti referred to Korkie as the "slow poison" because it started at an altitude of 1,465m at Fountains Park outside Pretoria and finished at 1,690m at the Herman Immelman Stadium in Germiston. It grinds slowly uphill the whole way.

Altitude and elevation aside, my mind shut out most of the struggles of that day other than the hot, slow trudge after passing Johannesburg international airport, and reaching the marathon mark. Then taking a right turn at the La Conga Roadhouse and crossing the concrete bridge over the railway, where effervescent Germiston Callies Harriers stalwart Fred Morrison was standing and encouraging us. He would not have recognised me but he and my father had been great political allies against the Nationalists. Finally, I was into the last 200m on the beautiful synthetic track and finished in 4:25.13. I was completely knackered. I had to lie down in the shade for a few minutes to regain my composure, before my family could drive me home. It was tough going and I could not believe Ben Choeu's winning time of 3:15.24.

The rising Wits runner Fordyce finished fifth in 3:23, and later told journalists he had used the race as a training run. These elite runners appeared as exotically gifted and talented as mythical Greek gods. If someone had read my palm as I was recuperating on my back in the shade and suggested that I would win Korkie five years later in a time of 3:14 and beat Choeu in the 50km JSE Marathon (now renamed City2City), I would have demanded my money back.

After lunch I needed a power nap, as I was feeling a little weary. In reality it wasn't just a little weariness, it was utter exhaustion. Total depletion. Never in my life had I ever needed a power nap. My wife was nursing a three-week-old baby and trying to amuse three-year-old Nicole, but I was as useful as a sack of potatoes. As I dozed off my left calf cramped. I'd never cramped in my life: it felt as though a crocodile had locked its jaws around my calf. My left foot also cramped and the pain was excruciating. Instinct made me reach for the toes so I could try to pull a stretch into the calf. Ouch! Something tore inside, permanently scarring my left calf muscle tissue. It is the only running injury that still lingers with me today.

Nevertheless, no gain without pain, or so my new clubmates told me. I mailed my Comrades Marathon entry that night. I retained a copy of my Comrades entry form and the race rules confirming the entry fee of R8. This entry fee covered 60 well-stocked refreshment stations, in addition to 70 sponging facilities. Finishers under 11 hours were guaranteed a medal plus a Comrades tracksuit badge and tag. The race was open to anyone over 18 as long as you were an amateur and had met the qualifying requirements, essentially a 4:30 marathon for novices or runners older than 65. There was no prize money. The winner and the first 10 finishers would receive gold medallions. All runners finishing under 7:30 would receive a silver medal, with bronze medals for all those bettering 11 hours. The modest entry fee represented an extraordinary value proposition to me. Over the next 30 years I would never encounter a sporting event that offered such amazing value for money, at less than 10 cents per kilometre.

The following week I managed five training runs, including a 45km Sunday outing with my new club, for a total of 90km. It was tough going because I was still hurting from the Korkie. In the week after that, I managed six training runs including another Kudus Sunday run of 32km, during which I experienced shin splints, sore knees and a particularly sore left foot. By mid-April I could not run at all. My doctor advised me to take a complete break from running for at least two weeks. On the assumption my injuries would improve, I would have four and a half weeks left to train for Comrades. No longer was I an indestructible 27-year-old, just another mortal jogger with only blind faith to counteract the aches and pains.

The break did me a lot of good. I managed weekly totals of 110km, 67km, 50km, 47km and 30km to round out my final Comrades preparation. On 1 June I was one of 1,332 novices in the field of 3,925 who lined up outside the Durban City Hall. Woody Allen correctly reflected that 90% of success in life depends on just showing up and that is true. But Johnny Halberstadt was more marathon-specific with his advice, which was to show up uninjured and not over-trained. I was injured and seriously under-trained.

When the starter's gun fired at 6am, runners covering the width of Smith Street, extending back hundreds of metres, began moving as one amorphous sea of humanity. The start of my first Comrades must rate as one of the most exciting moments I have ever experienced. It felt as though I was riding a tsunami of excitement underpinned by real fear. The following nine hours would be less zestful. Media reports suggested Halberstadt was set to rewrite the Comrades record books

The course took us up our first climb, Berea Road, and as the day dawned we were 10km out. At the 16km mark, on the climb up Cowie's Hill, the nagging injury to my left knee convinced me I should walk. This was dangerous as I still had 70km to cover, but my initial enthusiasm had deserted me. After walking for about five minutes my rescue arrived. Six fellow runners from Kudus came by and suggested I should jump on their bus. It was difficult to mobilise the knee but once I got going again I had a trouble-free jog for the next 50km, managing to ascend Fields Hill, Botha's Hill and Inchanga. There were some experienced Comrades runners in this Kudus bus who stopped at every refreshment station to rehydrate.

The camaraderie in the Comrades struck me as simply extraordinary. Spectator support was amazing, especially over the last 30km. Then again, a cheer of well-intentioned encouragement from spectators at the 60km mark to "keep it up, only 30km to go" had exactly the opposite effect. Oh, no! Don't remind me! But thanks anyway.

At the 70km mark near the Lion Park turnoff I trotted past a refreshment station where a disappointed young girl was pleading with her motionless and exhausted father.

"Daddy, Daddy, why aren't you running?"

I shuffled on realising how fortunate I was not to have my daughter Nicole on the course sharing a similar level of anxiety about her father. I had covered the previous 25km in tandem with my brother JP, when he declared that he had a commitment in Pietermaritzburg and could no longer dawdle with me. He took off towards Polly Shorts and finished 18 minutes faster than me, concerned that his University of Natal teammates would finish the beer stash he had contributed to if he loitered with me.

With 15km to go, I was walking solo again and happily resigned to getting to the finish within the 11 hour cut-off. Once again, another Kudus runner came to my rescue. Nobby Clark jogged up to me and insisted I join him. He was determined we would finish the Comrades together. Clark was running his ninth Comrades, and so we climbed Polly Shorts together. Once over the top of that monstrous climb I felt rejuvenated but Nobby started cramping, leaning on telephone poles to stretch his muscles. We plugged away and were in the stadium when his legs gave way and he collapsed. I helped him up and we made it to the line in 9:02. He headed for the medical tent; I staggered to the Varsity Kudus umbrella. I was beyond exhausted. I had absolutely nothing left.

My body was hurting and my mind was numb. I was vaguely in awe when told that the Wits runner with the long blond hair, Fordyce, had peeled off an up record 5:37.28 to beat Halberstadt. He'd covered the distance almost three and a half hours faster than me. I simply could not comprehend the magnitude of his performance, other than to mumble to myself that he was a freak. A few minutes later Fordyce himself came over to the Kudus gathering dressed in a pair of jeans with a tee shirt, windbreaker, sunglasses and his dry blond hair floating in the breeze as though he was taking a casual stroll. Not a sign of the distress or physical torture the Comrades had inflicted on the rest of us. Just amazing!

There were others in the Kudus camp who hadn't done too badly themselves. Gerald Nelson had finished 28th in a stunning 6:24 and Gail Ingram had finished fourth woman in 7:46, behind UCT student Isavel Roche-Kelly, who won the women's race in an exceptional 6:44. During my undergraduate days at Wits I got to know Ingram reasonably well. She played some hockey and squash but otherwise was a non-runner. Yet a few years later she had won the Two Oceans and had come close to a Comrades silver medal. There was a lesson in there somewhere for me, but it took me a few days to regain my composure and realise it. In the meantime I was delighted to have achieved my long-held goal of finishing the Comrades, as had my brother JP and brother-in-law Derek Youens.

My mentor from the 1976 Vaal Marathon (and now fellow Kudus runner), Dave Gurney, finished his 11th consecutive Comrades in a comfortable 10:03, and Hodgskiss casually completed his 11th Comrades in 7:13 to extend his silver medal collection to 10.

The other amazing athletes we were to learn more about and appreciate were the Ian Jardine blind runners competing in the Comrades with their pilots or guides, attached by a handkerchief held between the runners. At the end of the 11 hour cut-off, 93.4% of starters had completed Comrades, all made possible by 2,400 race organisers and volunteers who dispensed 45,000 litres of Coke and 209,000 litres of water, combined with extraordinary spectator support and encouragement. It was another Herculean effort by the Collegians Harriers, a modest amateur athletics club. The Comrades Marathon Association would assume the overall responsibility for the event from 1982 because of the phenomenal growth in participation and popularity.

The noble sentiment, expressed by Collegians Harriers, was that the Comrades was bigger than any club or individual, and it was time for them to hand the event over to an organisation whose sole focus would be the responsibility for the successful running of the event, the Comrades Marathon Association or CMA.

The Comrades Marathon was destined to become the biggest, oldest and one of the greatest ultramarathons in the world.

10

The aftermath

A few days after the sheer enormity of an event like Comrades, a more meaningful reflection occurs. Those few rest days provided an opportunity to recover from soreness and stiffness; digest the press; and review the athletic performances of the winners, and the extraordinary stories of ordinary people with some disability or disadvantage, who completed Comrades. The life stories within Comrades could fill a public library.

Once the dust had settled on the 1981 Comrades, the black armband lingered. Bruce Fordyce had won the Comrades wearing a black armband as an anti-apartheid protest. I respected Fordyce's courage to run with a black armband, knowing it would alienate some potential sponsors and fans but, simultaneously, the issue intrigued me. I did not understand it because it had not emerged in my Kudus running group before the Comrades. Perhaps I was inadequately informed?

Only once before had it been proposed that the Comrades should be linked to an event of a political nature. In his book The Comrades Marathon Story, Morris Alexander recalls a proposal that the 1981 Comrades was to be associated with the 20th anniversary of the Republic of South Africa celebrations. The Nationalist government had planned these celebrations to take place in Durban on 1 June. Intriguingly, the 1981 Comrades would be run from Durban to Pietermaritzburg, so all the action would ultimately be in Pietermaritzburg. The Comrades was initially run on 24

May, being Empire Day. From 1954 it was run on Union Day, being 31 May. After South Africa became a republic in 1961 Comrades continued to be run on the 31 May Republic Day public holiday from 1961 until the election of Nelson Mandela in 1994. From 1996 Comrades was run on 16 June, the anniversary of the Soweto uprising in 1976, until the action of the ANC Youth League alleged that the Comrades distracted from the importance of the celebration of National Youth Day. From 2009 the Comrades reverted to the last weekend in May. That aside, I am unaware of any official association between the 1981 Comrades and the 20th anniversary republic celebrations.

I still have a copy of my 1981 entry form and the official programme which makes no mention whatsoever of the 20th anniversary of the Republic of South Africa. There is a 'R20' logo on the left hand side of both without any words, no flags, no emblems, and no coat of arms. The Republic of South Africa is not mentioned at all, and the official Comrades results say nothing of the Republic of South Africa or any Republic Day celebrations.

Nonetheless, if the nexus between a Nationalist apartheid republic and the 1981 Comrades had been publicly promoted, I am confident my running club, Varsity Kudus, would have opposed such an association. Their opposition would certainly have resonated with other progressive-minded runners in the broader South African community. I would never have run in support of the Nationalist republic.

Since 1981, my experience of the entire Comrades community – runners, organisers, families, friends and spectators – is that they are a group of fair-minded individuals who respect human endeavour above race and gender. In 1974 the organisers, Collegians Harriers, convened a meeting of members to determine whether non-white runners should be allowed to participate. The Nationalist government had indicated that it would allow non-whites to participate as long as there were at least two overseas or international competitors. This was a golden opportunity for organisers to open Comrades to all. Disappointingly some 105 Collegians Harriers members voted in favour of retaining the male whites only status quo while 39 members voted in favour of opening the Comrades to all. Following the negative vote, a member of Durban-based Savages

Athletic Club was quoted as saying: "They deserve to see their Comrades Marathon wither and die."

Morris Alexander's *The Comrades Marathon Story* chapter on the 1974 race is titled "No Black Friday." The opening paragraph suggests:

> Before the 1974 Comrades Marathon there was a fine spirit of comradeship between the official White competitors and the unofficial women and non-White runners. This camaraderie was threatened in 1974 by outside attempts to force a racial integration on the race, an integration which would in any case have come about quietly and in good time – and probably very much earlier than could have been expected as likely only a few years earlier. A vociferous minority would just not accept that integration, like segregation, must not be forced.

Wits runners initially contemplated boycotting the event. In the build up to the 1974 Comrades, Wits University commerce graduate Charles Coville, did not realise he would be one of the most important figures in aiding the participation and profile of black runners in Comrades and Two Oceans. While serving his articles of clerkship, Coville was sent to an audit at the Marievale Gold Mine where the finance manager was Eddie Smit. Smit also happened to be secretary of the SA Amateur Bantu Athletic Association. He was Coville's point of contact for the audit. Smit told Coville about the marathon exploits of two Marievale employees, Vincent Gabashane Rakabaele and Michael Monaheng, who both had run sub-2.20 marathons at the SA Mines Marathon Championships although their world-class marathon times were disputed by the white athletics authorities. Smit was adamant the course was accurate and their times were correct.

Smit and Coville spoke a lot about running during the audit including the latter's infatuation with Comrades. Coville had already earned five medals for five consecutive Comrades and raised the idea of Rakabaele and Monaheng running the 31 May classic. Blacks had been running Comrades unofficially since 1935 without incident despite not being recognised in the official results and being denied a finisher's medal.

The Comrades proposal appealed to Smit, Rakabaele and Monaheng and thus Coville suggested they join the Wits University runners on weekend training runs, in particular the final 60km Sunday morning training run from John Bush's home in Florida.

Smit drove them up from Marievale to Florida, where they easily completed the training runs with the Wits runners. Coville recalls them suavely dressed in formal shirt and blazer for the post-run lunch at the Bush residence while the casual attire of the Wits students looked like they had just recovered from big hangovers and insufficient sleep.

Following the "no" vote by Collegians Harriers, Wits runners resolved to participate but to protest passively by wearing black wristbands. Fellow Wits students, including Bush and Denis Sacks, editor of the Wits Athletic Club newsletter "Track and Veld", supported Coville. In his editorial of the March 1974 edition Sacks lamented the Collegians' decision, pointing out that the form of protest was up to the individual. In his view, the only winner in the 1974 Comrades would be apartheid.

Although Wits students never advocated a boycott of Comrades, Coville opted to boycott the race and second Rakabaele instead. Before the race he received threats of having his car tyres slashed. The day before the race, Coville drove over the course with Rakabaele, Monaheng and Smit. At Drummond, Coville asked Rakabaele what he thought of the course only to be asked in return in which direction they would be running. Coville had omitted to mention it would be an up run.

And so on Friday 31 May 1974, with the full support of the Wits runners, Rakabaele and Monaheng lined up at the start of Comrades. They would be running unofficially and the plan was for Rakabaele to run with the Wits Comrades running star, Trev Parry. Coville and wife Maureen seconded Rakabaele while Smit looked after Monaheng. Confusion at the start resulted in Rakabaele missing Parry but chasing race leaders Ronnie Brimelow and Merv Myhill instead. Astonishingly Rakabaele led the race in the early stages despite attempts by Coville to slow him down. Needless to say he slowed anyway, but too late.

Coville recalls that after halfway there was a lot of singing and chanting from the black spectators and twice Rakabaele handed him a handful of coins given to him by some of the black spectators. Rakabaele finished, unofficially, in 42nd position to a rousing reception in Pietermaritzburg. Monaheng struggled with stomach cramps from drinking more fluid than he was used to but still finished in a highly respectable 76th position. Neither received medals. Consistent with previous years, all blacks were excluded from the official results. Despite the negative Collegians' vote ahead of Comrades, the race went off without a hitch. Blacks ran unofficially with whites and some twenty Wits students protested passively via their black wristbands.

Fortunately, in 1975, the Comrades organisers finally opened the event to non-whites and women. No longer would it be the exclusive preserve of white males. Incidentally, the Boston Marathon was only opened to women in 1972. The Comrades organisers finally took a leadership position in South Africa to show the nation how, on one day of the year, all South Africans could embrace the Comrades, the joy of life and one another, without the acrid and inhumane dogma of apartheid. The Comrades was on public display for all to enjoy, witnessing individuals stretched to their absolute limit, and the resulting camaraderie and mutual respect. It was a nakedly honest day, rich in human spirit, and the entire nation embraced it enthusiastically.

Rakabaele went one step further. He won an official medal by finishing 20th at the 1975 Comrades, followed by a gold medal run of 5:59 in 8th position in 1976. Rakabaele also put the Two Oceans 56km ultramarathon on the world map, and in the living rooms and hearts of most South African households, through his record breaking victories in 1976 and 1979 combined with engrossing tussles in the intervening years. Rakabaele became the star attraction in any running event he entered in South Africa and always ran with dignity and impeccable modesty. Everyone loved Rakabaele.

Coville subsequently had his domestic telephone tapped by South Africa's dreaded security police. He emigrated to Australia in 1978. Soon after arriving in Sydney and participating in local road running and marathon events, his level of dissatisfaction with the poor organisation of these events provided him with the impetus to establish Sydney Striders in 1980, now one of Australia's largest running clubs with over 800 members in 2014.

Returning to my 1981 Comrades debut and the black armband controversy, there was an opportunity to increase black participation in the Comrades, to assist with their development and training so that they might emulate the extraordinary results black runners were achieving in all distances up to the standard marathon. They were late starters in distance running only because of their enforced disadvantage under apartheid. In 1981, they were still at an enormous disadvantage compared to the white competitors.

I am not aware of any black runners who might have run the 1981 Comrades in the colours of Wits University or its alumni club, Varsity Kudus, despite the pioneering efforts of Coville and others in 1974. Both running clubs were vehemently opposed to apartheid and the Nationalists; yet, in those early days, our actions and deeds did not necessarily match our convictions. We were the product of an almost exclusively white university, Wits. None of us had graduated with blacks because of the Nationalists' education policy legislated through the Extension of University Education Act of 1959. In the 1981 Comrades, there was only one black runner in the top 10, Chris Mkize, and another two in the top 50. That was the reality of 1981. Those clubs that had assisted black runners since 1975 to join running clubs established within white communities were the real social pioneers and they were not necessarily liberal English university-based clubs like Wits, UCT, Natal, Rhodes, or Varsity Kudus. Ordinary community clubs like RAC and many others did not protest with black armbands; instead, they got black athletes into weekend road races with a few following through to the Comrades. Conspicuous absentees from the 1981 Comrades were the two top black athletes tipped as possible future winners, Rakabaele and Tjale. Their pedigrees were impeccable and their race results leading up to Comrades were breathtaking, yet they were both non-starters.

On reflection, there was probably some intrigue surrounding Fordyce's citizenship status in 1981. Born in Hong Kong, he avoided military conscription unlike Halberstadt and Robb (who had to do a military camp a few months before the 1981 Comrades) and all other white South African males. I was doing my very best to dodge the military draft after my initial training and a couple of camps. In the preface to Tim Noakes' *Lore of Running*, published in 1985, Bruce Fordyce and Arthur Newton are referred to as Englishmen, not South Africans. In the history of the London to Brighton, Bruce is referred to as "a South African-based Briton." Local Afrikaners would term this status as one of a *soutpiel*. This is not insignificant as in 1975 South Africans were barred from all international events, including the London to Brighton, following the IAAF's suspension of South Africa from international athletics. So Fordyce, born in Hong Kong, was able to run the London to Brighton as a Briton and return to Johannesburg as a victorious South African. It was his good fortune to be afforded the best of both worlds.

Between 1982 and 1990, the Comrades was run on Republic Day no fewer than eight times without another black armband in sight, despite the continued imposition of apartheid and several states of emergency being declared. During these years, commercial endorsements and logos competed for live television airtime ahead of political issues and black armbands.

In 1981, black South African athletes were surely amongst the most disadvantaged groups in the universal world of athletics. Black sheep in their native South Africa and black sheep internationally, until Mandela's release in 1990. They had no opportunity to seek fame and fortune abroad. Halberstadt caused enormous controversy in 1979 when he refused Springbok colours over the government's failure to grant a passport to fellow Springbok athlete Matthews 'Loop-en-Val' Motshwarateu. The then president of the South African Amateur Athletics Union, Professor Charles Nieuwoudt, referred to Halberstadt as a "sports terrorist." Halberstadt and Plaatjes subsequently abandoned their South African citizenship in order to compete internationally.

Although my initial goal was simply to run the Comrades once, the event had motivated me to continue jogging. I loved my early morning jogs, being outdoors and embracing the dawn beauty of the African Highveld. I had discovered these moments of outdoor solitude to be amazingly productive in terms of clearing the mind, reflecting on the day ahead with all the priorities, demands, staffing concerns and commercial issues. The extraordinary bonus was the spiritual enjoyment I started deriving from my dawn runs: witnessing early mornings through all the seasons, watching the city wake to a new day, hearing the bird calls. No one had told me about this richness in an early morning jog, the sheer beauty of nature and the uplifting beginning to another day.

My running was spontaneous and I could squeeze it into my family and professional commitments in the early hours of the day. I enjoyed being busy, and running seemed such a perfect fit. It defused the stress and stimulated my energy levels and career drive. I always felt good after a run. It made me become acutely time-efficient because I had no time to waste. My half-hour jog was a precious early morning indulgence so I had to be organised. Gradually my career started stimulating my running, and vice versa. It became a very harmonious yin-yang relationship. I could not imagine doing one without the other. They were highly compatible, requiring discipline, consistency and optimal time management. Ambition in one sphere stimulated ambition in the other. I could not contemplate being a full-time runner as such a one-dimensional existence held no intellectual appeal whatsoever. Luckily, most of my working hours were spent sitting behind a desk on an upholstered chair so there was no pressure on my legs. No black runner in South Africa would have enjoyed such workplace luxury. Most were employed in more physically demanding jobs.

The remainder of 1981 was a case of solid application and consistency on many fronts, including my family, KPMG, jogging and household maintenance. It was a productive and rewarding spell. My career was moving in a positive direction, my daughters were healthy, happy, stimulated and loved and my running gradually started improving. The fitter I got the easier it became, including recovery times and nightly sleeping requirements. Over the rest of 1981, I progressed from a nine-hour Comrades novice to a top-20 finisher in shorter, highly competitive road races around Johannesburg. My progress was a result of running almost every morning combined with weekend races, or long Sunday social runs organised by Kudus, plus a few useful training tips from some of the more experienced runners around Johannesburg.

Hodgskiss was instrumental in recruiting me into the Kudus cross country team. Although never my favourite event, I soon started to benefit from the anaerobic effort of running hard over tough courses on Saturday afternoons. The long run of the week was always scheduled for

Sunday morning. We would either meet at a Kudus member's home for a 20–25km easy jog, returning for tea and cake, or if there was a Transvaal Road Runners Association race close by, we would enter and jog that to achieve a similar distance.

Then Hodgskiss insisted we should run weekly time trials to improve our speed. The Pirates club in Greenside, 3km from my home, hosted an 8km time trial every Tuesday evening. Depending on my client commitments on a Tuesday, I could jog into the office and then jog directly to Pirates on the way home. I could almost run faster than the Johannesburg traffic, and with careful planning and timing, I would arrive at Pirates, warmed up, and ready to go, only a couple of minutes before the start. After an all-out effort over 8km, I would jog the 3km home as a warm-down and arrive only a few minutes later than usual.

Then there was the Sweat Shop in Braamfontein, a couple of blocks from Wits University, founded by Gordon Howie. I was reliably informed that Howie, assisted by Jax Snyman, offered the best running shoe service in South Africa. While purchasing my next pair of running shoes, I picked up a Sweat Shop training schedule for the 50km JSE Marathon a couple of months away. This was a free handout sitting on the counter, but I quite fancied the Sweat Shop training schedule for a silver medal (sub-3:45) although the race was being run uphill from Pretoria to the Wanderers, not dissimilar to the Korkie slow poison.

So, in addition to the cross country, Sunday long runs and time trials, the Sweat Shop training schedule would introduce me to session variations including hills, track and fartlek, as well as training principles like base load, incremental weekly distances, peak training and tapering. My running suddenly became even more enjoyable as the methodical planning of session variations and peak training appealed to my career mindset and personality. The most appealing aspect was that I had never run to a training programme, let alone a structured training programme, so I enthusiastically introduced this variety into my morning runs. Every run would now take on more significance, representing a small building block in my ultimate speed and endurance as a marathon runner. I was excited. In the years ahead my association with the Sweat Shop would greatly assist my rapid improvement as a distance runner. Little did I know how fortunate I was to lift that JSE training schedule from the Sweat Shop counter in 1981.

The highly informative 1981 JSE Marathon official programme mailed to all entrants beforehand included profiles of leading black runners, Hoseah Tjale and Thompson Magawana, plus articles written by running celebrities Fordyce, Kevin Shaw, Cheryl Winn (nee Jorgensen) and Alan Robb. The programme also included a cutting edge sports science article entitled "Five ways to improve one's Racing Performance" that suggested –

- Carbohydrate loading
- Drinking two and a half cups of coffee before the race
- Stretching before the race
- Drinking everything in sight during the race, and
- Blood doping.

The author was a passionate runner and enthusiastic sports scientist, Dr Tim Noakes.

Thirty years later I finally appreciated how the performances of world-class endurance athletes had been enhanced through blood doping and, to a lesser extent, caffeine.

Meanwhile my rudimentary running science took another big step forward in August when I purchased my first running watch from Dions Discount Store for R25.95. It was a Casio F310G, and the next day when I lined up for the start of the 50km JSE Marathon, I felt like an absolute pro. Fortunately, it turned out to be a successful outing for me. I finished in 3:26, comfortably within the silver medal time, and also achieved my first sub-three-hour marathon, passing through the 42.2km mark in 2:51.27. I was over the moon to finish 63rd out of 1,451 finishers and I felt better than after any of my previous races of marathon distance or more. The other highlight was meeting up with Brian Chamberlain, who had finished a comfortable sixth in 3:02. Chamberlain had an extraordinary running pedigree. He had won the 56km Two Oceans Marathon twice, in 1977 and 1978. In August 1977 he had set a course record of 2:18:30 in the Stellenbosch Marathon, and two weeks later, had won the national title in 2:19. We lived pretty close to each other and over the next few years would become good friends and training partners.

Back at our KPMG offices, Malin was aware of my enthusiasm to improve my standard marathon time after my first sub-3 result at the JSE. One day he suggested I should run with him at the Transvaal Marathon Championships in a month's time. He would guarantee me a sub-2:40 finish because it was a fast course. He was right: the route followed the first 42.2km of the Korkie ultramarathon but run in the reverse direction, so it was ever so gradually downhill. Jeff piloted me the whole way, talking non-stop. He got me to the finish in 2:37.40, a personal best by 14 minutes and an improvement of 47 minutes over my Golden Reef Marathon time a year earlier. The improvement bug had well and truly bitten and I was enjoying the experience.

In October I raced the Phillip Jones Memorial 32km hosted by Pirates in Greenside over a tough, undulating course. I managed to run my first sub-two-hour time for a 20-miler finishing in 1:57.01 in 22nd position. For the first time I finished ahead of Robb and Ernest Seleke, and only three minutes behind Chamberlain.

Next was the Dave Isaacs Memorial Half Marathon at Zoo Lake, hosted by Rocky Road Runners. I finished 20th in another PB of 73:29. That was significant because I was among a cluster of talented runners who trained together, guys like Fordyce, Franz, Tony Dearling, Dov (Yiddish for bear) Traub, Ian Laxton and Chamberlain. I had always aspired to join them, but felt I was not good enough. That was about to change. I had a word with Franz and he suggested I give it a go.

A week later, I again finished 20th in the horribly hilly Jeppe Glendower BMW 16km, clocking 55:09. Fordyce was only four places in front of me. I was amazed I could be so close to the Comrades' champion and record holder.

That morning I got to speak to Halberstadt and Tjale for the first time. I sheepishly introduced myself to Halberstadt and congratulated him on his sub-50-minute winning time and in the blink of an eye he established my time, my running goals and offered me some very positive encouragement. I was a novice runner and a total stranger to him but his enthusiasm, energy and generosity left a mark. In addition to being a freakishly good all-round runner, he had returned from an athletics scholarship in the US with a Bachelor of Science and an MBA. He was a smart guy.

My next conversation was with Hoseah Tjale, affectionately known as 'Hos.' He was simply an extraordinary marathoner and ultramarathoner. Soon after 1975, when racial and gender segregation in road running was abandoned, Hos started making his mark. A driver by occupation, Hos was given great encouragement circa 1977 by Len Keating and the Allen family of RAC. Keating shaped his first intensive training programme. He went on to win Two Oceans, Korkie, JSE and almost every major road race in South Africa with the exception of Comrades, where he finished in the top 10 no fewer than nine times, including second position in 1985 and 1990. Hot on the heels of Rakabaele, Tjale was the second black athlete to win a Comrades gold medal. Tjale and Halberstadt both had unorthodox running styles. Running behind Hos in a race made you believe he had cramped in both hamstrings and could only run another five paces before falling over. In reality, that was his natural running style and he could run like that all day, smiling.

The final race of 1981 was the 32km Tough One hosted by RAC. As its name suggests, it is a hilly 20-miler. However, the benefit of my consistent training combined with time trials, speed work and other variations was evident. I ran the second half of the race with Australian ex-pat Pete Connolly of Pirates and we finished together in 15th position in 1:58.03. Viv van der Sandt beat Tjale by six seconds to win in 1:47.48, but Halberstadt created the real news. He had only recently been deemed to be a 'professional' athlete and thus denied entry into this 'amateur' race. Nonetheless, he ran unofficially and came within one metre of shattering the course record, minutes ahead of Van der Sandt, but dramatically turned his back on amateurism in road running by walking off the track without breaking the tape. He would have stopped the clocks at 1:44.14. He was destined to run on the new professional circuit in the US with fellow South African Bernie Rose. The pro road running circuit would beat the sports boycotts in a similar fashion to professional golf and tennis. Henceforth, both Halberstadt and Rose would be precluded from competing in any amateur sanctioned running event in South Africa, including the Comrades.

As 1981 drew to an end I could not believe just how much fun I was having both in my professional career and, quite unexpectedly, in road running. In addition to my 2:37 marathon, I had managed to run 26.55 for the Pirates 8km time trial, 33.32 for a 10km race and 55.04 for a 16km race. My training diary reflects that I covered a total of 3,340km for the year, averaging 73km a week for the 46 weeks that I ran.

At the Kudus end-of-year prizegiving I received the trophy for the most improved runner, presented by none other than Comrades champion and record holder Fordyce. The talk around the table that night was that I should have a crack at running a silver medal time of sub-7:30 in 1982.

I was soon to have a more valuable and far-reaching conversation. I was in the change rooms after the weekly 8km time trial at Pirates when Plaatjes asked me what I was training for. Remembering that he had won the SA Marathon Championship at altitude only a few months earlier in 2:16, I felt terribly self-conscious when I told him I planned to run my first sub-2:30 marathon in March, at the Peninsula Marathon in Cape Town.

He immediately fired his next question: "What is your training schedule?"

I explained I had recently increased my training to 90–100km a week, working off a 50-minute weekday morning run (recently increased from 30 minutes), a time trial on Tuesday evenings, a one-hour steady run on Saturday, followed by Sunday long club runs with Kudus, or races.

Mark retorted: "Just be careful you don't run too many junk miles."

"What do you mean?"

"Well, if you hope to run a sub-2:30 marathon, you will have to average at least 3.30 per km so you must include several training sessions at a minimum of that speed just to get used to race pace."

He warned me against running for 50 minutes in the mornings at four minutes per kilometre or slower, and instead recommended warming up for 2km at an easy pace and then running for 20 minutes at race pace.

"Always finish strongly, running like you want to go further because you feel so good," he concluded.

I took note. Plaatjes was at the cutting edge. He was a determinedly ambitious athlete.

The unsolicited advice offered to me by Plaatjes would represent another major building block in my continued improvement as a distance runner.

Call back the past 3

Apartheid's ticking time bomb detonated on 16 June 1976. Nothing was ever the same.

The Nationalist government had managed to deal with a number of crises in the nearly three decades it had ruled South Africa with an iron first. It survived the Sharpville massacre. It outlasted the passive resistance towards the pass laws. It choked off *Umkhonto we Sizwe* with the mass arrest of the high command of the ANC's armed wing at Lilliesleaf Farm, in Rivonia, in July 1963, and the subsequent jailing on Robben Island of ANC leaders such as Nelson Mandela, Walter Sisulu and Govan Mbeki.

But the one thing the suppression of human rights could not do was stop the time bomb.

The buffer zone that the Portuguese had established around the perimeter of South Africa through their colonisation of Angola and Mozambique came to an abrupt end with the Carnation Revolution of April 1974 when army officers overthrew the right wing Portuguese government. Samora Machel's Frelimo movement seized power in Mozambique, giving the ANC a safe haven on South Africa's north eastern border, just 400km from Pretoria. Another white stronghold toppled.

On the same day in April 1976 a team from the Wits University Marathon Club was driving from Bulawayo in Rhodesia to the border post at Beit Bridge after competing in the Matopos 53km ultramarathon, when guerrillas gunned down four motorcyclists on the other main road heading south to Beit Bridge, from Fort Victoria. The bush war in Rhodesia drove Prime Minister Ian Smith to admit to advisors that, with hostile nations on three sides, indefinite postponement of majority rule would not be possible. Another buffer state of the apartheid regime was in trouble.

In South Africa, anger had been building for two years against the Afrikaans Medium Decree of 1974 which forced all black schools to use both English and Afrikaans in equal measure to teach school subjects. Black students identified Afrikaans as the language of the oppressor, but the government was determined to foist its language on the masses. The deputy minister of Bantu Education, Punt Jansen, arrogantly declared: "No, I have not consulted them and I am not going to consult them. I have consulted the Constitution of the Republic of South Africa."

In early 1976 the Reverend Desmond Tutu, Dean of St Mary's Cathedral in central Johannesburg, wrote an open letter to the Prime Minister BJ Vorster. Tutu warned that unless something was done urgently to remove the causes of black anger, he was fearful of what was likely to erupt because black people were growing increasingly restive under the oppressive white regime. Vorster dismissed the letter as propaganda engineered by my father's opposition political party.

Boom! An explosive mix of anger and frustration detonated on the morning of 16 June. About 20,000 black students marched from their schools towards Orlando Stadium for a protest rally. The police claim they threw stones. The students claim the police wanted to stop them whatever it took. Gunfire and rioting erupted and by the end of the day 23 people, including two whites, died in the maelstrom which swept Soweto before nightfall. It was the day that irrevocably changed the course of South African history

The Soweto uprising spread rapidly to other parts of the country and shook the fabric of South African society; it drove home the dangers of racial confrontation. In the two months that followed, more than 300 people died violently and thousands were arrested. Many young blacks fled the country to join resistance movements in Africa and elsewhere, and to undergo military training. In that short period, black militancy grew while white South Africa armed itself to the teeth. It took less than a month for blacks to realise that mass action would yield results, even though they were pitting their bodies against bullets; on 6 July the government announced that black Africans could nominate their language of choice for instruction in schools.

In January 1976 South Africa finally got television across the nation. For decades, South Africans had been denied television lest the population get a glimpse of how the rest of the world lived, without apartheid. It took the Nationalists that long to realise what a potent propaganda tool the medium could be. In the latter half of June 1976 the South African Broadcasting Corporation broadcast into the living rooms of many white South African families daily images of angry black youths throwing stones at police, barricading roads, and setting fire to government buildings. This had the desired effect of forcing most whites into a siege mentality, never allowing them to see the black point of view.

The British Actors Equity ban of South Africa, together with the draconian internal censorship regime, obliterated the chance to view any high-quality foreign programmes, other than ancient re-runs of the likes of *Star Trek*, *The Bob Newhart Show* and *The Sweeney*, excruciatingly badly lip-synched into Afrikaans. The one exception to the mediocrity was the annual telecast of Wimbledon.

A terrible sense of mistrust between blacks and whites followed the Soweto uprising. Black teenagers were prepared to boycott their schooling and slip over the border for military training for a guerrilla war against South Africa. Their parents were more willing to negotiate, not wanting their children to become mortuary statistics. Irrespective of the generation, the explosion had occurred. The resulting outpouring of black discontent with apartheid would never again be contained. South Africa's economy had been built on the back of cheap black labour: the level of black consciousness was such the workforce understood that withholding labour would effectively cripple the economy, despite the short-term hardship it would impose on their community.

However, the Nationalists thought they could forcibly suppress the growing resistance. Activists were targeted and on 12 September 1977 activist Steve Biko died in police detention under mysterious circumstances. Biko had founded the Black Consciousness Movement in the early 1970s, which promoted the "cultural and political revival of an oppressed people."

In 1973 the former medical student and student leader was formally banned and placed under house arrest in King Williams Town, his birthplace. Biko exerted considerable influence on the South African socio-political scene even though his banning order prevented him from travelling. In the wake of the urban revolt of 1976, and with the prospects of a national revolution becoming increasingly real, security police arrested Biko and transferred him to custody in Port Elizabeth. He was 30 years old, studying law by correspondence and extremely fit at the time of his arrest.

His death fuelled black anger, and international disgust with the Nationalist government was palpable. When Biko was buried in King Williams Town, 20,000 mourners attended the funeral, including diplomats from 13 Western nations. The police did their best to stop mourners from driving to the funeral from across the nation but, although they stopped some, they could not deal with a full-force flood.

International outrage demanded an inquest. Police alleged he had died as a result of a prison accident following a hunger strike. Evidence presented during the 15-day inquest revealed otherwise. Biko was stripped naked, interrogated for 22 hours, tortured, beaten and kept in leg irons for 48 hours, chained to a grille at night. An alleged scuffle with police and a blow to his head resulted in concussion and brain damage. He was not sent to hospital, but driven to a maximum security prison in Pretoria. He was slung into the back of a police van, naked and manacled, for an end-of-winter 1,100km drive. He did not survive the maltreatment, dying of a brain haemorrhage; he was the 20th person to die in security police custody in 18 months.

The Minister of Justice and Police, Jimmy Kruger, reacted by infamously commenting: "I am not glad and I am not sorry about Mr Biko. It leaves me cold."

There was no prosecution of those involved in Biko's death. The Nationalist government was circling the wagons against attack.

A few months before Biko's death, the white opposition in parliament split. My father allied himself with the dissident group, called the Progressive Federal Party, who sought the end of racial rule. In November he stood as the PFP candidate opposing Dr Piet Koornhof, the sitting member of parliament for Primrose since 1964. My father polled a mere 10% of votes, indicating nine of 10 whites either supported the status quo or feared that South Africa would degenerate into the chaos which had befallen so many other former colonies in Africa after independence. The National Party increased its majority, carefully manipulating electorate boundaries to maximise its grip on power, and to win 80% of seats in parliament, with 65% of the vote.

It is worth reflecting on the extraordinary life of Dr Koornhof. He studied theology at the University of Stellenbosch and completed his doctoral studies at Oxford University as a Rhodes scholar. As a cabinet minister in the Nationalist government, he held several portfolios during his parliamentary career. He was a strong proponent of apartheid, even to the point of proposing separate national teams for each ethnic group in 1973. He served as ambassador to the US from 1987 to the end of the Nationalist regime. In 1993, aged 68, he left his wife for his black secretary, 44 years his junior, with whom he subsequently had several children. Under the laws he helped draw up, he would have been imprisoned for this. It gets more bizarre: in 2001 he joined the ANC. He died in 2007, aged 82.

In 1982 the security police surpassed themselves. After two months of intensive interrogation that involved excruciating torture, including electric shocks, doctor-turned-trade unionist, Neil Aggett, hanged himself in his cell in Johannesburg's massive police headquarters at John Vorster Square in March 1982. In the cell opposite was another trade unionist, Auret van Heerden, a Comrades Marathon finisher and former chairman of the Wits University Cross Country and Marathon Club. He testified at Aggett's inquest about the sustained maltreatment that led to the physical and mental breakdown of his fellow detainee.

Aggett was the first white person to die in security police detention since 1963. It polarised the white community. Those who voted for the government considered Aggett a communist troublemaker who got what he deserved; the remainder thought the murderous Nationalists were herding the population over a cliff and started voting with their feet.

An increasing number of families emigrated, rather than let their sons undertake military service for a regime that had abandoned all pretence of humanity, legitimacy and adherence to law in its desperation to perpetuate its aspiration of white Afrikaner supremacy.

11

A silver lining

Things were going smoothly in January 1982. Too smoothly.

Just when I had got our Linden house feeling like a home, my accounting career progressing well and my running on the move, KPMG transferred me to its East London office.

The move came with the first of my silver linings of the year: I would be admitted to the partnership on 1 March, the same day I was to start in East London. At 28, I would be the youngest partner in the firm.

After our three years overseas, we had become accustomed to being close to our families so that summer break took on a more subdued atmosphere. We did not know anyone in East London and would never have moved there voluntarily. On the other hand, the maximum term of my secondment would be two years and the girls were not yet at school, so we viewed it as another adventure and decided to soak up as much of the Eastern Cape as possible. An added bonus was that we would be living right next to the ocean.

Apart from the packing up and readying our home for the rental market, I had to prepare for a handover of my clients in Johannesburg and to make a series of trips to East London to meet my new partners and clients. I also had to check out accommodation for the family. Amid all this I was still hoping to run the Peninsula Marathon. If ever one needed evidence of just how time-efficient and travel-friendly running is, this was the moment. Given a spare 30 minutes anywhere, all one needed was a pair of running shoes, shorts and a singlet and I could be out of the door and on to the road – anywhere, any time – within minutes.

I had started running with the hot-shot group from the Wanderers Club in Johannesburg on Saturday mornings and this further developed and stimulated my running. The group included Fordyce, Dave Wright, Franz, Dearling, Laxton, Traub, Ev Mons, Hugh Patterson, Tony Drury, Gerald Nelson, Alan Edwards, Chamberlain, Stuart Peacock, Dave Anderson, Ivan Glasenberg, Ken McArthur and Graham Lindenberg, who, between them, had competed well in all of South Africa's major races.

The running protocol was quite simple. Typically, they would run 15km in 56 to 58 minutes, including an easy start to warm up, and a few faster sections en route. Cruising pace would be about 3 minutes 45 seconds per kilometre. If you felt good, you went to the front and applied the pressure to push the tempo pretty hard while still maintaining the banter. It was always a moderate to hard run. The session also provided a wealth of running news and knowledge. In the pre-Google era, such running sources were invaluable.

I started some structured hill training in January and, for the first time in my life, I ran four consecutive weeks of over 120km per week. For February I had the Springs Striders 32km planned as my only flat-out race further than 16km in my build up to the Peninsula Marathon. I was not disappointed as I ran a PB of 1:49.56 and finished in 18th position in a high-quality field. My notes record the race as the run of my life and I was increasingly confident of going sub-2:30 at the Peninsula Marathon three weeks later. The following weekend I ran PBs for 8km (25.39), 10km (32.20) and 16km (54.25), all at altitude.

The week before I left Johannesburg, I visited Halberstadt at Adidas where he was assisting with their marketing on a freelance basis. He sold me a pair of Marathon Trainers at wholesale price, and also gave me a pair of grey LA Comp racing shoes, a couple of pairs of shorts, a few singlets and a couple of tee shirts. I walked out of the Adidas premises feeling like a world champion, totally energised by Halberstadt.

Rather than start at the East London office on 1 March, I negotiated some annual leave to ease the transition. At the start of March, Vern and I packed our little VW Golf with our two daughters and essential luggage

RUNAWAY COMRADE

and set off on the 1,600km drive to Cape Town, overnighting in Beaufort West. We spent three days in Cape Town before heading to Hermanus for a holiday. Our final leg would be the drive to East London, our home for the next two years. En route I still hoped to run a sub-2:30 on 6 March.

The Peninsula Marathon, run from Green Point Stadium to Simon's Town on a Saturday morning, had a reputation for being a relatively fast course. Despite a south-easterly wind starting to gust as we neared False Bay and slowing down all the fancied runners, the race went perfectly for me. I ran 2:26.01 for 12th place, picking up several places in the final 10km. Despite the headwind I ran the second half only a minute slower than the first 21.1km. I was thrilled with this result because it led me to believe I was capable of running faster after a few more years of consistent, smart training

My new friend and self-appointed mentor, Plaatjes, led the field home in 2:17.09. He'd set himself the goal of breaking the course record and wasn't as satisfied as I was. That is the kind of drive he had. None of us would ever guess he would go on to win the World Marathon Championship in Stuttgart in 1993.

My new 2:26 PB was in no small part due to the advice Plaatjes had offered me at Pirates a few months earlier when he advised me to break my training into shorter, harder runs as opposed to longer junk miles. Matthews Temane re-confirmed this approach to me a few years later.

When I reflected on my run, I recalled how my head sank towards my shoulders and my forearms dropped to my waist after 32km, thus depriving me of the ability to aggressively drive forward. I clearly needed to research strength training options for marathon runners, especially upper body. Although my running had improved dramatically over the past year, I lacked core strength. Since finishing school in 1970 my lack of physical exertion, particularly in the upper body, was evident. My hard-earned CA was more highly treasured by me than a six-pack torso and biceps, but I would have to do some work on the missing muscles in that area.

A few days after arriving in East London I figured out the reason for my transfer. We had four elderly partners, all approaching retirement, and one middle-aged partner who was extremely smart but driven to despair by the old quartet. Nothing had been done in the way of succession planning. The elderly partners were also reluctant to implement national policies, particularly in the human resources area. As an outsider, it appeared to me that they continued to operate in a colonial time warp.

The result was a generation gap between the old head and the willing young body of the firm. It was not hard to get the wheels turning in the right direction. Periodic performance appraisals, incorporating two-way feedback and career planning, did wonders for staff morale.

The client portfolio assigned to me included some very interesting businesses like the local newspaper, the *Daily Dispatch*. This was the newspaper edited by Donald Woods, a fiercely outspoken critic of the Nationalist government, climaxing in his escape from South Africa to Lesotho to avoid arrest and possible detention. He and Helen Zille were the journalists who exposed the tragic death of Biko at the hands of the South African Police.

Within a week of my arrival, I ran a 32km race and featured strongly enough to gain selection for the Border team to compete in the South African inter-provincial marathon championships five weeks later. I was flattered to gain representative honours. In reality the only running goal I had envisaged was running Comrades to hopefully earn that elusive silver medal. I was also recruited by the indefatigable Bob Norris to join the Old Selbornian Club, associated with one of the oldest and most prestigious schools in the Eastern Cape, Selborne College, established in 1872.

Apart from a new windsurfer, I also acquired a precious commodity in East London: time. The office was a five-minute drive from home in light traffic. I could accomplish 45-hour weekly professional obligations to KPMG and have plenty of time for family and running. My Johannesburg routine was usually 7am to 7pm, while in East London it was 8am to 5pm.

Unfortunately, the deceleration of my pace of life was mirrored in my running. I went to the inter-provincials in Port Elizabeth hopeful of a decent time but by 16km, I was 30 seconds behind my Peninsula Marathon pace and my legs grew increasingly leaden. I lurched through 32km four minutes slower than Peninsula and experienced the unlovely feeling of hitting the wall. I did not experience any cramping, I was not injured, and I was adequately hydrated and fuelled, yet ran only 2:35 and was utterly drained. My subsequent training log entry was "no fire."

Although I was essentially new to running, with just 19 months of regular training under the soles of my shoes, my physiological intuition has always been sharp. Although my health was good, I sensed I had overloaded myself with all the changes that had occurred in the previous two months, wiping out my vitality. There and then I decided not to run a single step for a week.

It left me just three weeks to finalise my preparation for Comrades and a wishful silver medal. I ran weekly distances of 104km, 108km and 46km and headed to Durban accepting that I was under-trained but at least fresh, healthy and feeling good.

After knocking off from work on the Friday evening, I got my kit ready and packed the trusty VW Golf for the Saturday haul to Pietermaritzburg with Vern and our two daughters. On the drive through the Transkei, I reflected as to why I should approach the race with some justified confidence and run under seven hours if all went well.

I had run consistently, without injury, since my Comrades debut a year earlier. Between 1 January and Comrades, I had managed to run a total of 2,100km compared with 844km a year earlier. My running speed had improved over all distances and my intuition was that the down run would be much faster and hopefully easier than an up run. I had not forgotten all I learned about physics at school.

Monday 31 May dawned damp and overcast. I started near the front of the field and bumped into Fordyce. We had not seen one another since I left Johannesburg at the end of February. Modest Fordyce exclaimed that the Saturday morning runs from the Wanderers had become more enjoyable since my transfer because there was no longer a hare in the pack.

"Like hell," was my ungracious reply. I reminded him that I had only ever heard him breathe hard once on all the training runs I had done with him. By the 10km mark I had picked up Anderson and he, too, started chatting to me like he was enjoying a recreational jog. We were running behind Eric Bateman and Bruce Matthews, both from Cape Town, and serious gold medal contenders. Matthews stopped to tie his shoelace and never regained his position. Anderson, too, eased off the pace although I was to see him and his disappearing back 60km later. I attached myself to Bateman because his stride was in sync with mine, and started to obey the advice of Chamberlain to concentrate for the entire duration of the race.

As I approached the halfway mark I re-joined the elite group of Fordyce, Robb and the Hillcrest Villages trio of Graeme Fraser, Tony Abbot and Derek Tivers. Robb had just completed a compulsory army camp on the Angolan border, a predicament that placed him at a significant disadvantage in attempting to secure a fifth win, yet he never raised the issue. He was such a stoic sportsman, admired and respected by all.

The pace felt remarkably comfortable and it coincided with my first exposure to these top athletes having a pee on the run. It would take me another year, and much practice, before I could emulate this feat and still keep shoes, socks and feet dry.

I passed through the halfway mark in 2:50 in 14th position. Although 25 minutes faster than my most optimistic estimate, I was feeling remarkably good and somewhat astounded by my presence at the pointy end of the race with the Comrades contenders. Nothing was ever said but there was definitely a pecking order. I was terribly self-conscious about not ending up in the casualty basket as an outmatched optimist. After Drummond, Fordyce removed his rain-soaked tee shirt and took off with other gold medal contenders. Because I had never run further than 56km without walking, I had the deepest fear that over the last 40km of Comrades I would be overtaken, tsunami style, by thousands of more experienced runners. The guys I had been running with had suddenly decided there was indeed a race called the Comrades, which somehow started at the halfway mark, and they were out of sight in no time at all.

In terms of hydration management, I drank water until the 50km mark, after which I switched to Coke and water. There were no gel sachets or oral forms of carbohydrates. It was at this stage that the guy I was running alongside beckoned to his spectating father, telling him there were lots of glass splinters on the road and he might need some shoes. I looked down at his bare feet. I did not recognise him, but I came to appreciate the barefoot running feats of Charlie Bantom. He finished in 6:33.

Beyond this point it was a pretty lonely run, passing three-quarter distance on the snaking descent of Field's Hill in 13th position in 4:22. I was still nervous that I would be humiliated and shuffled back out of the first thousand. I started to tire on the climb out of Pinetown up Cowie's Hill. Unlike cycling, crowds get sparse towards the top of hills in the Comrades and the opportunity presented itself for a short walk of, oh, 15 paces. No sooner had I stopped running then Anderson came powering past me. It must have given him the lift he needed because he powered through to the finish in 10th position for the final gold medal in a great time of 5:55. I soon got my mojo going again and picked up the pace, but it was not enough to prevent Joe Claase from overtaking me gracefully. He was already a Comrades gold medallist and it was soon revealed that he had already achieved great things with a defective heart valve. He underwent open-heart surgery and returned to the Comrades with a more efficient heart. Two years later when a journalist asked him if there was any noticeable difference with a new valve, he replied: "Yes, I can hear this artificial valve ticking away when I go really hard."

The climb up to Tollgate from the Westridge Park Stadium, with little more than 5km to go, presented me with another irresistible opportunity to give the crowd the chance to urge me to break into a run. I only stole a quick 15-second walk but, boy, did they get on my case. People power got me going again but, even so, Errol Ackerman soon came blazing past. I was now in 16th position with 5km to go and I resolved to fight to hold on to my position in the top 20. Actually, I held on to 16th in 6:04, not knowing I had a solid five minutes on the next runner, John Dixon.

I was amazed that only three runners had passed me over the final 22km. For this I can thank the crowds in Westville and Durban. Without their constant encouragement I would certainly have taken some more walks, but the fans would have none of that. Hard taskmasters, those Natalians.

Fordyce won again in 5:34.22, beating Robb by some seven minutes, but failing to break Robb's astonishing 1978 down record of 5:29.14, when he won by almost 20 minutes.

The performance that really wowed me was that of fellow East London runner, Kenny Wilkinson. He finished his 17th consecutive Comrades in

6:39 but just to highlight what an absolutely fine athlete he really was, he also made sure it was his 17th consecutive silver.

After finding my wife and two young daughters at the finish, I enjoyed a hot shower, a change into some dry clothes and a mug of warm vegetable soup. I struggled to come to terms with my three-hour improvement. It felt a lot easier than finishing in nine hours, as I had done a year earlier, and my body was in a lot less pain. We hung around for an hour or two at the finish but it was miserable weather for socialising. With two young daughters, a patient wife and the looming eight-hour drive, I decided to call it a day and return to East London.

Driving down the coast I felt that curious blend of humility and elation that is probably referred to as the runner's high. I had astounded myself with a 6:04 Comrades just 20 months after I started jogging. I was both elated and a little overwhelmed by what I had managed to achieve because I became aware of some level of physiological talent that lay within, way beyond anything I had ever expected. I was happy to embrace it. I had no difficulty at all driving the full distance broken by nothing other than a petrol stop and, by 10pm, we were all in the comfort of our own beds at home. Our third daughter Philippa was born in East London on 2 March 1983, exactly 275 days after the 1982 Comrades.

The morning after the Comrades I was in the office at 8am, pleasantly surprised to read the sports coverage afforded me by the Daily Dispatch. I was just a little slower on the stairs between floors.

Later that day I made the following entry in my training log:

"Finished 8min. 49sec. away from a gold medal. Unbelievable! Very happy with 16th position. Probably the run of my life! Will I run Comrades again?"

As I reflected on my 1982 Comrades effort I learned a little more about the 15 runners who had finished ahead of me. Henry Nyembe finished 8th in 5:53 and was the only black runner in the top 20. By 2014 there would not be a single white South African runner in the top 20 and my 1982 time would barely enable me to scrape into the top 30. However I was inspired by the fact that all of the 15 runners ahead of me in 1982 (except the winner, Fordyce) had full-time careers outside running and most were married with families. There were two medical specialists amongst the 15 – Bateman and Ackerman – and they were the guys I really drew great inspiration from in that they were able to mix it up at the competitive end of the Comrades despite their professional practices. I regarded them as kindred spirits.

Hell, yes, I'd give Comrades another go!

12

Snap, crackle, pop

I still remember the phone call. Bob Norris, president of the Old Selbornian Runners Club, was not happy. He wanted to split the running club from the Old Selbornian parent club because it refused to grant our six black runners full membership. It was happy for blacks to belong to the running section, but would not admit them as full members of the main club.

Bob advised that he and fellow marathon stalwart, the late Kevin Flint, would call a special meeting of the running club to propose a motion to form an independent running club with a single class of membership. All members would be equal. Without hesitation I gave Bob and Kevin my full support, but mentioned I would be unable to attend the meeting because I would be in Johannesburg on the night. The meeting went ahead and 46 runners, representing the body and soul of the section, elected to immediately leave the Old Selbornian Club and incorporate a new non-racial running club. It was called Oxford Striders, after the main street in East London. The *Daily Dispatch* gave us extensive coverage on page 2 on 19 June 1982. I spent the rest of my running days in East London with Oxford Striders and a great bunch of like-minded runners. Over the ensuing decade, Norris would also make a valiant contribution to the transformation of South Africa's political system.

Professionally, my career was ticking along although I was quietly missing the hurly-burly of the Johannesburg business world. Given the slower pace of life in East London, I had become extraordinarily time-rich in my new environment and resolved to make the most of this. The girls loved the beach and we'd spend our weekends fossicking around Nahoon Beach and the river mouth. I noticed a couple of windsurfers on the Nahoon River and, given my earlier interest in sailing, I checked it out. Within weeks I had bought a Dufour sailboard and was windsurfing while Vern and our daughters were building sand castles on the beach. I loved the thrill of sailing across the wind at speed, when the board would plane over the water. Little did I know this pleasure would soon be a source of pain.

My East London sojourn turned out to be a blessing in disguise for my running. Even though I was not the most knowledgeable person on the road, I realised my rate of improvement had been spectacular; yet I also knew I needed another couple of years of patient running to acquire a solid base before I could compete at the next level. East London provided that opportunity and the quality of talent at the front end of the races matched anything in Johannesburg.

My short morning runs would be along the Nahoon, on relatively flat terrain. Two or three times a week I would visit the gym at lunchtime and work on my missing muscles. The weekends consisted of a local race on a Saturday followed by a long club run on a Sunday. I averaged about 100km a week for the rest of the year, without injury or setback. I completed 1982 injury free, having covered 5,211km in training, an increase of 56% over the previous 12 months. In all, I needed just 6½ hours to run my weekly distance.

In August I returned to Johannesburg for a couple of days on a business trip and managed to squeeze in the 50km JSE ultramarathon. I was pleased with my performance, running 3:02 and finishing in 23rd position. My marathon split was 2:31. Unlike my Comrades experience a few months earlier, no runner overtook me beyond the marathon mark. It was another quantum improvement over my JSE debut a year earlier, and my post-race recovery was also quicker. My strength training was starting to work.

The race statistics make for interesting analysis when compared with the Comrades, in which Henry Nyembe was the only black runner in the top 10. Conversely, Willie Farrell was the only white runner in the JSE top 10, in sixth place. Choeu won in a sizzling 2:46, after passing the marathon mark in 2:17. The top 10 finishers in JSE were consistent sub-2:20 runners and JSE, unlike Comrades, offered prize money. This commercial incentive provided far more competitiveness at the front end of the field. Another consideration would have been the prolonged recovery period following Comrades of Rakabaele and Tjale, which would have had a detrimental impact on their capacity to win race prizes in the following months. These black athletes raced Comrades at some considerable opportunity cost. At the time it was essentially an elite event mainly for white males, and some white females. Fast forward the clock to the 2014 Comrades after the introduction of attractive cash prizes in 1995. The only white face in the top 10 was that of Swede, Jonas Buud, in 7th position. White South African males no longer feature in the top 20.

Back in East London, I ran a marathon each month as part of my training including the Ciskei (2:36), Old Selbornian (2:32) and Kaffrarian (2:31), always managing to run a negative split. (A negative split is running the second half of a race faster than the first half.) A surprise, second only to my 16th place in Comrades, was the Bongolo Marathon in Queenstown on 6 November. Locals told me just how tough this marathon was because it included several stretches of gravel road and a few testing climbs, including Long Hill. The red-hot favourite was local ace Solomon Pongolo, a delightful Xhosa who I had run many miles with. I knew this would probably be the only opportunity I would get to run the Bongolo so my attitude was to log a quality, long training run without pushing myself too hard. There was absolutely no upside in going for broke in the Bongolo.

The starter's pistol fired and we were away in near perfect running conditions. I soon settled into a four-strong bunch just behind the pacesetter. Maxwell Zuba and I moved ahead and pretty much ran even tempo, in sync, for the next 24km. No drama. The race favourite, Pongolo, was two minutes behind us and I sensed he was not having one of his better days. Suddenly I fancied my chances of a top three finish. As we approached 37km, my KPMG colleague, Gordon Shaw, appeared roadside and barked: "You gotta go *now!*"

I decided to apply some pressure. For the first time in the race I set the tempo and after pushing for 200m, Zuba dropped off the pace. With less than 5km to the finish I was the race leader, a new experience for me. I managed to hold on comfortably and entered the sports oval at Queens College to run a victory lap no one had warned me about. I ran down the main straight visualising the end of the marathon 100m away. It was not to be. At the line I was directed by a marshal to run another lap. When I finally made it home, I thought the 500m on the track was a very unkind welcome. I owed the win to Shaw. If he had not told me to move, I would not have done so. I still had no idea of tactics at the pointy end. My race splits of 79.32 and 79.00 converted to a winning time of 2:38.32, my slowest marathon of the year. The most enjoyable, too.

Zuba finished second, about 45 seconds back; I asked him what had happened because I had been following his pace for most of the race, and expected him to respond to my surge. He looked at me, offered me the most generous Xhosa smile and replied: "Ah, Bob, it was sudden loss of power."

At the end of 1982, the De la Motte family spent a fortnight in Johannesburg and I was able to train with elite runners like Chamberlain, Fordyce, Franz, Snyman, Edwards, Laxton, Dearling, and others. I instantly noticed how much quicker their training runs were than my East London runs. They were not running any junk miles. They were also highly sceptical of the fast times coming out of the Eastern Cape, suggesting the measuring wheel in East London must be yielding short courses. When Rogers Mbantsa ran one of the fastest half marathons of the year, followed a year later by a 62:17 by the then unknown Zithulele Sinqe, they wondered if the timekeepers knew how to correctly operate a stop watch. Eventually the evidence was overwhelming and the pedigree of Mbantsa, Sinqe and other Eastern Cape athletes had the Jo'burg boys murmuring respect, not muttering jibes.

I shared some of the Eastern Cape running intelligence with them because their knowledge of races in the region was limited. The Buffs Marathon, organised by the Buffalo Road Runners Club of East London, had a reputation for very fast times because it was a downhill course, falling 450m in elevation, with two short hills near the end. I planned to run it in 1983 for my next marathon PB, hopefully quicker than 2:26. I suggested to Franz that he bring a group from RAC and have a crack at the team prize. I hinted to Fordyce that his celebrity status would almost give him the keys to the City of East London. The Buffs Marathon seed was sown.

Disaster struck at the end of January. Training had gone well, and the Oxford Striders had targeted the team prize in the Buffs 21km night race. I was in good shape and looking forward to a hard run. The wind was gusting on race morning and I could not resist. I got out the windsurfer and headed for Nahoon Beach. I clipped into my harness and rode screaming beam reach after beam reach across the wind. It was totally addictive. When I could hold on no more, I headed towards the beach along a short section on the Nahoon River where the water was deep enough to sail right up to the bank. With a deft manoeuvre, resembling a sailing jibe, you could virtually step off the board onto the beach. The regulars were doing this throughout the morning and my turn had come to emulate them. About five metres before hitting land I pulled the boom and stalled the board dramatically, broadsiding into the beach so I could step off. Well, that was the intention. Instead I was catapulted onto the beach at 20 knots, landing upright but sideways on my feet until my right ankle snapped. I heard an almighty pop. I dropped like I had been shot. Then the pain hit.

I showed up at the start of the race with ankle strapped, propped up by a walking stick. Norris and Flint laughed their heads off at this practical joke, until they realised their team was one short. They could not believe my stupidity and offered no sympathy. Oxford Striders placed three runners in the top 10, but it was not enough. We were pipped by Ciskei Joggers for the team prize and I felt terrible. I had let down the team and myself because the ankle was clearly a mess, so much so that I knew I could wave goodbye to a potential PB at Buffs, and maybe even a top 10 at Comrades.

Vern was probably the only De la Motte who saw an advantage in the situation. She was seven months pregnant and had five-year-old Nicole and two year old Simone to care for. In the short term she could add me to the list, but when the baby arrived I would be able to focus on the family, not the Comrades.

I did not sleep for one minute on the Saturday night. My ankle was throbbing and, judging by the swelling, there was some significant haemorrhaging going on inside. The local hospital confirmed my suspicions the following morning. The ankle was cracked but so swollen they could not offer me a protective cast. I had also torn the ligaments. My GP, Dr Judge, subsequently confirmed a six-week break from running, during which time I would undergo extensive physiotherapy and rehabilitation.

In my sixth week of rehab, on the afternoon of Wednesday 2 March 1983, Vern went into labour and our third daughter, Philippa, was born later that evening. And there were more arrivals to come. My hints about the Buffs Marathon had been heard and acted on and, while Vern was recuperating, I was preparing the house for the arrival of Dearling, Sibisi and Franz, who would be spending the weekend. Mr Mum was soon to become Mr Dumb as I struggled to feed my daughters, let alone these highly-tuned athletes. A further complication was that I had agreed to second four-time winner Shaw, who was set to take on Fordyce.

On Friday afternoon my houseguests went for an easy jog along the Nahoon River to loosen up after the long drive from Johannesburg. Fortunately, they took off to the Buffs Club for race registration on Friday evening, encountering Robb and his Germiston Callies Harriers teammates. The Callies boys easily won an impromptu pre-race, carbo-loading, beer drinking event session – and I didn't have to cook. Less than 12 hours later, Robb lined up to run a comfortable 2:24 marathon.

Shaw went hard, very hard, from the start. He wanted to win the Buffs for a fifth time, and he wanted to beat Fordyce. I felt I had an understanding of Fordyce's racing tactics, holding back at the most comfortable pace he could without losing touch, and then unleashing his merciless kick over the final 10km, especially on the two climbs.

At 32km, Shaw was more than a minute clear of Bruce and then it suddenly happened. Bruce injected a turn of speed that left everyone else for dead. Over the final 10km he would gap the runners that were with him, including Sibisi, by more than four minutes. He closed down Shaw by 10 to 15 seconds a kilometre. I reciprocated the tactical advice Shaw had given at Bongolo: "Gordon, you have got to go as hard as you can."

Shaw dug deep, very deep. Fordyce was using every molecule of speed he possessed. He had pushed the pace from 3.20 per km to 3.05. I checked the splits with 6km left and, for the first time since the 32km mark, Shaw was holding a gap of about 40 seconds that Fordyce could not close. I yelled the news to Shaw but he did not say a word. He was utterly focused and achieved the race feat of withstanding the Fordyce Finish to win in 2:16.44. Fordyce crossed the line 34 seconds later in a new marathon PB. It had been no ordinary training run for him. He also realised that he had a formidable competitor in the 1983 Comrades, just 12 weeks away.

My houseguests from RAC ran off with the team prize, with PBs all round. Franz had never broken 2:30 previously but almost went sub-2:20. Even so, it was not his most memorable achievement as far as the spectators were concerned. As soon as he finished, he sat on the kerb and lit up a cigarette. I asked him how he could even think of such a thing and he horrified onlookers with his casual reply: "You will not believe how good it tastes after a marathon when it goes straight into your lungs."

Later that afternoon, we met up with Fordyce, and the other Johannesburg runners, and went for a stroll along Nahoon Beach. Sibisi had slept in my home. He had competed in the Buffs Marathon on equal terms with all other runners. He was a club member of RAC with the same rights as any other member, yet South African apartheid legislation prohibited him from walking on Nahoon Beach because it was designated "whites only." It was more absurd than living on the moon. We all walked on the beach – Sibisi broke the law.

My return to running was managed very conservatively, and greatly aided by a strapping technique I had been shown by Dr Kingsley Logan, which restricted the lateral movement of my right ankle. It took me four weeks to gradually increase my weekly mileage to 100km. I held my weekly training at 100–120km for another 10 weeks before I entered my first race, with great caution.

On 31 May 1983 the SABC televised the Comrades live for the first time. I watched the event from home and got a new perspective on the race and the gold medal contenders. My energy and sentiments were behind my KPMG colleague Shaw. When questioned in mid-May about his prospects of winning the Comrades, he said: "My training has gone pretty well and I reckon my chances of winning are as good as anyone else's." I really admired Shaw's frankness. He had nailed Fordyce in the Buffs Marathon and subsequently won the Allied 60km Ultra in 3:52 on 16 April, followed by a win in the Settlers 60km two weeks later on 30 April in 3:56. I knew he was uninjured and in good shape.

Fordyce had jogged the 56km Korkie in 3:59 (4.15 per km) and then merely a week later, raced the 56km Two Oceans, finishing fourth in 3:14, desperately disappointed that he had not made his move earlier and possibly won the event. Either way, Fordyce had tackled a very tough course and averaged 3.28 per km over the distance. Shaw had raced at a far more sensible pace of 3.54 per km.

In the Comrades duel, Fordyce chased down and overtook Shaw at 64km and put a further 15 minutes into him by the finish. He won this up run in 5:30, less than a minute outside Robb's down record of 5:29.14. He ran the second half in 2:39.57, exactly 10 minutes and 18 seconds faster than his first half, equating to a speed of 3.25 per km. This was faster than his pace for the Two Oceans, and even 12 seconds per km faster than he averaged five months later when he won the London to Brighton ultramarathon on a relatively flat, sea-level course, and set a new world record for 50 miles.

In *Lore of Running*, Tim Noakes describes how transfixed he was when he watched a recording of the 1983 Comrades: "for the screen bore witness to something that was intangible, something beyond words. Never before had the Comrades seen such poetic running, such effortless mastery and athletic perfection; indeed, such excellence."

Fordyce had cracked Piet Vorster's 1979 up record of 5:45 by eight minutes in 1981 and he had now sliced another seven minutes from the mark. It was an astonishing 4.3% improvement on Vorster's best.

Heroics and miracles aside, my great inspiration came from two runners in the 1983 Comrades. Errol Ackerman of Hillcrest Villagers, who had finished one place in front of me at the 1982 Comrades in 6:02, finished in fifth position in 5:55. Dearling of RAC ran 6:00 to claim ninth position and a coveted gold medal. I could relate very closely to their balanced lifestyles of busy careers and sporting prowess. My intuition also told me I had at least as much athletic talent as these two, and our body shapes and sizes were similar. I felt I had a really good chance of running a top 10 in 1984. There were two essential requirements. I needed to run negative splits, and I needed to galvanise my capacity to bite the bullet. The first 70km of the Comrades was relatively straightforward. The final 20km was the contest.

My time in East London had almost come to an end when I received a call from Franz. He told me that RAC were going to have a serious crack at winning the Comrades Marathon team prize, the Gunga Din, in 1984. They reckoned they could place four runners in the top 20. Dearling was the prospective top 10 runner, and Trevor Metcalfe, Alan Day, Mike Arnold and hopefully I, would get the job done. I relished this competitive proposal. Dick and Vreni Welch, both respected personalities, ran the RAC club which had one of the largest memberships in South Africa, a very strong Comrades participation rate, and was well integrated with strong support offered to its black runners. It would be sad to leave Kudus but they comprised mostly social runners or former champions now enjoying the fun side, whereas I was getting serious. We moved back into our home in Johannesburg at the start of October. We had made the most of our time in East London.

Now I had to make the most of my time in the high-octane business world and running scene in Jo'burg.

13

There's gold in them thar heels

My windsurfing injury made me faster. It seems a huge contradiction, but tearing up my ankle prevented me from running a single marathon in 1983. Instead, I had rehabilitated by running shorter races and slowly building strength. By the time I returned to Johannesburg from my stint in East London, I was fresh and fast and fit. Although 192cm tall, I weighed just 76kg and had a resting pulse rate of 38 beats per minute.

I signed up with the RAC club and committed to the Gunga Din bid. This seemed optimistic at the start of the year, but those of us who raced in the white strip with diagonal maroon stripe quietly felt we could give it a good shake. Dearling was our front-runner after his ninth place in the most recent Comrades. I was thought capable of improving my position from 16th in the 1982 run and we had strong back up in the seasoned pair of Metcalfe and Day, both able to run under 6:30. The Gunga Din winner is determined by the combined times of the first four runners from each club, so consistency was essential. Our only top 10 finisher was Dearling, so we felt we might sneak under the radar of clubs with more prominent individuals such as Hillcrest Villagers, Germiston Callies Harriers and Rocky Road Runners. RAC was still viewed primarily as a social club because of its size. The previous year it boasted 483 Comrades finishers, representing almost 10% of the total field.

Dearling advised me to join the Sweat Shop training run every Wednesday evening from its Braamfontein outlet next to Wits University.

He was convinced that this 23km tester had improved his endurance enough for him to make his breakthrough in 1983. We had read about Australian world champion Robert de Castella adding a long mid-week run to his training regime, and Plaatjes had returned from the University of Georgia with a similar idea. Fordyce himself was a Sweat Shop run regular. I needed no further convincing and joined the group.

I settled into a 100km a week routine for the last two months of 1983. On weekdays I ran a 7km loop at 6am around Emmarentia Dam, plus a couple of hills, always mindful of Plaatjes' advice not to run junk miles. The Wednesday evening Sweat Shop run gave me a further 23km, and the Saturday morning run from the Wanderers was never further than 16km but, taking 55 minutes to complete, it was a high-quality training run. Sunday runs were between 20km and 30km, depending on the races in the neighbourhood.

I relished being a part of the vibrant Johannesburg running scene. There was no loneliness to being a long distance runner. As well as socialising with clubmates past and present, I made contact with clients involved not only as sponsors but participants. I was one of 30 partners in the Johannesburg office of KPMG and I found the running fraternity to be a bountiful networking opportunity.

On 27 November I ran my first race in RAC colours. It was the club's own 32km race, notorious for its hills and aptly named the Tough One. Ernest Seleke won in 1:44 and I finished 14th, seven minutes later. The hills towards the end punished me but I nevertheless went home happy because I'd helped RAC win the team prize, and beat three Comrades top 10 finishers in Deon Holtzhausen, Anderson and Dearling.

A week later, I jogged the Soweto Half Marathon with Dearling and the late Patrick Laurence, a political journalist with the *Rand Daily Mail,* and an outspoken critic of apartheid. He had been arrested in 1973 for interviewing Robert Sobukwe, the leader of the Pan African Congress, but his willingness to push the boundaries had earned him quite a following. At Nelson Mandela's first media conference after his release from prison in 1990, Mandela exclaimed "Patrick Laurence! I have been reading your articles for years," and walked over to embrace him.

At the following week's Sweat Shop run I was feeling particularly inspired because Plaatjes and Fordyce were there and the pace was brisk. After a brief drinks stop halfway through, it got even faster. The last 4km included the long and punishing haul up Jan Smuts Avenue from the zoo to the crest of the ridge, and another shorter but steeper hill leading back to the Sweat Shop. I attacked the hill past the zoo and had everyone but Plaatjes under pressure, with Fordyce running right on my shoulder, sucking in big gulps of air. I made an entry in my training log that evening: "Pushed Jan Smuts hard – had Fordyce breathing." The run took us 83 minutes.

On New Year's Day I looked at a 1984 planner, blank apart from a Comrades Marathon note on 1 June, and considered my build-up over the next five months. I thought a lot about Fordyce and what made him such a formidable competitor. Although he was born a year after me, he completed school aged 19 and had been a full-time university student ever since. He had prioritised his running ahead of his academic options. This was a brave decision but had yielded three wins in the Comrades, two London to Brighton victories and a world record for 50 miles. He had, in effect, earned a doctorate in ultramarathon running, perhaps even a professorship.

He had elected to live the life of South Africa's first full-time Comrades professional, even though the race did not award prize money. Given his intellect, I believed that his knowledge of the Comrades race with all its nuances would surpass anyone else's by miles. No one but he had the time and single-purpose obsession to indulge so meticulously in one event. The road between Durban and Maritzburg was his home ground, and he left no one in doubt to his territorial claim. He had been embraced by South Africa as a popular, articulate winner. He had a strong rapport with the Comrades Marathon Association, which organised the event, wrote regular columns for the print media and developed an alliance with sports scientist Dr Tim Noakes.

Between his cross country running at school and his nine years at university, he had been running for a decade. I conservatively estimated he had run at least 30,000km. (The total subsequently published in *Lore of Running* amounted to 36,419km). By comparison, I had logged a lifetime total of 13,365km, little more than a third of the distance Fordyce had in his legs. I longed to be able to fast forward two or three years' worth of training to get closer to my true potential, with improved strength and speed. Even so, as I gazed at the 1984 planner, I ambitiously added to my Comrades entry: top 5, sub-5:50.

I devised my training plan of some 3,400km over 21 weeks:

- 2 weeks at 140km – gradual increase in workload
- 6 weeks at 160km – including a 32km race and a standard marathon.
- 5 weeks at 140km – relatively easy, including the 56km Korkie
- 4 weeks at 200km – peak load – highly vulnerable phase – no racing
- 4 weeks – taper from 160km to 80km, including speed work.

My quantitative and psychological goals included a PB for the standard marathon and improved speed endurance; running the second half of the 56km Korkie faster than the first half, at faster than 3.40 per km (Comrades racing pace), to finish strongly with something left; and as many wins as possible over previous Comrades top 10 finishers to reinforce my confidence.

Planning is easy. Execution is what matters.

As always I was flat-out at work and there was no space on my calendar for illness, physiotherapy or gym rehabilitation if I picked up an injury. Things had to fall in place for me if I was to earn a gold medal and run under six hours on the road to Durban.

By mid-January, I had increased my weekly distance to 160km, the magical 100-mile week. My office commitments entailed some challenging late nights and I'd had to skip a couple of morning runs. By the end of the month, it was time to step up to the marathon and record a qualifying time for my Comrades entry. Plaatjes was happy to jog the Benoni Marathon with me and we decided to run at 3:45 per km pace and aim for a negative split. This would replicate the pace and the tactics I hoped to use in Comrades.

We passed through halfway in 81.23 and then picked up the tempo. As we entered the Willowmore Park Stadium, with about 300m to go, an official caught a glimpse of Plaatjes and yelled "Stop him". It turned out he was not wearing the required licence number on the front of his running vest. We crossed the line together in 2:36.37, after a second half split of 75.14 but the real drama was about to start.

The overzealous officials knew the rules but not the faces. They had no idea they were dealing with the national champion, a man the race organiser had given a free entry to only hours before. The authoritative left hand certainly wasn't clapping in sync with the promotional right hand in Benoni that day. Words were exchanged and Plaatjes was called to appear at a provincial disciplinary hearing a few days later. As we walked away, a young boy approached Plaatjes bashfully, clearly seeking an autograph. Instead, Plaatjes flashed him a broad smile, gave him his finisher's badge and said a few encouraging words. It was so much better for the image of running than an official scowl.

My next flirtation with race pace was the fast, flat Springs Striders 32km. A hard effort over 32km did not pose the same nervousness and recovery dilemmas as a marathon. You could really go for it. I viewed the Striders as a long time trial, albeit with a frantic start in which you had to take care not to fall and be trampled. In no time at all we hit 8km and it was a PB, but it did not stop there. I recorded PBs at 10km, 15km, 16km, 21.1km, 25km, and finally made 32km in 1:45.48 in 10th position. Ernest Seleke won the race in 1:39.47, beating Plaatjes by 48 seconds. Six weeks later, he would become the first South African to run sub-2:10 for the marathon, at Port Elizabeth. My time equated to a sub-2:20 marathon at altitude, and my confidence soared.

My next target was the Peninsula Marathon in Cape Town in three weeks' time. I aimed to lower my marathon PB of 2:26.01 and record negative splits. The organisers had complied with the suggestion of marathon champion, Bernard Rose, to switch the direction of the point-to-point race from Simon's Town to Green Point, to avoid the prevailing south-easterly wind. Unfortunately, the weather did not cooperate on race day and at 12km, we ran smack into a fresh northwester. Rose did not run the marathon.

With eventual winner Ron Boreham, followed by Jasper Ward, well out in front, no one in my group wanted to push the pace into the headwind. They knew they were running for third, at best, with no prospect of a PB in sight. I did a fair bit of the pace setting and worked hard to finish fourth in 2:20. Despite running a PB, it was very hard work into the headwind. The traditional direction would have been so much better.

The 56km Korkie followed three weeks later. I wanted to place in the top 10 with a negative split. I believed this was a crucial aspect of a good performance in Comrades. Others felt I was capable of more. On three separate occasions, I had bumped into former Wits runners and each told me I had a decent shot at winning the Comrades. Hmmm! The fire in my belly was glowing brighter.

The Korkie started in pouring rain, and Tjale made an early break. I settled into a group containing Fordyce, Robb, Holtzhausen, Anderson and Ian Emery, and we ticked along at a 3min. 35sec. per km pace. Before halfway I sensed the pace was starting to fall off a little. I lifted the tempo because I was set on running the second half faster than the first. We passed through the 28km mark in 1:40, still 1.34 behind Tjale. I was running steadily at 3.28 per km and, in the process, dropped the others. Tjale, too, picked it up and led by two minutes at the marathon marker.

We were both going well. I chipped away at his lead, closing the gap to 100m at 50km. But chasing Tjale is a frustrating process. He has a clipped style with very little leg lift and, from behind, it looks like he is cramping with every step. His head rolls from side to side and you constantly think he is about to fall over. I fell into the trap and told my brother JP, who was seconding me, that I would nail him in the next kilometre. Uh-uh. If I was the hammer, the nail kept moving further away. When Tjale crossed the line in 3:16.20 he was 41 seconds ahead of me. He shook my hand and his face split into a toothy grin in delight at controlling the race. I had my dreams; he knew his victory was never in doubt.

Even so, I was satisfied. I had run the final 14km in 47.11; this was 26 seconds faster than Fordyce had clocked over the corresponding section of the Two Oceans the previous year. I was healthy and super-fit, and my recovery was rapid. The following day I weighed myself. The scales read 73kg, my leanest ever.

After Korkie, I cut back in both distance and intensity apart from the Wednesday Sweat Shop gallop and the Saturday morning run from the Wanderers, where Laxton, Traub, McArthur and Glasenberg would keep us honest. They did not run ultras and were always sharp and fast.

By the end of April I had completed the planned 17 weeks of distance training with health intact. At the start of the year I had worried about surviving this phase. In reality, I had thrived. All that remained before Comrades was a four-week taper and some intelligent speed work, during which I lowered my 8km time trial best to 25.25, at altitude. When I flew to Durban on 31 May, I had logged 3,405km in training compared with Fordyce's 2,713km and knew I was in the best condition of my life. I felt I had the measure of the top 10 contenders, excluding the ethereal Fordyce. I lifted my ambition to top three, and wondered if I was in sufficiently good shape to apply some pressure to the defending champion in the final quarter of the race.

The only person who knew what I was going to attempt was my brother-in-law Derek who asked me on race eve what I honestly felt I could do. When I told him I was going for top three and, if the opportunity presented itself, a crack at Fordyce, his eyes bulged in disbelief. I swore him to secrecy – although I subsequently learned he told my sister before they went to bed, and she mirrored his astonishment.

As always, the media coverage was huge. *The Star* newspaper in Johannesburg interviewed seven experts, including some race winners. Of those polled, only Dr Tim Noakes did not pick me in the top 10. In the *Natal Mercury*, athletics writer Grant Winter was particularly brave and reckoned I was the biggest threat to Fordyce.

Getting the carbohydrate drinks I favoured required an operation of military complexity and precision. The race rule regarding seconding was clear: "No seconding from, or the utilisation of, any mobile vehicle (bicycle, etc. included), will be permitted along the route."

As Fordyce had showed in his previous runs, it was critical to receive assistance en route, over and above the 60 well-stocked refreshment tables provided by the organisers. I needed two motorbikes and four volunteers to take back roads to fixed points on the race route to hand bottles to me. My KPMG partner Morris, he of our 1976 Vaal Marathon debacle, sprung to the rescue. He had a friend who farmed outside Pietermaritzburg, and Morris borrowed two of the farm motorbikes. Plaatjes volunteered to ride pillion. Gary Butler, a chartered accountant from KPMG Durban, roped in friend Paul Denhoed to crew the other bike. Bearing in mind this was two decades before Google maps, I had to buy a set of 1:100,000 survey maps covering the area. We had a planning meeting and decided my seconds would meet me every 8km after 20km. All I had to do was run.

There was no seeding so I had to pick my way through the other 8,512 runners to the front of the multitude. The traditional Max Trimbourn cock crow resounded from the speakers before the starting pistol cracked. Despite the initial rush of desperadoes sprinting to the front for a moment of fame on live television, I got a clean start. It was still dark in Pietermaritzburg at that hour and I could privately compose myself for the 90km trial which would fill the next 20,000 seconds of my life. That first dark hour is a wonderfully introspective experience, yet at the same time the energy is palpable. These spiritually adventurous moments are rare yet special. We were all connected like a giant umbilical cord gently snaking its way along the Old Main Road downhill to Durban.

After an hour, we emerged from this nocturnal experience that almost replicates weightlessness to the clarity of dawn and the brutal reality of the challenge ahead. We had covered 16km and were squinting into the sunrise at Umlaas Road. I was rolling along with a seasoned group including Fraser, Abbott, Holtzhausen and Lemos, trailing the leading group of John Hamlett, Kevin Shaw, Chris Reyneke and Velemseni Nyandeni by two minutes. Our pace of 3.46 per km was comfortable and the weather was cool. Those around me were chatting away but I kept uncharacteristically quiet. I wanted to concentrate.

Over the next two hours I tried to run as economically and efficiently as possible. I was conscious about my arm movement, the position of my hands relative to my chest and the lowest possible foot lift. My only apprehension was the start of the real race at the halfway mark at Drummond after 45km, where contenders surged away from pretenders. It represented everything I had trained for in the past year and I was about to throw my body and courage into a zone and a challenge never previously experienced. My credo has always been: you only live once.

Reyneke went through the halfway mark in 2:44.20. I crossed in 2:48.14 in fourth, 1.48 ahead of Fordyce. I soon moved into third, which earned me the dubious distinction of being targeted by the SABC. A huge motorbike pulled alongside and the expert commentator on the back yelled: "So, number 7026, what is your name?" Some expert.

I soon passed Shaw to take second, four minutes behind Reynecke. I knew nothing about him but I should have: he had finished ahead of me at Benoni. In any event, I was delighted to have him up front. I knew Fordyce was coming, and Reynecke must have known too, because he really hit the gas pedal. All the splits being provided to Fordyce would be to the race leader, so I opted to ghost along behind the pacesetter.

I had analysed Fordyce's two previous down runs on tape and felt he was spent by Mayville, about 5km from the finish. He had said publicly he did not enjoy the down run as much as the up, and his marshmallow legs at the finish at Old Kingsmead was further evidence. On both occasions he led for the final 20km, running the second half at speeds of 3.44 per km (1980) and then 3.36 per km (1982). I felt good and decided to take him on. The time had arrived for me to run the biggest negative split of my life. At Hillcrest there was no change in the gap to Reynecke, with Fordyce 1.55 behind me. We were all bombing along a fast downhill section at 3.05 per km so changes weren't possible.

Reyneke ran stronger longer than I had expected. I chased him through Winston Park and Kloof, where my seconds clocked me through one 5km stretch in 16 minutes, if the marker boards were accurate. Near Kloof, I started to sense Reynecke coming back. I wanted to hold him there for a while to rest before making my bid, but he swerved suddenly off the road for a toilet stop. I inherited the lead by default. Oh shit! Now Fordyce would get constant, real-time feedback from every spectator with a stopwatch of the gap between us. By contrast, I would not enjoy the same benefits. The race organisers did not provide any information or assistance to the race leader and mobile phones had yet to be invented. I simply had to push on as hard as I could. There was no place to hide.

Little did I know but my promotion to leader nearly resulted in the premature end to Plaatjes' running career. Morris was so excited that, after a drinks rendezvous, he popped the clutch before Plaatjes was ready, somersaulting him off the back of the bike. Fortunately the future world champion was unhurt. Morris would eventually rise to KPMG's global board of management. Not a bad pair to have in your corner.

I entered Pinetown after the descent down Field's Hill and enjoyed the flat section before tackling Cowie's Hill. In my mind, Cowies was a Himalayan-type pass since my 1982 Comrades ordeal on its slopes, so I was euphoric to crest the climb without any difficulty, sponging myself at the summit and reflecting on the remaining 16km. For the first time I realised I had a real chance to win. A one-hour grind lay ahead that would be equally challenging for Fordyce who had not been able to close the gap since halfway. Tactically, I knew I had to reach Mayville ahead of Fordyce. What I did not know was that I had left a gap in my planning, by failing to adequately scout the Westville terrain I was about to encounter.

There is no video record of my struggle into Durban or Fordyce's relentless chase. Viewers across the nation watched as I grimly strode towards 45th Cutting, with Fordyce nowhere to be seen. After switching away from live Comrades coverage at this critical juncture, and broadcasting a pre-planned insert about the SABC production of the telecast, they returned to live Comrades coverage to see Fordyce in the lead not very far from the Old Kingsmead Stadium. Television viewers around the nation had absolutely no idea of what had happened.

They had to wait until the following day's newspapers to read about the drama at 45th Cutting.

The lap of the Old Kingsmead Stadium was an overwhelming experience. I was feeling like I had just lost the Comrades while the crowd was treating me like a triumphant runner-up. I experienced both devastation and elation.

Fordyce won in 5:27.18, a down record. Full credit to the reigning champ: he had prevailed under enormous pressure. I crossed the line in 5:30.59 with a big smile and immediately shook hands. He had won but I had given him a very serious workover, pushing him to a new record.

He had run the second half in 2:37.16, an astonishing 13 minutes faster than his first half, and, 30 years later, it remains the fastest second half in the history of the down Comrades, eclipsing even Shvetsov's second half 2:37.33 run in 2007 when he set a new record of 5:20.41. Fordyce averaged 3.31 per km (a further 2.3% improvement in his 1982 speed over the same distance) equating to a 2:28 standard marathon, plus an extra 2.6km at

RUNAWAY COMRADE

the same pace. I ran a second half of 2:42.45, equating to a speed of 3.38 per km and six minutes faster than my first half.

The Fordyce Finish equated to a second half acceleration of 7.5% over his first half. Illustrated in the context of a sub-4 minute mile, he had run two laps of 62.3 seconds followed by two laps of 57.6 seconds. Breathtaking stuff.

The consolation prize, originally my aim in conjunction with a top 10 finish, was winning the Gunga Din with my RAC teammates. Dearling ran 5:55 for 13th, followed by Metcalfe's 6:08 in 30th and Day's 6:11 in 36th to wrap it up.

I talked to journalists, had a shower and sat around soaking up the Comrades atmosphere. After the presentation of trophies and medals, I had a quick supper at a Durban steakhouse before catching flight SA518 at 9.00pm to Johannesburg, where my VW Golf awaited in the airport car park. I unlocked the front door at 10.45pm and was greeted by my wife. My three daughters were fast asleep. I had a kitbag with some soiled running gear, a Coca Cola towel presented to the top 10 finishers, a couple of medals and a tired body. I felt desperately empty, like I had contested an egg and spoon race but popped the egg out of the spoon just before I crossed the line.

After what seemed an eternal night, it was dawn and I felt more exhausted than when I had crossed the line 18 hours earlier. Suddenly our bedroom was filled with the joy of Nicole (7), Simone (4) and Philippa (2), who had watched me on television the day before and wanted to see my medals. Smothered by my three daughters and their excitement and pride in my Comrades loot, I realised I had already won one of life's most precious prizes.

It took me a while to dissect exactly what had happened. Over the following weeks, months even, I was able to piece together the puzzle and come up with some ideas but the ultimate answer remained the same.

Run faster.

14

Pissing blood

I was pleased with my second place, but I had absolutely no idea how pleased those around me would be. On Monday 4 June I walked into the office and was overwhelmed by the celebration. My desk was covered in telexes from every KPMG office in South Africa and the women in the typing pool had decorated my office with congratulatory cards and celebratory paraphernalia. All my partners were swinging by my office for a quick chat and a two-minute analysis on the race with the sole objective of wanting to know how I could beat "that little bugger Fordyce." This was not derogatory. In South Africa, this is a phrase indicating high regard and respect. My support team had instantly grown from four to 400, just within the confines of KPMG.

I was all but unknown in the media hub of Johannesburg and when the journalists called, I had to explain my very recent association with distance running and the Comrades. So it was almost a relief when I took a call from Glynn Williams from the East London *Daily Dispatch*. Mindful that my first Comrades breakthrough happened when I was living in East London in 1982, the East London running community still retained an interest in my running, having fostered my improvement and recovery from my windsurfing accident. I didn't have to introduce myself to Williams. I could discuss the future, not the past. He knew where I had been, having interviewed me after my first marathon win at Bongolo.

The net result of all this interest in my Comrades race was zero billable time to lunchtime. Given that I had targets to meet, my morning was the equivalent of a batsman who has been at the crease between start of play and lunch and not scored a single run. Morris saved me. He stuck his head around the corner and said I would be joining him for lunch at the Rand Club.

The few city blocks between KPMG's offices and the Rand Club felt like the last 500m of Comrades. I had lost both my big toenails through an entirely unnecessary shoe decision and my calves felt seriously over-inflated. Lunch provided a great opportunity for Morris and I to compare race day stories and experiences. I had only seen him for a few minutes at the finish. Not only was it chaotic, he had the added challenge of returning the motorbikes to Pietermaritzburg, and then driving some 600km back to Johannesburg. The effort of my support crew of four to assist me in the Comrades was enormous and I gained an appreciation of their problems, criss-crossing back roads to gain access to the race route and nearly losing Plaatjes. It brought me back to earth.

I also called Dr Noakes at UCT for his feedback. In my view, any information from the nation's leading running expert would be useful. I was therefore totally surprised when he told me I had overheated. That was never on my mind at any stage during race day, neither during the 90km ordeal nor afterwards. Although it had been a warm, clear day, I had consciously sponged myself with water and at no stage had I felt that I was heat stressed. I would take his observation on board and research it further. From experience, I knew that I ran faster in cooler weather but that would apply to most runners.

I believe the ideal marathon temperature is about 12°C and we were running into Durban at about 27°C, so it is probable we would all have gone faster if it had been cooler. Gratefully, I made notes and recognised that I would have to research how I might be able to avoid overheating in the future. In effect, Noakes said big guys heat up more quickly that smaller runners do, so I would have been at a disadvantage. The corollary was that cool, wet weather on race day would suit bigger runners over their smaller competitors. I believed I had learned something and remained grateful to Noakes for his willingness to take my call and talk with me in such detail. Robb, at 183cm and 65kg, was considerably taller than Fordyce at 166cm and 52kg, and had run his astonishing 5:29.14 in 1978 in cool, damp conditions.

On Wednesday evening, RAC hosted its post-Comrades aches and pains drinks at the clubhouse in Craighall Park. We celebrated all manner of Comrades achievements, with the club having 495 finishers, Priscilla Carlisle finishing second, and our Gunga Din team prize. In club running in the mid-1980s, the Gunga Din was the ultimate team trophy. No fanfare, but four strong runs by Day, Metcalfe, Dearling and De la Motte achieved a club first. It had the added bonus of offering the four of us an international ticket to run a race of our choice. In October 1984 Metcalfe and Day competed in the London to Brighton, finishing seventh and eighth respectively. Race organisers still remained sympathetic to South African athletes, notwithstanding the IAAF ban on South African athletes.

The other unexpected development was becoming an instant media celebrity in the local market. It seems crazy that this would happen to me merely for leading the eventual winner for two hours before being caught, but this was sports-crazy, endurance-crazy, Comrades-crazy, internationally-isolated South Africa. The television broadcast had iden-tified me as an accountant and I received job offers, including one from a global sports shoe company which could not understand why I had no interest in becoming its finance director and working flexible hours to allow for training. It was difficult to explain that running was merely my recreational outlet and, in career terms, I was totally fulfilled as a KPMG partner, with enormous opportunity ahead. At the time I was probably earning more than the managing director of the shoe company, but there was no need to make that point.

I did not see any longevity or career alternatives in my running, even if I had won the 1984 Comrades and broken a 50-mile world record en route. The managing director of another shoe company got hold of me, inviting me to name my price to run in their shoes. Once again, it was hard for him to understand my logic. I had never run in their brand before. I could afford to buy a new pair of running shoes every week if I so desired. Most importantly, I would never consider being contractually bound to any manufacturer of sporting goods for good reason. Running was something I did of my own free will and I did not want to be obligated to anyone.

Speaking offers and race invitations poured in but I was busy at work and had to decline most of them. I had long decided against forgoing time with my family over weekends by entering races in faraway places like Cape Town or Durban. Preferably, a race needed to be easily accessible so I could be back home by mid-morning. I even considered Pretoria to be out of the question.

All these approaches gave me an insight into a Comrades economy that I was ignorant of. The first live television coverage of the race in 1983 led to the rapid growth of this phenomenon. Cameron-Dow writes that Fordyce left Wits at the end of 1983, after nine years as a full-time student, with an incomplete academic record, to devote himself fully to the sporting career that was dominating his existence. The race itself did not offer any prize money. The money was to be made in the aftermath of his triumphs. In 1984, he became a full-time Comrades competitor. He had already released a Comrades video, published a book, gone into business with Noakes and Rose to manufacture a sports nutritional supplement called FRN, and wrote weekly columns for South African newspapers.

In the running and sporting community, he was the public face of Hertz, Edblo mattresses, Leppin nutritional products, Asics Tiger shoes and Sorbothane shoe inserts. He also launched a Comrades 'Gold Team' training programme, in conjunction with Dearling and Anderson, selling tailored training programmes to aspiring Comrades runners at R245 a pop.

Inevitably, he had become a much sought after, highly articulate motivational speaker at many corporate functions, on good commercial terms. It was told to me that when he trailed me by 100m as we approached 45th Cutting, his helper Franz yelled out: "See that gap? Well, it's worth R100,000 to you." A motivational plea, yes, but Franz was a KPMG-trained accountant with a good financial aptitude. Whatever effect it had on Fordyce, I had spent every physical cent and a similar message would have had no effect on the De la Motte will. I had no desire to rely on running achievement to earn a living, and just as well.

The persistent question I had to field for months was how I was going to beat Fordyce. Only five months earlier my personal goal had been to finish in the top five to cap my Comrades involvement. My running horizon did not extend beyond 1984 and one of the gold medals awarded to the first 10 across the line. Between my family and my career, my life was enjoyably busy. However, my Comrades time of 5:30 and a near defeat of the defending champion and world record holder had been a revelation to everyone, most of all myself. When I ran my 6:04 time in 1982, most considered it a good effort but unlikely to be repeated. In other words, a fluke.

Now, abruptly, my status had been elevated to that of contender. I have thought long and hard about what I would have done had I prevailed in 1984, and think I would have emulated Dave Levick. He won Comrades once and, having satisfied his ambition in that area, focused on his engineering career. The Comrades Marathon was always going to be a sideshow for me but it is in my nature not to leave any stones unturned and I re-evaluated my interest in challenging for a win. If I did not run another Comrades, I would leave a personal itch unscratched and probably be accused of being afraid of Fordyce. I knew I'd give the race a decent crack again, but not to the exclusion of all other priorities.

Unexpectedly, my physical health nose-dived after Comrades. My big toenails had disappeared and my calves remained tight and swollen for days. However, the biggest issue was sinusitis. My first jog was nine days after Comrades and I spluttered the whole way. Before the end of June I saw my GP about my lingering sinus problem and he sidelined me from running for a week.

On 4 July I received an unexpected surprise in being selected for the Transvaal team to compete in the JSE 50km Marathon in August. I started running again the next day, but only managed another 10 runs before acute sinus congestion stopped me in my tracks again. I was told I needed to see an ear, nose and throat specialist.

I resumed training after completing a course of antibiotics. I ventured no further than 7km in the early mornings and at the end of the ninth week after Comrades, I had averaged a very modest 50km per week but still lacked good health and vitality. My appointment with the specialist resulted in day surgery at the Rosebank Clinic in early August to have my sinuses drained under general anaesthetic. It was an enormous relief to know that the source of my breathing problems had finally been dealt with, but I had some big work deadlines coming up, which also kept me off the road.

I had committed to participate in a series of fun runs organised by TFC travel chief executive, Cliff Foggitt, to raise funds for the Cripple Care Association.

The first of these was a joint promotion with South African Airways to celebrate the 50th anniversary of the airline, with a 22km run from SAA's original hangar at Germiston to the main Johannesburg airport.

Other than eight invited runners who would raise funds for Cripple Care, only SAA employees could participate. The deal was that a variety of sponsors would pay for every second by which the guest runners would better 80 minutes. I wasn't in great shape but managed 78.10 on a warm afternoon. SAA surprised us with two domestic tickets which could be used on any flight on which they had spare capacity. I had heard favourable reports about the scenic beauty of the Winelands Marathon in Stellenbosch in mid-November, and thought it would be a great opportunity for Vern and me to escape to the Cape for a weekend, in addition to getting in a high-quality training run.

The other running highlight of 1984 was Blanche Moila being the first black female athlete to be awarded Springbok colours in her favourite discipline, cross country. Blanche epitomised the traits of amateurism and being a good sport in every sense. She competed against world-class athletes like Sonja Laxton, Zola Budd and Colleen de Reuck whilst pursuing her professional career as chief professional nurse in the psychiatric unit at King George Hospital in Durban. During her competitive years, she won more than 50 races in cross country and over distances ranging from 1,500m to 21.1km, setting many records en route. She has completed the Comrades ten times and been the recipient of multiple awards including the State President's award for lifetime achievements in 2001. In 2010, Blanche was inducted as an Ethekwini Living Legend for services to the community and her inordinate contribution to athletics in South Africa, particularly amongst disadvantaged communities. Blanche observed that

South Africa was a nation obsessed with sport, yet there seemed to be so little glory in it for women.

Meanwhile, I had Fordyce on my mind. He had worked desperately hard to dethrone Robb, and deservedly so. He then had to deal with Halberstadt, who many thought was capable of unleashing something special; like the way Robb ran the down race in 1978, and Fordyce the up race in 1983. When the Halberstadt meteorite burned out, Fordyce had to contend with Tjale, but he always seemed to have him worked out. Tjale's competitive runs for much-needed cash and his top placings in both Two Oceans and Korkie combined to dilute his Comrades effectiveness. He had been a real workhorse on the distance running scene over many years and raced many more intense marathons than his ultra-distance peers. Although Tjale could never be ignored, I believe Fordyce was always quietly confident he would win any duel to the finish with him. Then there were the Hillcrest and Durban boys like Fraser, Abbott, Tivers, Biggs, Lemos and Van Staden. They all represented solid, top-five potential, but were unlikely to get close to 5:30. The Cape Town running scene did not present any looming threat to the Fordyce reign so it was back to Transvaal and the school of high altitude distance runners.

Apart from Rakabaele's pioneering top-10 run in 1976, and the emergence of Tjale in 1979, black distance runners had chosen to concentrate on the shorter distances up to the marathon. The plethora of weekend races offered cash prizes to podium finishers, and often down to tenth place. Beyond the standard marathon, only the 56km Two Oceans and the 56km Korkie offered modest cash prizes, Two Oceans more generously than Korkie. The Comrades did not pay any money, and the gold medals awarded to the top 10 runners in the 1980s were actually alloy discs that had been gold plated. The monetary incentive for a black runner to compete in Comrades was zero. The only guarantee was very sore legs for weeks and a slow recovery.

South Africa's top marathoners in 1984, like Plaatjes, Gibeon Moshaba, Seleke, Sibisi and Magawana, did not consider Comrades. Had there been a first prize of, say, R100,000, I suspect the action at the pointy end would have been a lot more intense. It would have taken a few years of adjustment, but the top 10 would have looked considerably different. When prize money was introduced in 1995, black runners switched their focus in numbers. By 2012, there was not a single white runner in the top 10 in the Comrades and Two Oceans.

The pool of possible challengers from the Highveld was actually a puddle. No black runners, let alone Russians, just Deon Holtzhausen, Ian Emery, and me. Fordyce would have been confident about Holtzhausen and Emery but he was wary of me, and unsure of what I might do next. To tell the truth, so was I. This made me less vulnerable to Fordyce who not only had the measure of his rivals on the road but also in their heads. He was brilliant in managing them and had effectively hypnotised the lot. I remained fiercely independent and headstrong, unwilling to acquiesce to groupie status. It would be a prickly relationship between us from then on. I had absolutely nothing to lose. Fordyce had everything to lose. The game was on.

Shortly after deciding to engage Fordyce on his preferred battlefield between Durban and Pietermaritzburg, Nick Lanham of Adidas asked me if I'd be interested in running in their shoes. He didn't know how good his timing was. I'd been a New Balance man but the trouble was getting shoes for my rather large feet. Gordon Howie of New Balance had diversified his business from running shoes to include football boots to cater for the black community's obsession with the sport. Shortly before Comrades, he had invested a considerable amount in his first consignment of boots. The offset was a lower inventory of running shoes and I ended up running in the excellent model I had used for ages, but a half size smaller than usual. It cost me both my big toenails.

I had already got to know Lanham through Brian Chamberlain and I warned him of my aversion to contracts, stating I would run in his shoes only as long as they suited me. His message to head office in Cape Town must not have been clearly received: they drew up a contract and forwarded it to me. I still have the original, unsigned document in my files. I told them I would not be interested if they were not prepared to trust me to uphold my word.

Adidas also asked me to prepare a Comrades training programme, covering the five months from 1 January 1985 to race day, to help runners achieve a silver medal time of less than 7 hrs 30 mins. The programme

My father "Frenchy" enlisted in the South African Irish Regiment, World War II, 1940.

Yvonne Liebenberg my sporting mother on Leopard Rock, Oribi Gorge.

Frenchy wearing his tin hat in the North African trenches near Mersa Matruh, shortly after being decimated by General Rommel's Afrika Korps at Sidi Rezegh on 23 November 1941.

1970 Boys U16 800m Champion – East Rand High Schools Athletic Association.

Vincent Gabashane Rakabaele winning the 56km Two Oceans in 3:18.05 in 1976. History on two fronts – new record and first black winner.

Alan Robb winning the 1978 Comrades in a record 5:29.14. The first runner to break 5:30 – the Roger Bannister of Comrades.

RUNAWAY COMRADE

Hoseah Tjale punishing the trailing cyclists in the 1982 Two Oceans.

Hoseah Tjale winner of the 1980 Two Oceans in 3:14.30. Arguably South Africa's top amateur ultra runner in the 1980s.

RUNAWAY COMRADE

Indestructible 22 year old with Vern in 1976 before my humbling marathon debut.

1984 Korkie 56km Ultra with Gordon Howie (Sweat Shop) and Vreni Welch (RAC) after finishing second in 3:17.01, only 41 seconds behind winner Hoseah Tjale.

August 1985 50km JSE with runner-up Thulani Sibisi.

March 1986 56km Korkie with runner-up Hoseah Tjale.

RUNAWAY COMRADE

Leading the 1986 Comrades beyond the 70km mark.

RAC's historic first Gunga Din team winners 1984. L to R: Tony Dearling, Alan Day, Trevor Metcalfe, Bob de la Motte. Note the chromed tin hat in the centre of the trophy.

Comrades 1986 – 125 seconds too slow.

Ironman Western Australia, 2004 – 10:30 M50 debut. L to R: Simone, Philippa and Nicole share my joy.

Cape Epic 2009 – summiting after a one hour portage on day six.

Hurting at the end of 216km Gran Fondo Sportful Dolimiti, Feltre, Italy, June 2008 – net elevation gain of 5,400m and a snow storm at Passo di Rolle – 1,970m.

Summiting Col di Sampeyre (2,284m) en route to winning M50 cat – 249km Gran Fondo Fausto Coppi, Cuneo, Italy, June 2008 – net elevation gain of 3,710m.

14 August 1993: Mark Plaatjes of the USA raises his arms aloft as he crosses the line to win the marathon at the World Championships at the Gottleib Daimler Stadium in Stuttgart, Germany. Plaatjes won the gold medal in 2:13.57.

2014 Boston Marathon (aged 60) finishing in 3:06 – 9th in my M60 category.

The De la Motte family join the Chicken Run to Australia, June 1987. Vern with Philippa (4) Nicole (9) and Simone (6).

would be distributed as an insert in the December 1984 edition of *SA Runner* magazine. I willingly obliged on a pro-bono basis. I stood to receive a couple of free pairs of running shoes that effectively cost them nothing. Of more appeal to me was the networking opportunity the Adidas community offered. In my opinion, Adidas road running shoes in the early 1980s lagged behind their excellent track and field shoes, and were a step behind the scientific innovation of the new American manufacturers like Nike, New Balance, and Brooks, but I was happy to be associated with the company and the project.

I kept a watchful eye on Fordyce and noted his 4:50.51 victory in the AMJA 50-miler in Chicago. It was only a minute faster than I had passed through the 80km mark in Comrades 14 weeks earlier. Fordyce missed his own 50-mile world best by a mere 20 seconds. It represented an extraordinary back-to-back performance roughly three months after Comrades. His powers of recovery appeared to be astonishing, let alone his mental strength.

Five weeks away from the Winelands Marathon I knuckled down to some serious roadwork. I reeled off a succession of 100km weeks and gradually got the good feeling back. At the end of October I jogged to and from a tough 16km race, in which I clocked 53.01 for eighth, with the added satisfaction of having run a negative split. It was the best I had felt since Comrades, and my diary entry offered hope of going sub-2:30 at Winelands in three weeks' time.

The drive from Cape Town airport to the Lanzerac resort outside Stellenbosch soothed the soul. The marathon started right outside the property but the mind games started in the *Cape Argus*. When I opened the newspaper I was greeted by the headline: "No-one to beat Bob de la Motte – Fordyce."

So, when I lined up and looked around I spotted defending champion Willie Afrika, also Karel Julies, Eric Coetzee, John Brimble, Bruce Matthews, Nigel Evans, Graeme Dacomb, Karel Liebetrau, Eric Bateman, Graeme Lindenberg, Leon Otto and others who were all probably in better shape than me. Matthews said he felt he had a 2:25 in him and I assured him I would not be setting out at that pace. Afrika and Matthews took the lead, while I settled into a group including Julies, Coetzee and Brimble.

We overhauled Matthews at halfway, Afrika was over the horizon and I was 50m behind Julies in third. We were both laughing; passing through a coloured community, the spectators started sledging me in hilarious fashion while urging him on. I decided to show them, and surged up to his heels while he tried to shake me off.

The pace picked up and I held it better than Julies, who drifted back with 2km to go. I finished just ahead of him in 2:24.52, thanks to another negative split. I remarked to him as we walked away from the finish that it was as if he'd known every spectator personally, so vehement was the support for him. With the happiest smile imaginable he confirmed that my observations were correct. In the Winelands region, he assured me, *everybody* knew who Karel Julies was. Great guy.

Naturally, the headline the next morning read: "Afrika wins in an upset." I had a good laugh and got down to some planning. I was clearly a marked man in Fordyce's book and I accepted my training would be under constant surveillance. He was king of the up run whereas I had only attempted it once, finishing nearly 3½ hours behind him. Nevertheless, I thought the training schedule of 3,400km I had adopted for the first five months of the year had worked well, and there was no need for any major changes. All I would do was refine it to incorporate some of my observations from 1984.

My stepped approach to the 1985 Comrades would include many of my 1984 events:

- 16 January – hard 25km Nite Race
- 10 February – hard 32km Springs Striders
- 17 February – easy 42.2km Hillcrest Marathon (including Comrades route familiarisation)
- 2 March – 42.2km Buffs Marathon, East London (sub 2.20)
- 24 March – 56km Korkie plus 4km – steady
- 21 April – 53km Bergville plus 7km – steady
- 28 April – 42.2km Golden Reef Marathon plus 8km – steady

On 30 December RAC held its final club run for 1984. Surprisingly, Fordyce showed up for the casual 32km. We didn't talk much and the rivalry was palpable. Little did I realise, his visitor status would soon be converted to full membership because his student membership of the

Wits club had expired. One of his unfulfilled Comrades ambitions was to win the Gunga Din.

The first week of 1985 went to plan. I started my Nutri-Sport vitamin supplements that Halberstadt had pioneered and I was testing out different models of Adidas shoes to see which worked best for me. I realised that lots had changed over the year. Only 12 months previously, I was an inexperienced Comrades runner with the potential to place in the top 10. The Sweat Shop and Wanderers training runs had been the backbone of my improvement. These runs had been going for years before I joined in and the core runners had friendships pre-dating my arrival. Fordyce had been one of these core members, so understandably the relationship he enjoyed with these guys pre-dated me by years. I understood it would be more appropriate for me to train elsewhere. I also wanted to do my running away from the vigilant eyes of the Fordyce camp.

Here is my training diary for week two of the year:

- Monday to Friday – 5.15am runs with Chamberlain 10k.
- Tuesday pm – easy 8km loop around Emmarentia.
- Wednesday pm – 23km with Chamberlain.
- Thursday pm – 15km loop around Parkview Golf Course, felt good.
- Friday pm – easy 8km loop around Emmarentia.
- Saturday – Wanderers 17km with about 12 others, including Fordyce.
- Sunday – steady 32km. Plaatjes, Wright, Chamberlain and Dickson met at my house. We jogged to Cecil Payne stadium and back, including a 21.1km race at steady 4 min km pace.

Although my training distance was right on target, something else was going terribly wrong. I started urinating blood on Tuesday morning after my run. This continued the whole week. It was worse immediately after a run than during the day. My weight had dropped to 75kg. By midweek I was so concerned that I made an appointment to see Dr Ivan Cohen, a renowned running doctor based on the Wits campus, on Saturday after my training run at the Wanderers. He examined me and noted I was in excellent physical condition. He tested my urine in the rooms and thought the blood might be related to my shoes and a very hard heel-strike interfering with my kidneys or bladder. He suggested drinking

RUNAWAY COMRADE

more fluids before my morning runs, and referred me for a blood test on the Monday morning.

I awoke with an excruciating headache. For the first time in four years I neither had the desire nor energy to slip into my running kit and head out the door for the 5.15am jog. I could not run one step. I did not know then, but it would be six weeks before I was able to run again, and my 1985 Comrades was already over. My boundless energy had deserted me. The office was an absolute grind. When I walked a few city blocks to the pathology offices for my blood tests, I literally dragged my feet. They filled vial after vial and tested me for everything including bilharzia.

Tuesday was no different. No running. No improvement. At 10am, I had an appointment at a Johannesburg clinic for some X-rays via an intravenous myelogram, following which the radiologist performed an ultra-sound.

The tests were all negative. They showed nothing wrong. No kidney problems, no oedema. Dr Cohen was puzzled. The readings were normal but I clearly was not. I had never felt worse in my life. He referred me for another battery of tests, and a few days later I was admitted to the Kenridge Hospital for a kidney and bladder probe (intravenous pyelogram) under general anaesthetic. By the following evening, I was throwing up and my appetite had completely disappeared. I struggled into the office a few days later to learn the second round of tests had yielded no more helpful information than the first.

My personal assistant Bev decided it was time to get involved and asked me some pertinent questions in her husky smoker's voice.

"So this doctor suggests your health is fine?" she queried.

"That's what the indications are."

"Does the smartarse know that your eyes are jaundiced and that you are pissing blood?"

"Well, I am not sure, Bev."

"Call him up straight away, he needs to know."

I made the call, using the most diplomatic language possible. At some point in the discussion he asked me if I had done a bilirubin test for hepatitis.

"Doctor, I have needle marks all the way up the vein on my left arm like an intravenous drug addict. I'm not sure which blood tests I have taken or missed."

When I told Bev I was heading down to the pathology offices again for a bilirubin test, she did not raise her head. She just muttered something about smartarses. Back at the pathology offices the staff and I were starting to develop a friendship; my third visit in less than two weeks.

A day later the urologist called.

"You've got hepatitis A. Yes, hep A. It's infectious. Leave the office straight away and see your GP immediately."

My GP, Dr Ivan Barlow-Rademeyer, rose to the occasion. He saw me on the spot and was just as astonished as I was with the results of tests that had been done to evaluate the health of my liver. Simply, my badly infected liver was in dire health. My bilirubin count was 86 compared to the average range of 2–26.

Apart from the shock of what this meant for my overall health, from a running perspective this news was catastrophic. The liver stores glycogen and produces new glucose units, essential energy sources in marathon and ultramarathon racing. My fuel tank for marathon running was severely perforated and the road to recovery would be equally enduring.

The doctor's priority was to immunise my entire family against the possibility of hepatitis A infection. Fortunately, I did not infect anyone in my home or my workplace. There was no medication available at the time for hepatitis A, but luckily the liver has great recuperative powers if nurtured carefully because it is the only organ that can self-repair. My GP stressed the importance of diet and the dangers of alcohol. He suggested six weeks off work, to which I retorted that I had already been ill for two weeks so it would be more like four weeks in a worst-case situation.

As bad as it seemed, I was enormously relieved to receive the long overdue diagnosis. My own health – and as far as I was concerned, the medical world – had failed me devastatingly. When the exotic banks of tests consistently return negative, the most awful fears start niggling away at your optimism. The possibility of cancer crops up, and you start imagining your body melting down.

The big unanswered question was how I had got hepatitis A in the first place. My GP said there was typically a 30-day incubation period, which put me right in the middle of our summer holiday the previous month at Morgan Bay on the Wild Coast. Hmmm.

A week later, the owner of the Morgan Bay Hotel phoned to ask after the health of the De la Motte family. When I told him I had been diagnosed with hep A, he revealed I was one of 20 guests at the hotel with the same condition. The source of the infection had been traced to a kitchen worker who assisted with the preparation of fresh salads and fruit. She had passed it on to all of us.

The word spread rapidly through the running community. Journalists called and club mates and friends visited. Fordyce himself phoned. There was no need for him to make the call, and he also had the courtesy of telling me that he would be joining RAC. I appreciated that.

By the end of the week, I had lost faith in conventional medicine and visited a homeopath. After a week in bed and some homeopathic treatment, my gastroenteritis abated. This had haunted me for three weeks and I could finally eat a piece of fruit and drink a cup of black tea. My weight was down to 71kg.

I resumed work, initially for half a day only. By mid-February my stomach had settled back to near normal and despite my perforated liver, my urine was a little clearer. I called Dr Noakes at UCT and sought his opinion on returning to running without further damaging my liver. He advised six weeks before returning to run at 80km per week. Halberstadt called a couple of times to encourage me to maintain the strongest positive outlook. There was never any doubt with him. He was such an uplifting and inspirational individual.

When tests confirmed my liver was in strong recovery mode, I resumed running on 4 March. I decided on a 10-week recovery phase followed by a 12-week preparation for the 50km JSE Ultramarathon, which would be the big test of my recovery from hepatitis A. Comrades would have to wait another year.

Sports physiotherapist Clive Lipinski structured some gym sessions for me. I'd break my 5.30am morning run with a 20-minute stop at a local gym. It was a brief but intensive visit. My specific strengthening routine included 100 sit-ups, triceps and biceps work, leg presses, leg curls and leg extensions. I would jog the final 1km home, which felt like the final 10km of Comrades after my muscle-searing workout, and flop into the pool.

A few weeks later, I volunteered to assist with a refreshment table at the 56km Korkie and, when the last runner had passed through, I joined the tail-enders of the race and jogged the final 32km to the finish where I learned that Helen Lucre had created history by running the first sub-4 hour Korkie winning in a record 3:56. Even more astounding, I learnt that Fordyce had won in 3:21.48, almost five minutes slower than my runner-up time the previous year. He ran the final 14km in an impressive 47.17, consistent with my observations of how he preferred to race ultramarathons: control the race pace at a moderate tempo and then burn up the competition in the second half. And that's exactly what he did at Comrades that year, as I watched from the confines of a television studio.

My big race day in August approached quickly. I had received the all-clear for my 12-week block of intensive training, which was more about quality than quantity. My programme included six weekend runs of between 30km and 34km. The rest were between 20km and 25km, complemented by the Sweat Shop and Wanderers sessions.

I estimated a time of 2:51 for the 50km, but was unsure if I had what it would take to crack the top 10. The JSE paid handsome prize money for the top 20 finishers which attracted most of the elite black marathon runners. I had told journalists the day before the race that I would be delighted to finish among the top 10, and I wondered if I had not been a little bit brave in saying so. The field was full of marathon hotshots with standard-distance PBs I could only dream of; guys like Choeu, Petrus Kekana, Gibeon Moshaba, Sibisi, Michael Rakabaele, Sam Ndala and Bernard Buthelezi. As if these marathon speedsters were not enough to worry about, the field also included Comrades elite runners like Tjale, Tivers, Holtzhausen and Lemos.

The JSE started outside the Wanderers Stadium in Johannesburg and traditionally finished at The Fountains in Pretoria. The Fountains was a public park managed by the conservative Pretoria City Council, who decided to take a Nationalist stance and insist the facility remain whites only. By now, road running was completely non-racial and the organisers had to quickly find another venue for the finish that would still measure 50km and honour the Johannesburg to Pretoria tradition.

The race patron was Finance Minister Barend du Plessis, and he engineered a solution that was not only politically acceptable, but a propaganda coup. The event would finish at the largest military complex in Africa, Voortrekkerhoogte. The defence force was committed to suppressing black aspirations in South Africa yet opening their sports grounds to the event and allowing participants of all races to use change rooms, showers and toilets, projected a benevolent image.

There was another twist to the finishing saga. The switch to Voortrekkerhoogte introduced a significant climb near the end, followed by a gentle 1.5km descent to the stadium. It made the course a little tougher and slower, right at the end. It would work to my advantage.

At 6.30am on Saturday 3 August, the brass bell of the Johannesburg Stock Exchange sounded to more than 4,000 runners in Corlett Drive outside the Wanderers Stadium. I loped through 8km in 26.25, possibly a little fast, but still trailing leaders Holtzhausen and Ndala by nearly half a minute.

The pace picked up approaching 15km as the guys around me really wound it up on the gentle downhill sections. We were tearing into the downhills at three minutes per km, and I could only just hold on. Luckily, the course had some undulations that slowed them down. At the halfway mark I was enmeshed in a group of eight runners chasing the leading group of three, which included Moshaba. I didn't need all those years at university to work out there were 11 of us chasing 10 gold medals. This meant someone would have to crack, so I thought I would contribute to the surges coming from our group. I hung in on the downhills but when the road tilted upwards, I dictated the pace and pushed hard. After three or four of these uphill surges, my rivals realised my legs were strong; they were not going to drop me in a hurry. I passed through 32km in 1:48 in ninth place, with my group starting to fragment. The following 10km stretch was a hot slog, with dust thrown up by vehicles driving on the dirt shoulders of the Old Main Road. Much to my surprise, I had managed to drop all the runners in my bunch including Choeu and Kekana, runners I had never beaten previously. In 1981, Choeu had set a world best time of 2:48.52 for 50km in winning the up JSE.

I felt I had a top 10 in my grasp when I strode past the standard marathon marker in 2:23 in fourth place. It was tough going but I was feeling reasonable, albeit 50 seconds behind the leading trio. My guess was that 2:13 marathoner Moshaba had the race in the bag. Richard Mayer captured his ungainly style perfectly in the book *Three Men named Matthews*.

"Gibeon Moshaba was the archetypal black South African road runner. His protruding jaw, his square head and awkward style, with his unmistakable pigeon-toed right foot strike made him look like a journey-man competitor to Temane's master athlete. Moshaba was nevertheless a formidable athlete. Mentally and physically he was as hard (*thata* in his native Pedi) as any of the rocks in the mine where he worked. South Africa has not produced another athlete who could justify being termed the quintessential roadie more than Moshaba."

Over the next 4km I would experience the glorious uncertainty of sport. My race pick Moshaba, and Nkoane blew up within metres of each other and I reeled them in without any trouble. With 4km to go, I was second and knew the remainder of the route well. After reaching the Iscor Circle, the lowest point of the course, there was a steady climb up to Voortrekkerhoogte where the road levelled out for about 1km. When I caught my first glimpse of race leader Sam Ndala, it was clear he was taking strain. I knew we would soon swing right for the final 500m climb of the day before descending into the finish. I was preparing for a battle with him on the climb but, astonishingly, he also slowed and I passed him before the climb. At the top, I was a minute clear and could savour the last couple of minutes.

In the past seven months I had engaged Rudyard Kipling's two imposters, triumph and disaster. Every disappointment I had experienced after my January diagnosis of hepatitis A was overshadowed by my new-found joy. I crossed the line in 2:50.45, watched by my wife, my parents and my seven-year-old Nicole who, excitedly, jumped into my sweaty embrace.

If my rise from fourth to first in the final 4km was a surprise, spectators were shocked when the runner-up appeared. It was my RAC team mate, Thulani Sibisi, who had absolutely sliced through the field over the last 15km. Unlike the Comrades Marathon, the rest of the top 10 were all black. Lucre was the first woman in 3:27, less than a minute outside her 1984 record.

I recovered well from the JSE and I fronted up to Dr Barlow-Rademeyer's rooms for my final clearance from the effects of hepatitis A. I lay down and he probed and pushed my abdomen, muttering assuring noises until ... "what do we have here?" His fingers had located a small bulge protruding from the left hand side of my abdominal wall.

I admitted I had first felt something a week previously while bending over to tie my shoes. He diagnosed an inguinal hernia and recommended surgery sooner rather than later.

It transpired that my abdominal weak spot, which most boys are born with, had been stressed beyond capacity during my exuberant gym sessions in March and April. Given my work commitments through to the end of the year, I had neither any interest nor any desire to run any more races, so I booked the operation in October.

The Nashua Johannesburg Marathon passed the KPMG office in the city, so I organised a refreshment table staffed by volunteers from the office. We thought we'd provide more than drinks and rigged up a serious sound system to add some music to the energy of the marathon. On a jog before the race I asked Kenny Jacobs, a regular winner up to the 32km distance, if he had any special requests and without hesitation he answered: "Bruce Springsteen, *Born in the USA.*"

Well, with Springsteen echoing in his ears, he finished third in his marathon debut in 2:17 behind winner Plaatjes, and Sinqe. A year later, he would be dead from an accidental gunshot wound in his thigh. He was still alive when the ambulance arrived, except it was a whites only ambulance. The assistance they offered was to call a black ambulance. He was dead when the black ambulance arrived.

Plaatjes had a battle with the Nashua race organisers beforehand, when he got wind of Fordyce being offered R20,000 appearance money to participate. Plaatjes had won Nashua on two previous occasions, setting a world best for a marathon at altitude in 1984. He went on to win the South African marathon title in a national record, and followed up with the national cross country title. He was South Africa's leading distance runner but it took a threat of withdrawal before he got paid appearance money too. It was a subtle reminder of how the racial game was still being played, as well as the overwhelming attraction of Comrades.

No sooner had I started some gentle cycling and swimming after my hernia surgery than the wound went septic. An impressive wound it was, too, because there was no keyhole surgery in those days. My first attempt to run after a course of antibiotics was painful. The second day was much easier and I jogged the Des Blake 15km run with 1966 Comrades winner Tommy Malone and Kudus running mate Mike Brown. That was the most wonderful thing about running in South Africa at the time. Regardless of the speed you wished to run, you would always be assured of good company and lots of banter. Driving home from the Des Blake run I stopped in Emmarentia to buy a Coke and the Sunday papers. As I was leaving the store, Nancy Whittaker greeted me and introduced me to her husband Dr Roly. I had not met Fordyce's mother and stepfather previously. Although I did not immediately recognise them, I appreciated their courtesy.

I ended the year with another 4,630km of running to my name, and with the health and condition that I hoped would enable me to have a crack at the 1986 Comrades. I resolved to run only one race in my Comrades build-up, the 56km Korkie. Regardless of how I performed at Comrades, it would likely be my last. Intuitively I knew I would not be in a position to keep the candle burning at both ends in the context of other priorities like my family and a successful career with one of the best professional services firms in South Africa, KPMG.

Domestically, I had a real concern. Vern and I had almost separated while living in the US but returned to South Africa with a resolve to make it work. Vern was much happier living closer to her family and with three daughters she was an extremely busy mother and homemaker. Between career, daughters and running, I did not make time for sufficient emotional investment in the marriage. There was never any disharmony in our home but an enormous void was opening in our relationship. Family and close friends who knew us well could sense that. It was eating away at me. Our marriage was under constant stress.

I had a great career and big plans for Comrades but I also needed to be a more attentive husband in 1986. I knew it would be my last serious tilt at Comrades as an amateur weekend warrior.

15

Talking a good race

That's showbiz! You soar emotionally from your debut as a television commentator and then you come crashing down when the hairdresser given the job of tidying you up for your on-screen appearance points out that you have developed a bald spot.

The hepatitis had not only trashed my liver, it had led to alopecia. I had no idea that I was losing hair until my lunchtime appointment with a barber on 27 May to trim what I thought was a full head of hair, ahead of my debut as a talking head on the SABC during the Comrades Marathon.

When he started fussing in dismay behind me, I asked if anything was wrong. He wordlessly angled a mirror to reflect the back of my head. Staring back at me was a bull's eye of white skin, 3cm across.

On the way home I visited Dr Rob Dowdeswell and was advised that the stress my body had been exposed to following my hepatitis had caused alopecia. I was less than delighted to hear that many alopecia sufferers lost an entire head of hair overnight. I anxiously checked my pillow as soon as I woke up for the next few days.

My involvement with the telecast of the 1985 Comrades came about from a call to Kim Shippey, who was in charge of SABC sport. I suggested that the live telecast of the 1984 race left plenty of scope for improvement. The print media had lambasted the 1984 broadcast as being well short of satisfactory. I sensed Shippey knew that much.

He wanted to know my angle and I suggested I assist in any way possible. I knew the top runners pretty well. I understood the tactics and I had a reasonable feel for the event, having just run one of the fastest times in Comrades history. He indicated that he was interested and would get back to me nearer the time.

In early May he invited me to a meeting at the SABC television headquarters in Auckland Park to discuss the broadcast. He chaired a planning workshop comprising the production team and the main commentators. I was invited to table my suggestions and to participate on equal terms with these professional media personnel. Shippey was clearly determined to improve the Comrades production, not least because it was the single biggest sports broadcast of the year in South Africa.

It dawned on me during the workshop that Shippey was referring to me as a member of the broadcast team. Neither of us had mentioned any on-camera involvement during our previous discussion, but that clearly was the role he now had in mind for me.

The technical broadcasting challenges were explained. The mobile television camera crew would work out of the back of a *bakkie* (light flatbed truck) and beam a signal to the helicopter hovering overhead. This, in turn, would redirect the signal to the local television station for national broadcast.

The helicopter would have to refuel after four hours in the air, risking a blackout during the most exciting part of the Comrades, as had happened the previous year when Fordyce was chasing me down during the final two hours and the live television coverage had been temporarily discontinued, just before the major drama of the day at 45th Cutting. The SABC had neither the budget for another helicopter nor a second piece of equipment to relay the signal to the studio. A refuelling stop would be made.

We would do the commentary straight off the live screen in a little portable studio office on a hill outside Pietermaritzburg, without any communication to the various camera crews, whether roving, fixed, or in the helicopter; or access to official timing clocks, runner identification and information as to who was exactly where on the course. Mobile telephony or cell phones, let alone the internet, had not yet arrived. Our resources were primitive.

On Tuesday 20 May I took two days' days annual leave and shared a minibus ride to Pietermaritzburg with the SABC crew, including Jan Snyman, Edwil van Aarde, Chris van Tonder and Larry Lombard of the *Sunday Times*. We met the rest of the Comrades broadcasting team, including the living encyclopaedia of running statistics, Riël Hauman of Cape Town, at the Capital Towers Hotel.

Hauman came prepared with an extraordinary depth of statistics and information. My contribution would be my current Comrades knowledge and personal insights into most of the contenders through friendships and research.

I had taken time in the few weeks before Comrades to identify my top-30 men and top-four women. I called every one of them and collated some interesting information and insights:

- The extraordinary multi-sport achievements of Danny Biggs who, after seven years, was one unit short of completing his four-year university course, and had been conscripted to start his military training in July.
- Siphiwe Gqele, trained by Thys Ferreira, ran a 2:13 marathon at his second attempt; followed by a Two Oceans 56km win in 3:11.54. He enjoyed steak and fruit with lots of milk.
- Graham Fraser had been a first-grade tennis player before taking running more seriously.
- Steve Hollier had been a semi-professional footballer in Zambia. When he arrived in South Africa in 1981, all he heard on the radio was Comrades. He started running.
- Alan Robb, four-time winner, stopped skydiving after 30 jumps. He said he had not been sufficiently motivated for the past few years, but was keen to give Comrades another serious shot again in 1986. His favourite food was anything with a Castle Lager
- Derek Tivers had lost his wife the previous year. His motivation in 1985 was to return to Comrades to show that he could do it again. He trained mostly with Hillcrest teammates, Graeme Fraser and Tony Abbot. His favourite food was steak with a few milk stouts on Friday evenings.
- Hoseah Tjale, a messenger and handyman with Hoechst, ran because it was what he did best in life. He predicted a slower winning time than

the previous up run because of the change in seconding rules. Tjale trained solo except for track sessions with Joe Crouch. He relaxed by going to church on Sundays and his favourite food was maize meal.

- Eric Bateman finished eighth in Two Oceans in 3:21 after a marathon PB of 2:22. His commitments as a lung-chest medical specialist, with four young kids, dictated his training time. Typically, he ran at 5am in the dark through the hilly Kirstenbosch and Constantia areas of Cape Town. He played the guitar and enjoyed mountain climbing and hiking.
- Bruce Matthews had been a keen windsurfer and surfer before concentrating on Comrades. He finished nineth in the Two Oceans and 14th in the Comrades in 1983 and 1984. He was strongly motivated to finish in the top 10 for that elusive gold medal.
- Tony Dearling, co-owner and managing director of the Sweat Shop, ran his first Comrades when he was 18 and 91kg for a bet. Twelve years later, he won gold, finishing ninth in the 1983 Comrades. He ran with Dov Traub most mornings.
- Helen Lucre was selected for the New Zealand basketball squad before arriving in South Africa in 1980. In 1983 she won Two Oceans, JSE and Korkie, all in record times. In February 1985 she ran a marathon PB of 2:47. She enjoyed fish and fresh salads washed down with a beer.
- Lindsay Weight had won Comrades the two previous years and often ran 170km a week. She had recently completed an honours degree in science at UCT and was studying for her masters in sports science under Noakes. She was a vegetarian and lived on cheese and salads.

The most astonishing revelation was that only one athlete was utterly committed to winning: Fordyce. Robb was keeping his powder dry for a serious crack at the down run the following year. Tjale had probably done too much racing in the lead-in to Comrades. Everybody else committed only to top-10 aspirations. It struck me that Fordyce would have to encounter some form of disaster not to win. Not for nothing did he wear the Comrades crown.

It took hours to track down the athletes but it was worth the effort to learn of their diverse interests, preferences, physiques and training routines. The only runner on my list who eluded all my contact attempts was Ian Emery. We always seemed to miss each other. It transpired my research covered nine of the top 10 men and the top three women. The only male gold medallist I failed to identify was Villiers Oberholzer.

Fifty hours before the start of the race, the SABC contingent was launching into a 4am dress rehearsal of the first hour of broadcasting. This would give the technical crew 48 hours to sort out any glitches. Fortunately, all went well. Sound and images from all cameras plus helicopter worked perfectly. We settled into our makeshift studio with a small single monitor for the broadcast and by 8am we were done.

I got changed into my running kit and headed out for a 32km run. I wanted to run down Polly Shorts and then return home the same way as part of my research, but I got lost. That's how sketchy my knowledge of the up run was. Instead of finding Polly Shorts, I headed out towards Richmond.

Race morning was surreal. We were confined to a small makeshift studio on top of a hill outside Pietermaritzburg, looking at a monitor without any sound. We were totally disconnected from the crackling energy that emanates from the thousands of hyped-up runners congregated outside the Durban City Hall.

The race progressed almost to script.

As expected, Fordyce won in 5:37 but he did not look good at all. As I watched the race unfold and saw Fordyce deteriorate near the end, I thought back to Tjale's comments about the impact of the new seconding rules precluding any helper or spectator from running even a single step alongside an athlete. The new rule was referred to as "stand and hand." In all his previous wins, the same team of minders and knowledgeable athletes had superbly supported Fordyce. They would ensure he had a proper drink and would run alongside him, keeping him informed and cajoling him to fulfil his goal.

It was a winning team formula. I had witnessed it in action, close up. However, the new seconding rules outlawed this level of assistance. If any supporter or spectator ran alongside any competitor, the runner risked disqualification. Fordyce's body language in the closing stages of the race was that of a domestic pet that had been left at home alone. He was missing the company he had grown accustomed to. His winning time was about seven minutes slower than 1983, and he went straight to the medical tent.

Nevertheless, a win was a win and Fordyce had chalked up his fifth in a row to create Comrades history. Although not at his best, he ran the second half a sizzling eight minutes faster than the first. It is worth noting that he took the lead from Tjale with 27km to go, and put a gap of almost six minutes between them by the finish, with Tjale running even splits.

Lucre ran a smart race to take the women's title in 6:53, eight minutes ahead of Weight. She had created history as the first athlete (men included) to win the grandslam of South Africa's major ultramarathons – Two Oceans, Comrades, Korkie and JSE. Helen subsequently made an invaluable contribution to the Rainbow Nation through her extensive community work and her foster-parenting of Lucky Hadebe who turned into a world-class 800m athlete. Like Blanche Moila, she was subsequently inducted as an Ethekwini Living Legend for services to the community and her inordinate contribution to athletics in South Africa, particularly amongst disadvantaged communities. Helen is one of road running's greatest ambassadors, a true living legend. She epitomises what the sport represents in its true form.

On 2 June 1985 the *Sunday Star* published a great compliment:

Nice one, Bob

"Bob de la Motte, runner up in the Comrades last year, may have been missing from the action out on the road between Durban and Pietermaritzburg on Friday but what a pleasure it was to hear his knowledgeable and well-informed commentary on television.

His relevant observations contrasted sharply with the drivel that accompanied the progress of Fordyce and the gold medallists up Polly Shorts."

A few days later, the *Financial Mail* carried this comment in its review of the SABC's race coverage: "Bob de la Motte was a real find – he rapidly became indispensable and set an overdue example to the professional commentators."

It was my 1985 Comrades consolation to learn that my research and insights into the race had resonated with viewers and non-runners.

A few weeks later, I received a cheque in the mail for R350 for my participation in the Comrades broadcast and an invitation to attend a debriefing workshop at television headquarters back at the SABC. The workshop was an eye-opener because they listened to all constructive feedback. Snyman and Shippey received strong endorsement for their decision to include Riël Hauman and myself in the live broadcast.

They were delighted with the positive feedback but wanted to keep improving. I made 12 constructive suggestions, with a final observation regarding the blatant free advertising when the cameras lingered on advertising banners for a car rental company and a technology company with no runner in sight. A few months later, I was not surprised to learn that one of the cameramen had been taking backhanders in return for product exposure.

Shippey asked me to nominate a commentator to take my place in 1986. My suggestions included Jax Snyman, Dave Wright, Ken McArthur, Ian Laxton and Bernie Rose.

And with that, my television career ended.

16

The fastest Comrades

itius, altius, fortius. The Olympic motto proposed by Baron Pierre de Coubertin translates from Latin as "faster, higher, stronger." Well, two out of three ain't bad. Mercifully, I wasn't going to grow any taller, but I had to become faster and stronger in 1986, particularly the latter.

I thought daily about how to improve my odds of beating Fordyce on the down run. One of the things that came to my attention was the difference in the Fordyce physique between 1982 and 1986. He had clearly done a ton of strength and conditioning work. Little wonder he could survive longer at pace than anyone in those brutal final 10km.

My strategy for the year was to improve my second half speed in every event I ran. Yep, the old negative split fixation again. However, now it was as much about mental training as physical. I needed to possess the mental capacity to turn it on and run faster second-half splits to the end. Fight fire with fire, right?

This would also be a great way to camouflage how my training and condition might be progressing in the build up to Comrades. I would start out very slowly with back marker friends, and then power away in the second half, still finishing out of the prizes and visible race statistics. I would be lost in the crowd, but get an invaluable interval training opportunity. I would also avoid running too many time trials where my times would be published, and I would substitute my own training runs in lieu of the Sweat Shop and Wanderers runs. I needed to do the bulk of my running away from the Fordyce camp.

My 1984 training schedule had worked brilliantly but changes clearly had to be made. However, I kept them to a minimum, apart from adding the necessary strength sessions. My five-month Comrades build-up would involve:

- Gym sessions three mornings a week until mid-March.
- Mid-week runs of 21km until end March, then increased to 32km.
- Weekly distance of 120km gradually increased to 160km by the end of January.
- Eight weeks at 160km to mid-March.
- Easy week before and after 56km Korkie on 23 March.
- Four weeks of 200km in April, no speed work or hill sessions.
- Four-week taper in May, 180km, 150km, 130km and 90km.
- Weekly track sessions and hill repetitions in May.

If all went according to plan, I would achieve a total running distance of 3,400km as I had done in 1984, but I would also be stronger.

Straightaway, I established a routine, leaving home by 4.45am to complete a 12km loop to Albert's gym, followed by a 20-minute workout and the 2km grind home with dead legs. After a quick swim, followed by a shower and family breakfast, I would load up Nicole and Simone and head for the office via Auckland Park Preparatory School, a private girl's school that voluntarily integrated black children. APPS classes started at 7.30am and I was at my desk by 8am.

On Wednesday evenings, I would run the RAC 21.1km circuit with an extra loop, and on Saturday mornings, I ran a 17km loop from our home in Northcliff, trying to replicate the course variety of the Wanderers run. I tried to organise my calendar to allow two lunchtime runs through Hector Norris Park, around the goldmine dumps and tailings dams, followed by a quick swim and shower. The entire routine would take less than 90 minutes, both healthier and shorter than a typical business lunch. I had major client deadlines but fortunately, these did not clash with Korkie on 23 March and Comrades on 31 May. However, I did plan to take a week's leave at the end of April to recharge my batteries after four weeks of 200km and a busy spell at the office.

I also had to deal with my rivalry with Fordyce. It was a natural, competitive rivalry and never once did I feel it degenerated into friction or resentment. It was as much intellectual as it was physical and emotional. I enjoyed this subtle game of mental chess. The mind games were a tangible element of the race build-up, as subsequently confirmed by Cameron-Dow in his Fordyce biography. His description was pretty accurate.

"Although Fordyce and De la Motte, both members of RAC, sometimes trained together, such runs were non-confrontational in an athletic sense but increasingly combative in subtle communication. Fordyce would be the last person to violate the rules or spirit of sport but, within such rules (or laws) and spirit he is a fearsome competitor. The pre-Comrades message given to De la Motte was, "Maybe you can win (the 1986 race) but it will cost you an arm and a leg."

At the end of January, I again used the Benoni Marathon to qualify for Comrades, cruising through in 2:48. I weighed 76kg, my resting pulse was 39 beats per minute and my only concern was whether the seven hours of sleep I was getting each night were enough.

I kept adding pieces to the puzzle, including a reconnaissance of the final 20km of the down run. My lack of familiarity of this section had cost me dearly two years earlier, and I wanted to resolve this. A week into February I flew to Durban and stayed with Norman 'Guru' Wessels, a senior member of the Adidas team in Durban and twice a top-10 finisher in the 1970s. The next morning I ran the last 35km of Comrades to the Old Kingsmead stadium with a group that included future eight-time Ironman world champion, Paula Newby-Fraser. The outing barely took two and a half hours, after which I showered and flew back to Jo'burg in time for Sunday lunch with the family.

The following weekend, I ran the Magnolia 21km with the intention of a sub-70 minute finish with a faster second half. The course was flat, fast and gentle on the body. Even with a pit stop behind a bush, I clocked 69.34.

For the next five Sundays, I alternated 32km and 42km runs, all at easy pace with lots in reserve at the end. I finished off with an easy 40km RAC club run. With the 56km Korkie one week away, I knew I was going to enjoy the outing. I could feel my fitness improving.

I wanted to win Korkie, but I kept everyone guessing. I had also been invited to run the Two Oceans and the journalists did not know which, if either, of the two races I would go hard at. Most tipped Tjale to win.

The race started at 6am at Centurion Park because the Pretoria City Council still refused to open public ablution facilities at The Fountains to black athletes. This meant a steep 2km before the slow poison grind to Germiston. Whenever I think of that race, I remember that apartheid slowed the winning time by at least a minute because of that initial climb.

For the first hour, the group I was in floated along 50m behind the leaders. We were enjoying the cool weather when, at 18km, Tjale interrupted our momentum by zooming past. No one else seemed inclined to chase so I went after him and pulled up on his shoulder. Tjale threw in the occasional surge but I was fine, even though we weren't loafing. We were running uphill at altitude at a speed of 3.25 per km.

After 33km, Tjale accelerated and I covered, but when he backed off he slowed a bit more than previously. I decided to let him do some chasing and went hard for 2km, building a 12 second advantage. I knew about Tjale's persistence, so went hard again. The gap between us grew steadily and I passed the standard marathon mark in 2:27. At 50km, I had a five-minute advantage and knew it was in the bag. I ran the final 14km in 47.07, easing off because my mind was already in recovery mode. I even joined in the chatter among a group of cyclists who had decided to follow me. I won in 3:14.07, having run the second half two minutes faster than the first. Tjale finished in 3:19, but any elation I felt was quickly suppressed when we heard that Robb was told on reaching the finish that his father, Hector, had died. He left immediately and a subdued atmosphere permeated the stadium. We all felt for him.

I had to wait for the awards function and I was sitting in the grandstand with my dad and Wally Hayward, when Mark Etheridge of *The Star* approached to inform me that the road running cognoscenti believed I had blown my chances for the Comrades Marathon by running so hard.

I smiled to myself. I had a pretty good idea as to the source of that opinion. I suggested to Etheridge the cognoscenti should have a chat to Fordyce about his build-up to his 1983 Comrades victory. He raced the 42km Buffalo Marathon flat out in a PB of 2.17, then jogged the 56km

Korkie in 4 hours for a silver medal and a week later, raced the 56km Two Oceans, finishing fourth in 3:14. Eight weeks later, he set a Comrades up record of 5:30. The mind games didn't work too well that day.

Actually, I needed a good, hard run. I hadn't raced a single event other than Korkie and I had 10 weeks to recover. It was a calculated and considered risk on my part. Although run at altitude, the Korkie course is far gentler on the body than the Two Oceans and I had eased off over the final 7km. My recovery within 24 hours and over the next week was excellent. And I had the added confidence boost of successfully race-testing my choice of shoes and drink for Comrades.

I had tested a variety of models before settling on the Adidas Marathon 84, designed for shorter events, but my feet seemed to cope well. I finished without blisters or other problems and that particular pair was packed away until 31 May. My drink was 50g of Caloreen powder mixed with one litre of water, sweetened with a powdered mandarin flavour. Caloreen was a glucose polymer high-energy product, distributed by Roussel Laboratories. Training friend, Dr Eddie King, had told me about using Caloreen in his triathlon racing and spoke well of the product as a doctor and an athlete. On the strength of my Korkie experience, I decided to use the same formula for Comrades.

The next morning, I headed out for a gentle 8km recovery run and bumped into Chamberlain en route. He asked me what training I had done on the Sunday and I replied that I had run Korkie. He presumed I had just run part of it as a Two Oceans taper, but I 'fessed up that I had not only run the full 56km but won.

Chamberlain said nothing but the look he flashed me was full of scepticism. I therefore enjoyed the mid-morning discussion when he phoned to say he had read the papers and no longer felt I was talking the product of the south-facing end of a north-bound bull.

At lunchtime, Morris and I settled into the Rand Club for lunch and a discussion of Comrades seconding logistics. There were no restrictions on seconds at Korkie and I found the regular, up-to-date splits invaluable because they allow you to immediately react to what you can't see behind you. It is always better to be the chaser than the pacesetter at Comrades for two reasons: you can use your eyes and you get constant time updates from spectators who click their watches when the leader passes and call out the seconds to the pursuer. Unfortunately, I'm a front-runner.

The following weekend, Fordyce praised my Korkie effort in his column in the *Saturday Star*, suggesting my effort at altitude would have matched the 50km world track record of 2:48 held by Briton, Jeff Norman. He also referred to the excellent Korkie record of 3:11.24 of Johnny Halberstadt. His reference to statistics and records got me thinking and playing around with some numbers. The 50km track record referred to by Fordyce was of no interest to me. I could not imagine anything more boring than running 125 laps of an athletics track. Halberstadt's Korkie record of 3:11.24 was out of my reach, even adjusting for a more difficult start to the 1986 race.

However, when I looked at Fordyce's 80km world best of 4:50.21 in the 1983 London to Brighton, my heart started beating faster. The average speed needed to better his mark was 3min. 37.5sec. per km. I had run uphill at altitude for 56km at 10 seconds per kilometre faster, and I felt that if I turned around and ran another 24km downhill, on the same course, I could have done it. I confidently believed the 80km record was within my reach but when I considered it in the context of my everyday commitments outside of running, I knew I'd never have the time to dedicate to it.

I did get a big smile out of Dan Side's satirical piece in *The Star* on the pressure for the Comrades to go professional.

Oh spare a thought for these poor "amateurs"

Shakes Twodice was suffering from insomnia sleeping on his Lowblo mattress stressed out about the pressure of being an amateur athlete.

All the high finance decisions are driving me crazy. I can't make up my mind which shoes to endorse. I got a big offer from Crikey and I can't decide whether I should leave Pussycat. Sometimes I wish I was Zola Budd and ran barefoot.

"Then there are all those races I have to enter and not win, so as not to ruin my chances of winning my umpteenth Packrats Marathon. I don't want to be a winner like Bobbin de Moat was in the Porky and leave my race on another course. It's hell holding back all the time, especially when I feel like being up with the front-runners. But I don't dare take the chance of, uh, winning. The thought of taking first place in anything but the Packrats sickens me. It would ruin everything.

"Then there's the problem of supertax. Sometimes I think of turning professional like Johnny Helluvastate. But think of the money I would lose. Poor Johnny has to go to the States to find himself a race to make some cash while I've got all the training runs I need for the Packrats right here in my own backyard. And big cheques to go with it."

Three weeks after Korkie, Vern and I travelled to Bergville with Rob and Jill Dowdeswell, which allowed me to jog the 53km Bergville to Ladysmith race, and tag an extra 7km on the end for my first 60km training run, to push my total for the week to 200km. The reward for running 60km in four hours was a freshly baked country scone with homemade strawberry jam, provided by the townsfolk.

That was followed by a 50km corporate relay around Johannesburg. It worked perfectly for me. KPMG entered several teams and mine finished second. I ran the first 10km leg and jogged the remainder of the course with Plaatjes to achieve a comfortable 50km outing, with the benefit of refreshment tables and great company.

At the end of April I flew to Durban for another recce of the race route. Starting from Cato Ridge, I ran the final 60km of the Comrades course in 4:20 with 'Guru' Wessels, and others. Along the way, Guru suggested I wear a baseball cap to avoid squinting into the sun. He recommended I cut out all unnecessary cloth, retaining just the webbing to provide shade while allowing heat to escape. It was my final long run before a month of tapering during May.

I thoroughly enjoyed my week's annual leave, cutting back on training and spending a few days in Durban where I ran the final 15km from Cowies Hill to Old Kingsmead with Lucre. Later that day, I measured my pulse at 36. I also discussed the new seconding arrangements with Lanham. No more running alongside your athlete. It was strictly "stand and hand". The logistics were onerous. We needed:

- A Toyota minibus to get the crew to Durban. My mobile pairs were Ev Lanham and Stuart Morris, Charles Bryant and Jean-Paul de la Motte, and Paul Burman and Rob Dowdeswell.
- Three motorbikes and six helmets
- Six two-way radios and back-up batteries
- Eight identification flags to help me spot my seconds among the crowd

- 32 drinks bottles, plus Caloreen, Coke and Clifton
- 12 wine coolers.
- 30 sponges in Ziploc bags.
- Three backpacks
- Three sets of survey maps
- Six notepads and pens
- Nine stopwatches
- Three pocket calculators
- One large Adidas umbrella for the meeting point at the finish.

It all came at a cost. Fortunately, Adidas provided my team with kit and reimbursed some of my expenses; RAC contributed to my accommodation; McCarthy Industrial lent us a few motorbikes; and Toyota loaned us a minibus.

Our observation of the slick Fordyce support team in 1984 had taught us a few things. I needed to get vital time gaps in addition to drinks. The mobile team would split at the appointed stop. One would head towards Pietermaritzburg for 500m with a drink and a stopwatch, and the other would head towards Durban for 500m with a cold sponge. Because they had two-way radios, I could collect a drink and, 1km down the road, a sponge and a time gap because I anticipated Fordyce would once again be stalking.

The highly restrictive seconding rules were expected to have a bigger impact on Fordyce, who had been extraordinarily well seconded in previous races. We also anticipated the crowded final 10km would be a logistical nightmare for my seconds, right at crunch time. The plan was to try to get to me every 4km.

I cruised through the final weeks before the race, achieving a PB of eight and a half hours sleep one night. The taper was going well and my focus was on staying healthy, taking extra care to avoid sneezing kids and clients.

The Comrades Marathon Association had made a few adjustments to the course. It was 700m shorter, with more sections on the smoother, flatter highway. Fordyce had said it was potentially 10 minutes faster. Another of his mind games, but worth investigating. He also proclaimed that no one who held a full-time job would win the Comrades, inferring that only he possessed the credentials of a full-time, professional athlete capable of winning. What were the rest of us supposed to do? Pack our kit away and pack him on the back? No way, Bruce!

The usual expert panels unanimously picked Fordyce as the most likely winner and all included me as a top 10 finisher. One article suggested: "Bob de la Motte is being tipped in some quarters as the man most likely to do the impossible ... beat Fordyce in the down Comrades."

Robb was quoted as saying that it was a two-horse race.

"Either Bruce and Bob will run a good time, or kill each other."

On 28 May my training log confirmed my level of satisfaction with my preparation and I calculated a hypothetical Comrades time of 5:21. I kept this information to myself. I started with my 1984 time of 5:30 and adjusted for various factors, including a shorter course of some 700m (or three minutes); more running on the motorway in the second half (one minute); faster first half tempo for the leading group (two minutes); and my all-round improvement and ability to achieve negative splits (three minutes). All good theory and hypothesis.

Instead of staying in Durban or Maritzburg, we checked into the Thousand Hills Hotel in Drummond. Lanham drove me over the route and I made notes, estimating my possible running speeds over nine discrete sections of the course. The first split was from the start to the 80km-to-go marker, and every 10km after that. I optimistically thought it would be possible to run the final 10km of the course in 35:24, the same as the previous 10km split.

We then called in to the Durban Exhibition Centre to complete my official Comrades registration. This was the first Comrades Expo, called the Comrades Experience, and the venue was decked out with booths showcasing running merchandise and Comrades memorabilia. The most interesting exhibit was the Asics stand. Their shoes contained a gel in the heel and the sales reps were dropping raw eggs from a height of about 1.5m onto a piece of this gel to demonstrate its miraculous shock-absorbing qualities.

For the an ultramarathon event, the 1986 Comrades entry fee amounted to a very modest R15, but the race rules included two paragraphs of particular interest:

> **Seconding**
>
> The No Seconding Rule will be very strictly enforced by the 1986 Comrades Marathon
>
> - No mobile seconds of any description will be allowed on the route.
> - No non-competitor may accompany a runner along the route (for any distance at all).
> - Any transgression of the No Seconding Rule may be reported to the Race Referee by a traffic officer, a marshal, an official or another competitor. The penalty will be at the discretion of the referee and may include disqualification which will be invoked at the finish until 5.00pm.
>
> **Advertising**
>
> We would like to draw your attention to Rule 8, which appears on your entry form. It reads:
>
> No advertising or sponsorship will be permitted except by the Organisers.
>
> This rule will apply for the duration of the race, i.e. from the start in Pietermaritzburg up and until you have left the exit from the finishing pen at Kingsmead Cricket Ground.
>
> VERY IMPORTANT – ANY INFRINGEMENT OF THE RULES WILL DEFINITELY RESULT IN DISQUALIFICATION.

After completing my registration, and on the point of heading back to Drummond, a radio announcer from Radio Port Natal summoned me over the public address system to his open-air studio for an interview. The last thing I wanted to do on the eve of Comrades was to be grilled by a radio DJ who would no doubt ask me about beating Fordyce. I had no intention of making any public predictions. Instead of ignoring him and leaving, I asked Lanham to thank him for his offer but to decline. Instead, the ego-driven announcer publicly declared: "Bob de la Motte's manager has demanded a fee before being interviewed."

I could not believe what I had just heard. Public broadcasts like that can never be unsaid or deleted. All I could think to myself on the way out was that I had been stitched up.

The next morning after breakfast, I recalculated a hypothetical Comrades time based on my course survey. My calculations suggested that whoever ran 5:23.30 would win Comrades. If I ran the absolute perfect race, I believed I had a good chance. However, despite my eternal optimism, I could not see how any runner, Fordyce included, could clock 5:20 over the 1986 course we were about to race. In the afternoon, Lanham once again drove me over the second half of the course. I thought I had a much better feel for the contours than I had in 1984. Later that evening, I meticulously inked those 5:23.30 race splits on the palm of my left hand.

There was no seeding of any Comrades runners in 1986. It would be a mass start of all competitors without any structure or grading based on ability. This was Comrades, the people's race. Unsure of how chaotic the start might be, I arrived at 5.30am and spent the next 10 minutes negotiating my way through a human sea of 10,552 competitors. By 5.40am, I was in the second row and declined the offer of a magnanimous Krugersdorp runner, in pole position in front of me, to swop places.

I stood at the start line emotionally charged yet simultaneously anxious. *Chariots of Fire* by Vangelis was blasting away over the sound system but the experience was surreal, more like scuba diving in the silent depths of the ocean with neutral buoyancy than being one among thousands of runners, all bursting with energy and fear. The starter's pistol brought me back to reality.

About an hour into the race, and running through a magical dawn as we descended Polly Shorts, I had established my bus of runners. Deon Holtzhausen, Athol Dand, Michael Rakabaele, Chris Reyneke and a few others were bound together by that invisible bond which seems to work in running the way pelotons work in cycling. Weaving and bobbing along the poor road surface of the first 50km, we stuck together like magnets. Fordyce was trailing me by less than 200m. He had never been so close to the front end of the race, so early in the Comrades. He was running exactly how I thought he would.

Running through the corridor of ululating Zulus at Inchanga Mission, I was a little distressed by the change in sentiment. Two years earlier, the encouragement had been effusive and indiscriminate. This year, the chants were chants of assertion with raised clenched fists, demonstrating the identity this group had found. Shortly before halfway, Holtzhausen and I were enjoying the serenity of Drummond and the Valley of a Thousand Hills when we rounded a sharp bend and saw a khaki-clad, burly Natal farmer and a rather large baboon, standing side by side watching the

Comrades. Holtzhausen and I looked at each other in disbelief, and then returned to the task at hand. We definitely were not hallucinating.

The halfway point at Drummond was terrific. It is like a mountain climb stage in the Tour de France, generating a din and a wave of excitement. It was extra special for me as I caught a glimpse of my daughters and parents. I ran through halfway in second position in 2:44.30, trailing Eric Quibell by 1.39. My left palm had a biro-inked time of 2:45. I was on schedule and unperturbed by Quibell. I hoped he might remain in the lead for another 20km, like Reyneke in 1984. Uncharacteristically, Fordyce, Tjale and Biggs trailed me by a mere 50 seconds. Fordyce was determined not to lose sight of me.

The race pace fell away quite suddenly after the crowd support at the halfway mark. Unfortunately, this meant I had no option other than to overtake Quibell to maintain my momentum. Tactically, I knew that Fordyce would prefer to slow the race down as much as possible, lulling all rivals into a false sense of easy running before unleashing his sting over Cowies Hill, with 20km to go. He would focus on a win regardless of time, whereas I had adopted the attitude of aiming for a record time. Consequently, I knew I had a long solo run ahead because Fordyce would not be willing to lift the tempo. There and then I had a choice. Either I could make a race of it and stick to the record tempo of my left palm, or I could ease back into the Fordyce group and take my chances playing cat and mouse.

I chose to race.

The down run only really begins after the 50km mark at Kearsney College and the thunderous applause from hundreds of well-dressed schoolboys lining both sides of the road. That short, tree-lined stretch of road is one of my favourite parts of the course.

After this point it becomes important to block out spectators and all other distractions. The concentration is intense and the trick is to lock into an efficient, hypnotic rhythm referred to as being in the zone.

With 30km to go, I checked the splits I had printed on my left palm. I passed the marker in 4:10, two minutes ahead of schedule. I was exactly where I wanted to be, running close to my race plan and feeling well in

RUNAWAY COMRADE

control. My seconds were keeping me informed about Fordyce and the moment to race him would soon arrive.

With 14km to go, he finally surged, dropping Tjale into third and pulling up next to me. I had been the pacesetter for the previous 30km and, inexplicably, he started talking incessantly mentioning what a fast race it was and what incredible times we were going to run. I was quietly amused given that we had not spoken a word since his message to the media after my 3:14 Korkie win in March, never mind the Comrades race splits of 5:23 that I had inked onto the palm of my left hand. The entire media world and live television cameras were only metres in front of us filming every move. If I ignored him I would certainly earn the tag of grumpy or unsporting Bob so in a flash I offered him a handshake with the retort that the race was far from over and whoever lost would have to pay for lunch. Let him think about that one for a minute or two. Next thing his left arm reached up and around my neck for a bear hug. I didn't think it appropriate to be horsing around at this critical stage of the race especially running at a new Comrades record pace. I had been outsmarted and his tactile antics towards other challengers in his future Comrades wins would be referred to as his "kiss of death."

We continued to belt along and passed through 80km in 4:51.49, less than a minute outside his world record. Neither of us had any interest in that statistic at the time although Noakes picked it up in his live television commentary.

We had both taken some hefty punishment and the serious part of the race was now underway. If non-elite runners think there is no pain at the front of the race, they are wrong. The race hurts everyone badly and Fordyce and I were hurting. Racing him was intense. He ran on my heels like he was trying to benefit from my slipstream, while I steeled myself for the inevitable attack at 45th Cutting or Tollgate.

We hit 45th Cutting and leaned into the 300m climb. Fordyce picked up the pace. I responded and held him for the first 100m. He kicked again and opened a gap of 20m – and immediately the media truck wedged itself between the two of us. Losing the visual connection was a huge disadvantage, especially when the gap is small, the obstacle is a large truck spewing fumes, and you don't know whether you are holding the pace or losing ground. The driver no doubt thought he was doing the best thing for his passengers but it was an unfortunate event.

Noakes told television viewers: "I just can't emphasise enough that we are now seeing Bruce really at the peak of his powers. He's running a phenomenal race. For Bob to be that close, it just shows what a fantastic run he has had today. There is no other runner in the world who could stay this close to Bruce on a day like this."

I ran the last 8km as hard as I could, including the testing climb up to the top of Tollgate. I was running more strongly than I had in 1984. But Fordyce simply outmuscled me. As he approached the Old Kingsmead Stadium, he was handed a wide yellow kidney belt that he wrapped around his waist proclaiming the name of one of his sponsors, a sports nutrition company, and completed his victory lap in defiance of the Comrades advertising rules.

He won his sixth consecutive Comrades in a record of 5:24.07. I crossed the line in 5:26.12, also inside the previous record, and Fordyce was waiting. We embraced, I ruffled his dry hair and proclaimed to the media: "This man is an absolute genius. He is not even sweating."

I had just run the race of my life, covering the second half three minutes faster than the first. Fordyce had also run the race of his: he would never win another down run and the supersonic Fordyce Finish had prevailed again. The 1986 record of 5:24.07 would stand for 21 years and over the next 28 years, only four Comrades winners would run faster than my 5:26.12. I think we had both given the Comrades our best effort.

Immediately after crossing the finish line and shaking hands with Fordyce, I was handed a written request to provide a urine sample for a drug test. I could not easily satisfy the request because I was in a state of near dehydration. Over the next while I had a Coke, a cup of soup, two cups of tea, and an ice cream, and then repeated the cycle. My doping official stuck to me like Velcro, regardless of whether I was showering, dressing, talking to my family or the media. Luckily at about 4.30pm, more than five hours after crossing the line, I entered a portable toilet with my minder and filled two vials with urine, darker than usual due to the presence of dead blood cells from the pounding of the down run.

Fordyce had challenged the Comrades' establishment with his brazen sponsorship display but, despite media speculation, there was slim chance of the Comrades champion being disqualified. I never heard a murmur or any suggestion among any of the runners that a protest would even be lodged. We were there to race the Comrades not the billboards. There were other inconsistencies. The media tower at the Comrades finish line was wrapped in banners proclaiming "Rothmans – the greatest name in cigarettes." It was the dumbest thing I ever witnessed in the Comrades, the CMA taking cash or benefits in kind from a tobacco company. Yet I do not recall a single journalist or sports scientist denouncing this ill-considered endorsement by the CMA.

The winning time I had predicted of 5:23.30, after surveying the course two days before the race, was only 37 seconds faster than Fordyce clocked and we had raced in unfavourably hot conditions. Emphasising the high quality of the race, Tjale also bettered 5:30, earning third place in 5:29.02, while Helen Lucre won the women's race in 6:55.01.

On the club front, RAC made a clean sweep of the team prizes. Fordyce and I were strongly supported by Dearling (5:55) and Metcalfe (6:02) to win the Gunga Din by 42 minutes in a record 22:48.37. The RAC women (Lynne Spence, Lowell Fourie, Priscilla Carlisle and Janet Sherrard) won the Dinner Gong and the veteran men (Trevor Metcalfe, Clive Allen, Piet Mokola and Ross Wood) won the Vic Clapham Trophy. The team results served as a tribute to Dick and Vreni Welch and their hard working RAC committee for their generous contribution to club members and South African road running. We were well cared for.

That evening, I celebrated at Paul Lenferna's Garfunkels restaurant with my first beer in 16 months since my hepatitis A. The beer didn't go down well. The taste seemed alien. I didn't blame the brewer but myself. I was utterly spent and not in the mood for celebration. Just two weeks later, to the hour, a car bomb detonated outside the restaurant in protest at the Nationalist government declaring a state of emergency, killing three and injuring 69, some of them restaurant patrons.

I drove the family back to Johannesburg with very sore legs. I knew I had given the Comrades my best shot and was unlikely to run it again at a similar level of intensity. My Comrades curiosity and my love affair with this punishing event had passed. So, too, had our washing machine. I loaded it with my running kit and the family's dirty laundry but it responded with a death rattle.

My audacious tilt at the Comrades Marathon as an amateur weekend warrior was over.

Call back the past 4

My eyes were wide shut in the leafy, genteel northern suburbs of Johannesburg. City suburbs were reserved for whites and the only black people who could overnight in Johannesburg slept mainly in backyard servants' quarters – but only if they had a stamp in their pass book granting the temporary right to do so.

The majority of the population had to make the daily trek to work from the satellite townships reserved for blacks, coloureds and Indians. The Afrikaans word *apartheid* translates to apartness, and that is exactly what the government of the day enforced. I can only imagine the revolutionary fervour the separate areas legislation evoked among the blacks who comprised about 80% of the population. They got a daily reminder of the relative luxury of the white suburbs during their commute, whereas I had no idea what life was like in towns like Soweto, Lenasia or Coronationville, where other races lived. Most whites had no need to go there and had heard horror stories about the crime in such places. Simply speaking, they were too scared to venture there from their enclaves of privilege.

When Mark Plaatjes asked me if I knew my way around the non-white townships, I admitted I was as ignorant of them as my neighbours. We had been discussing running in a new addition to the fixture list, the Soweto Half Marathon, so Plaatjes decided I was in need of an eye opener.

That's how I came to spend a Sunday afternoon having tea in the Plaatjes family home in Coronationville, discussing the hypocrisy of the system. The government had classified the family as coloured, or mixed race, and they were restricted to a particular residential precinct. They were barred from living in a white area, no matter how wealthy they were.

For that matter, they were barred from living in a black or Indian area, too.

Public perception was that the Afrikaner Nationalists had a soft spot for the coloured community because, as the saying of the day went, many of them had a "touch of the tar brush". During the preceding 200 years of colonialism, many a lone farmer would have taken to co-habiting with a local woman. Consequently, there was open speculation as to which prominent Afrikaners, politicians included, had the odd strand of DNA with an origin they would prefer to scour from their thoughts. The derogatory reference was to call such a person a *boesman* or bushman, inferring he or she was related to the indigenous Bushmen or Khoisan tribes which roamed southern Africa before European settlement.

The Afrikaners were so sensitive about this they devised a test to determine who was and wasn't racially pure. The consequences were not as extreme for the "impure" as during the Nazi era, but the similarity was chilling. The Nationalists' test required a critical item of equipment: a pencil. This was inserted into a person's hair. If it fell out, the person in question was considered white. If the hair curl was so tight that the pencil remained in position, the person was categorised as coloured. Coloureds whose genetic combination produced an appearance more European than African were encouraged by their kinsmen to "try for white." Astonishing, but absolutely true.

The Christian wife of former South African president, FW de Klerk, dismissed the coloured people as "non-persons, the leftovers, the racial misfits." If you think she and her ilk had trouble slotting the population of the nation into the four racial pigeonholes created by the legislation, it got a whole lot more farcical.

The large Indian population of South Africa were shoved into the Asian category. Like their coloured counterparts, they were consigned to live in their own areas, without the vote, and to attend their own schools and universities. In Johannesburg, this was an area called Lenasia, popularly contracted to "Lens." Regardless of whether you were a heart surgeon, a bishop, a nurse, a teacher or a street sweeper, if you were of Indian descent, you were consigned to Lens.

Chinese people were another challenge. Asian by origin, clearly, but because their skin pigmentation was closer to European, they were allowed to live in certain white areas and permitted to attend white universities. Many Chinese were industrious merchants and highly successful.

But don't go confusing Chinese with Japanese in this crazy system. The Nationalists developed selective colour blindness in categorising the Japanese, who were deemed to be honorary whites with exactly the same privileges other than the right to vote.

So there we were in the glorious Highveld afternoon sunshine, enjoying the company of Plaatjes, his girlfriend (now wife) Shirley, his older brother Ralph, and his mother. Shirley was a hit with my daughters with her wicked sense of humour and infectious laugh, and on the drive home my girls wondered why we hadn't been to visit before. It was not easy trying to explain the inexplicable to my young daughters who had no idea that the government treated people differently. Their confusion reinforced our dissatisfaction with the way things were developing in South Africa.

Push came to shove for many South Africans when President PW Botha was scheduled to make a ground-breaking speech in 1985, outlining a commitment to major political reforms. With internal rebellion at an all-time high, and foreign boycotts chewing chunks out of the economy, Foreign Minister Pik Botha hinted that the president's speech would announce drastic changes, including freeing Nelson Mandela with a view to negotiating a resolution. Hope was high at the start of the address, broadcast live in South Africa, Britain and the US, but the optimism of a nation was shattered by a recalcitrant old warmonger.

A decade later, Pik Botha revealed what had happened. It is on public record.

"In August 1985 President PW Botha had delivered what has become known as his Rubicon Speech in Durban. The world had been waiting for good news, important announcements on dismantling apartheid and releasing Mr Nelson Mandela. I myself drafted that part of the speech in which the phrase 'today we have crossed the Rubicon' appeared."

"President Botha retained the sentence but removed what had preceded it, namely the release of Nelson Mandela and the government's intention to dismantle apartheid. The effect of the speech on the world, and on many South Africans, was that of a bucket of ice water in the face."

A defiant president warned the rest of the world not to "push him too far" and that he was not prepared to take "white South Africans, and other minority groups, on a road to abdication and suicide."

The speech led to tighter international sanctions. The first casualty was South Africa's short-term banking facilities, called up by Chase Manhattan. The easiest option for Chase Manhattan would have been to roll over the funding, but at an inflated margin to reflect the increased political risk. It would have been a great financial outcome for the bank. Instead, it called up the facility, precipitating possible financial calamity for South Africa. Britain had the most significant economic interest in South Africa, but it was a New York banker who ultimately pushed apartheid to the edge of the cliff. The South African currency tumbled. Trade, travel and cultural sanctions and boycotts were imposed. South Africa was isolated globally, the pole cat of the world.

PW Botha's government had prepared for the inevitable backlash with its customary venom. He and his cohorts seized total control, forbidding any dissent from within or without. He severed the chords of the voice of reason. In March 1985 his police shot dead 21 protesters in Uitenhage near Port Elizabeth. On 6 May trade unionist Andries Raditsela died in custody from traumatic head injuries, less than 48 few hours after being detained under the Internal Security Act. Another 11 political activists were either killed by unknown assailants or went missing. In July the government imposed a state of emergency, giving it total powers of suppression. During the first six months of the state of emergency, more than 5,000 people were detained and 575 people were killed in political violence, including political activist and lawyer Victoria Mxenge. Organisations were banned, meetings prohibited and restrictions placed on the media.

Some things were beyond the Nationalists' ability to control. Foreign exchange dealings were suspended for three days in July when the value of the rand dropped to below $0.40c. In August the government froze foreign loan repayments in retaliation for the Chase Manhattan action. A month later, members of my father's political party, the PFP, led a delegation of businessmen and prominent opponents of apartheid to visit the ANC in its exile base in Zambia to discuss the future, infuriating the Nationalists. In December the Congress of South African Trade Unions (COSATU), representing 500,000 black workers, was launched. The dyke was springing more leaks than the PW Botha government had fingers.

Yet the government-controlled SABC continued to pump its sanitised version of affairs onto our television screens. Whites who declined to read between the lines in the newspapers had little idea of the extent of the cracks in apartheid's facade. Most thought everything was under control. I was not one.

One day, I worked out a correlation between the military effort and the Comrades Marathon. The Defence Force had 500,000 recruits, many clearly on the offence in distant Angola, consuming 20% of the annual budget with the end goal of maintaining white supremacy in South Africa. The 1985 Comrades Marathon had 8,149 finishers. Imagine the race being started 61 times in succession, with the same flood of humanity surging forward each time. The road between Maritzburg and Durban would have been jammed with people in khaki, with no space to run. That's the commitment that the Nationalists had made to retaining power ahead of education, health care and much-needed infrastructure like power and water.

In March 1986 the black residents of Winterveld protested against the detention and torture of their children. Word spread that the chief of police would address them about their concerns and 5,000 assembled on a soccer field. Instead, they got the riot squad in armoured vehicles. Stones were thrown and bullets came back. With minutes, 11 lay dead, predominantly women and children. By nightfall, hospitals had treated 200 for wounds and the police had arrested 1,000. The two police officers who commanded those involved in the massacre were promoted, including Brigadier Andrew Molope. His actions also promoted him to status of target. Three months later, ANC insurgent Ting Ting Masango assassinated him.

The violence was not confined to the townships. Bombs detonated in central Johannesburg on either side of New Year's Day 1987 and police raided English-language newspapers, seizing documents related to an advertisement calling for the unbanning of the ANC. In May the secret police bombed the 11-storey headquarters of COSATU in downtown Johannesburg. The building did not topple but it was suitable only for demolition. By June an estimated 26,000 opponents of apartheid had been detained during the previous 12 months. Many had been tortured during interrogation; some were murdered. The black townships were effectively under military occupation, cordoned off by barbed wire and patrolled by soldiers and dogs.

Even the most ignorant of whites could not ignore the deterioration of law and order. They knew the revolution was nigh. They reacted by voting with their feet and emigrating or, mostly, by giving total power to the Nationalists to prevent South Africa degenerating into just another black dictatorship. After all, did not the country have a few atomic bombs in its arsenal as a measure of last resort? The May 1987 election removed the liberal PFP as the official opposition, replaced by the Conservative Party which wanted to simply obliterate black resistance. Between the National Party (52.3%), the Conservative Party (26.6%) and the ultra-conservative Herstigte Nationale Party (3.1%), some 82% of white South Africans who voted had endorsed apartheid. By any measure or interpretation, the pro-apartheid support within the white South African community was simply overwhelming.

The suppression of a free media prevented us from knowing at the time that security forces had arrested Masango for the assassination of Brigadier Molope, plus three of his fellow ANC soldiers for various acts of armed resistance. They were charged with high treason and, when the news of their impending trial finally broke, were known as the Delmas Four. Consistent with the earlier arrests of ANC activists and their subsequent convictions, the death penalty was the inevitable outcome. Yet this would not be another simple show trial. The Delmas Four grabbed headlines around the world when they insisted on being accorded prisoner-of-war status in terms of the Geneva Convention.

In association with their legal representative Peter Harris, Masango, Jabu Masina, Neo Potsane and Joseph Makhura asserted: "We cannot plead not guilty. Although we are, in fact, guilty, our acts cannot be seen in purely criminal terms, just as those who killed the enemy in the fight against fascism in the Second World War were not tried for murder.

"The acts we committed were carried out against an enemy that has made us victims in our own country and taken any rights that we had away from us. Our rights to land, to move freely, to work in a fair manner, to be educated, and a range of others. This government is murdering our youth and has our leadership in prison.

"The people we killed were at the forefront of the apartheid regime's attack on black people and they deserved what happened to them. While we have killed and each of us has to deal with that inside ourselves, we are not murderers. We are not normal criminals."

Radical blacks and reactionary whites were polarising. Their un-declared war was moving closer to an endgame most expected to be horrifically violent.

Almost anyone in South Africa who had money for a gun was buying one.

17

View from the moon

Don't tell me the sky's the limit when there are footprints on the moon. The aphorism looks smart on a bumper sticker; it inspires when you chat to one of the 12 men who actually left their footprints there.

Ten days after the 1986 Comrades, I found myself having dinner with the sixth man to walk on the moon, Edgar Mitchell. Let's just say his walk on the moon brought me back to earth.

No sooner had I returned to Johannesburg, from my all-or-nothing bid at winning the big C, than I was packing for Paris. A few days of R&R in the French capital would be followed by a KPMG marketing forum at Chantilly, north of the magnificent city. KPMG colleague Theo Jager was an enthusiastic walker and the four days we spent traipsing around Paris was exactly what my legs needed.

The forum proved awkward for the facilitator, whose slick American repartee did not go down well with the conservative Europeans. After a couple of days he indicated he would invite a friend of his, who happened to be in Paris, to join us for dinner as an ice-breaker.

That's how I came to be sitting at a table, 10 days after Comrades, chatting to Mitchell. He was the pilot of Apollo 17 in 1971 and he intrigued me with his intellect and sensitivity, a wonderful mixture of engineer and artist.

Landing on the moon, walking on the moon for nine hours, and then having to return to earth was an experience for which nothing in his life had prepared him. He recalled how overwhelmed he was while standing on the lunar surface and looking at planet Earth, which resembled a fluorescent golf ball drifting through the dark sky. He developed a global consciousness, an intense dissatisfaction with the world and a compulsion to do something about it.

It got me thinking, as did a week in Europe immersed in the cultured, cosmopolitan fabric of Paris. The free press and freedom of speech without any evidence of violence made me realise just how unjustly our society was being suffocated in South Africa. While I was flying back to Johannesburg, the bomb outside Garfunkels in Durban detonated. By the time I was back home in Northcliff on the Sunday, I was unknowingly subject to the restrictions imposed by the Nationalist government's State of Emergency. That evening, with great trepidation, I spoke to Vern about my lack of faith in the South African government and my reluctance to have our daughters grow up in such an unjust, violent society. She agreed with me. We needed to make other plans for the future of our daughters. We agreed to research Australian possibilities.

It was as if Mitchell's view of Earth from the moon had confirmed my view of South Africa from France. Vern and I both wanted to emigrate but could not share our thoughts with family or friends until we had researched the feasibility of our idea. We agreed it was time for us to shape our daughters' futures beyond South Africa. That was the sole reason for our decision because we were extraordinarily privileged in all other facets of living in South Africa

Although KPMG was doing remarkably well in an economy powered by gold, which was rising past $400 an ounce, I felt like I did not belong in the South Africa of 1986. On one hand, the Comrades Marathon provided the richest evidence of the potential for all South Africans to co-exist peacefully, yet the government was intent on ruling with the might of its army and police force.

A short while later, Gavin Evans, a journalist with the *Weekly Mail*, contacted me. He was doing much of the front running for the End Conscription Campaign in the Johannesburg area and asked me to join with other South African personalities whose names would appear in small print as a footer to a full-page advertisement in the major daily newspapers. It read:

> ### We call on the government to recognise freedom of conscience
>
> We note with grave concern that the emergency regulations prohibit the expression of opposition to conscription. This not only bars the End Conscription Campaign from voicing one of its central concerns but also silences thousands of South Africans who are struggling daily with their consciences.
>
> As this is a matter of crucial importance and drastic consequence to many citizens of this country, especially in these strife torn times, the manner in which they are prevented from expressing their feelings is a serious violation of the fundamental right to freedom of speech.
>
> We call on the government to recognise the right of all South Africans to express their opposition to military conscription. We call for an end to the silencing of the End Conscription Campaign.

Evans reassured me that ECC had obtained clearance from the best legal brains in the country. If we put one foot out of place the Nationalists would pounce, using all their powers under the State of Emergency. I gave Evans my consent to add my name to the protest advertisement. While my conscience was proudly associated with such a protest in a very public manner, I was aware of my professional commitments within my apolitical firm, KPMG.

Intuitively, I believed that the vast majority of my partners shared my political values. However, the unwritten rule was that such matters remained private and out of the public arena. None of my senior partners ever spoke to me about my association with strongly anti-government organisations and my anti-apartheid quotes in the media. I took their silence as a quiet endorsement of my activities.

Researching a possible move to Australia was not easy. We had to check out the Australian government's requirements for immigrants, then job prospects, housing affordability, schooling, cash flow and finally, if all the variables could be aligned, timing. There were two significant dates that would dictate the announcement of our family's decision to emigrate: the time required by the Australian Embassy to process our application;

and the six-month notice period required under my KPMG partnership agreement.

I visited the Australian Embassy on 21 July to ascertain whether we would qualify to emigrate on the points system, independent of a job offer or sponsorship from Australia, and obtained the necessary application forms. It seemed pretty straightforward. Over the next week, Vern and I completed the paperwork and I confidently returned to the Australian Embassy on 29 July to submit our application. It was rejected.

Not because my surname of Lenferna de la Motte sounded un-Australian, but because the officials required originals or certified originals of all birth certificates, academic qualifications, professional memberships, and our marriage certificate in long form. It took me another month to procure those documents from the government bureaucracy before I lodged our complete application to begin a new life in Australia. Little did I realise it was nothing compared with what we were about to experience.

While we waited for a decision, Vern and I decided I should visit Australia to assess the housing and job situations. Buying a house would be a challenge because of the weak South African rand and exchange control regulations. We would be moving with modest financial resources despite the fact we were living like royalty in South Africa. I booked a two-week trip to Australia for the beginning of October to check out Sydney, Melbourne, Adelaide and Perth, where I would connect with Ross Norgard, who I had met at the KPMG forum in France in June.

I applied for a tourist visa, as all South Africans were required to at the time, and thought that would be it. On 19 August I received a call from the Australian Embassy in Pretoria advising that they could not grant me a visa because of my profile as a South African sportsman. I requested an interview and managed to secure an appointment in Pretoria for the following day. I received a very cool reception by an official of the Australian Embassy who wanted to know the real reason for my visit to Australia.

I had to reveal what had been a closely-guarded secret and admit I was on a fact-finding mission as a precursor to emigration. The interviewing official was not necessarily convinced but drew some comfort that I had never owned a gun and had no intention of ever owning a gun. I feared my application was about to be denied until he looked up at me and said: "We will grant you a tourist visa but if, during your visit, you participate in any running or sporting competitions as a South African you may seriously prejudice any subsequent application you might make to visit or live in Australia."

He explained he took me on trust, as it was not out of the question that I might show up at some ultra-event in Australia and embarrass its Labour government to the delight of South Africa. I asked him about the likely emigration visa processing time and his reply was less than encouraging. The Australian government was slowing down visa applications from South Africans as a protest, and the time taken to process the documents had blown out from three to nine months. In addition, South African Airways were banned from landing in Australia so the Qantas connection would have to be made in Harare. Phew! So much for a quick exit from South Africa.

At the start of September I received a letter from Adidas advising me they had paid R900 into my trust account at the South African Amateur Athletics Union office, comprising R300 for winning Korkie, in addition to being the first Adidas runner to finish, and R600 for the Comrades Marathon for being the first Adidas runner to finish. While these amounts may appear to be modest, Adidas had no obligation to pay me a cent. They had also made a contribution of R1,650 towards my Comrades out-of-pocket expenses.

From my side, I had prepared detailed Comrades training programmes in 1985 and 1986, for no payment, as an insert to *SA Runner* magazine. We operated on a gentleman's agreement without any written contract. I regarded myself as an independent runner with a mutually beneficial association with Adidas. The pivotal connection was Nick Lanham. Without him at Adidas, I doubt I would have developed the relationship. There were many positives about my relationship with Adidas despite my belief that their road running shoes, at the time, were certainly not leaders in terms of scientific innovation.

I had cut back on my running, managing between 70km and 100km a week including The Sweat Shop run on Wednesday evenings. My Comrades Cold War with Fordyce was well and truly over. With everything happening in my life I never for a moment considered defending my JSE 50km title. My candle, which was previously burning at both ends, had almost melted. Instead, I seconded Dowdeswell in the race. He was doing some research and invited me to his hospital in September. Somehow, I was coerced to breathe into a very complex piece of equipment in his laboratory used for spirometry testing. These tests measure how well the lungs take in and release air, and how well they move gases, such as oxygen, from the atmosphere into the body's circulation. Even at altitude I had a peak expiratory flow of 12.1 litres a second (or 726 litres a minute), with a total lung capacity of 10 litres. This was 25% above average and, partly, helped explain why I enjoyed such great stamina and endurance.

Soon after, I flew to Sydney on my Australian reconnaissance visit. It was a breathtakingly beautiful city that reminded me of a contemporary London. My morning jogs took me over the Harbour Bridge around Kirribilli, back over the bridge, around the Opera House then back to town through the Botanical Gardens. I met accounting contemporaries, including colleagues I had worked with in London in 1979, and Tim Potter, the KPMG Johannesburg partner who had emigrated to Australia the previous year. Sydney was a vast international city but so clean and well organised.

Melbourne reminded me of London in winter. It was a wonderfully sophisticated city but not to my liking with a young family in the wings. A jog around attractive Adelaide evoked thoughts of a 20th century Cambridge.

My last stop was Perth. The city centre sat on the banks of the broad Swan River and I made full use of the paths which lined the waterway. It was absolutely stunning and had a tranquil feel about it, a slower pace of life compared to Sydney and Melbourne. Intuitively, I felt I could relocate my family here, before even speaking to anyone about a job, schools and housing.

Over the next few days, I researched the academic and professional requirements to convert my CA status to Australia and checked out the job and property markets. I met Norgard, Michael Carrick, and other Perth associates, plus a couple of contacts who had previously flown the

Johannesburg coop. The honest feedback I got emphasised there would be a measure of trauma associated with migration, irrespective of how smoothly it might otherwise occur. Some families could not cope and others might never recover. It was a high-risk move.

On my last day in Perth, I was jogging around the Swan River when I caught up with another runner and we struck up a conversation. He explained that he had started his trip in Melbourne, on a bike. Michael Waterfield was a retired medical doctor who had cycled the 3,400km across the Nullabor Desert in 28 days at an average of 120km a day. He was jogging around the river to loosen up.

Later that afternoon, on the return flight to Johannesburg, I sat next to an English engineer. In his younger days, John Payne had run a 2:17 marathon and just missed out on Olympic selection for England. I continued to be amazed at the extent to which running opened so many doors and friendships. My accounting associates in Perth indicated that they would have an opening for me, albeit at less than one third of my South African earnings, if I could get a visa within a year. Norgard's Perth practice of KMG Hungerfords was set to merge with Peat Marwick Mitchell as part of the global KPMG merger proposal. The PMM client base and conservative professional ethos was more similar to our South African firm than the entrepreneurial KMG Hungerfords.

I returned to our house in Johannesburg with a sense of relief to share the results of my trip with Vern. Our single biggest asset, together with our single biggest liability, was our relatively new home in Northcliff. The property market was understandably subdued – indeed, gun-shy – in South Africa's draconian State of Emergency. If we could not sell our home, we would not be going anywhere. That was dilemma number one. Number two was how to break the news to my partners at KPMG.

When I returned to the office, I was summoned to the chairman's office. It transpired he and my closest professional ally, Stuart Morris, had been at a KPMG conference in Vienna and one of the attending Australians had told him how sorry he was to hear the South African firm would be losing me to their Australian associates. I can only imagine the embarrassment and disappointment that this would have caused. In hindsight, I deeply regretted that I had not shared my personal dilemma with Morris beforehand. The damage had been done. I resigned from KPMG that day without the faintest idea of whether or when our Australian migration visa might be processed. I drove home staring into an abyss for the first time in my life.

Back at the office my KPMG partners had to decide whether to ask me to walk out the door and take leave for six months, or allow me to work out my notice period to 20 April 1987. Deep down, I knew just how disappointed my partners were. I had pursued my career with passion, ambitiously and enthusiastically. They had reciprocated with untold opportunity. The Johannesburg managing partner at the time was Len Verster. I knew Len pretty well. He was a larger than life character, taller than me and considerably wider with strong features, resembling Gerard Depardieu. When, as a 22-year-old, completing my articles of clerkship and sitting that much-dreaded FQE, he had been my mentor. We even shared the same personal assistant, Bev, who helped Johannesburg's medical fraternity diagnose my hepatitis. He wisely let the dust from my bombshell settle before enquiring when I might be leaving. He had a substantial business to run, with 30 partners and more than 400 professional staff looking after many of South Africa's largest corporations. My client portfolio would have to be re-allocated with minimal disruption to clients and staffing, but the question was when?

The truth was that I did not know. All I could do was to reassure him that even in the event of some miracle on the part of the Australian Embassy, I would not leave before six months. It could well be a year. He suggested it would be appropriate for me to be extricated from the financial intricacies of the KPMG partnership at the financial year-end of 28 February. Beyond that date, he would continue to pay me at the equivalent rate of my profit share on a monthly basis until I left. We agreed this was unlikely to be before the end of June, and I undertook to let him know as soon as I heard anything from the Australian officials. Len was a good man.

Having agreed the basis of my departure from KPMG, it was business as usual for me. My clients kept me busy, my daughters had school assemblies and concerts, we had a home to look after with the inevitability of a pending sale, and I was trying to keep fit. Those early morning tranquil runs around Northcliff into the smudged Highveld dawn on the horizon, and the scent of jasmine accompanied by exquisite African birdcalls, soothed my soul. Maintaining robust health was now critically important for our uncharted future in Australia. We would be starting from scratch.

Although my orientation was focused on our future in Australia, I would in all likelihood still be around for the 1987 Comrades and decided I could make it my swansong, hopefully a top 10 finish. One difference to previous years was that my training was not only going to be running. Perth had struck me as a great place to cycle and I started supplementing my runs with a few short rides; I enjoyed the introduction of a different discipline.

At the end of November our Northcliff home went on the market and I was involved in a fundraiser for Operation Hunger with a number of other runners. After a barefoot dash down the final straight of the rain-soaked turf, Thulani Sibisi grabbed my left arm and said: "Bob, you mustn't go to Australia."

"Why not?"

"Because we need people like you in this country."

I was lost for words. Internally, I tried to justify my decision to emigrate to Australia as protecting my daughters from the horrors of apartheid and the inherent levels of violence in South Africa. But Sibisi's disappointment was palpable and I felt awful. I had let him down.

As the 1986 running year drew to a close, I could reflect on PBs in every distance from 8km to the Comrades, other than the standard marathon which I had not raced. Although I had not won Comrades, I had bettered the old down record, and run one of the three fastest times in the history of the race. During the year I had run a total of 5,959km.

No such definites in the other aspects of my life, unfortunately. We had no control over the timing of our Australian move and, in my universe that amounted to torture. We were also caught up in a court case involving the assault of a black driver. A few weeks earlier, Vern had been driving home, mid-morning, when she witnessed a highly irate and aggressive white driver force a delivery vehicle off the road. The white guy pulled the black driver out of his vehicle and began assaulting him. Vern and other witnesses immediately called on the white assailant to stop beating the black driver, who had not retaliated in self-defence. It happened outside a local school and the school principal was also soon on the scene. The white driver disappeared before the police arrived at the scene and the unanimous opinion of all witnesses was one of unprovoked assault.

Vern called the black driver's employer and advised that she had witnessed the assault. If he wished to press charges, she would agree to be a witness, along with many other whites on the scene. We were subsequently advised that the case was scheduled for 10 February 1987 at the Randburg Magistrates Court.

Realising that our days in South Africa were numbered, we decided to enjoy South Africa, our families and our friends to the maximum extent possible. I knew that at some stage in 1987 I would have to re-invent myself in Australia and restart my career.

It would make the Comrades seem like light work.

18

Runaway Bob

My strong running performances in 1986 resulted in me being invited to a few big races in 1987, including the Peninsula Marathon and the Two Oceans. Unlike 1986, when I was intent on running the Comrades as fast as I could, I decided that my remaining few months in South Africa would include as much fun as possible. Hopefully, I could get into shape for a sub-2:20 Peninsula on 7 March and run a comfortable sub-four hour Two Oceans on 18 April. If all went to plan, my final Comrades on 31 May would be a fun weekend for the whole family. I would run it without seconds with the sole objective of soaking it all up. A top 10 finish would be the ultimate bonus.

In January I achieved my 32km-long run by running to and from the Roodepoort 15km, and enjoyed a reasonably strong run of 49.36 for ninth place. A week later, I made a deal with Alan Edwards to attempt the Lindsay Saker Biathlon, comprising a 10km run and a 25km cycle. It was nothing more than a fun diversion, some cross training, and a little variety. Edwards and I cycled to the start and then I did a 5km warm-up before the 10km run. After paying my entry fee, I lined up for my race number to be inked on my biceps: the official expressed his disbelief that I had such skinny arms.

After running with the leaders for 3km, I broke away and completed the 10km in 33.04, with a two-minute lead. I dropped my helmet on the way out of the transition area and had to make a U-turn in my clip-clop bike shoes before setting off on the three-lap, 25km ride. I had very little experience on the bike and fully expected a bunch of guys with big thighs to come zooming past me.

On the out-and-back circuit I got regular views of my pursuers. It was as though I was reliving my childhood, playing cops and robbers, with myself as the latter, trying to get away. I never thought I would be able to stay out in front, but I managed to hang on and won by a minute in 76.10.

That afternoon, although I had clocked 120km for the week, my training diary entry was "If only I could swim?" There was a short-course triathlon scheduled for 15 March at Emmarentia Dam and I resolved to give it a crack despite the fact that I had never had a swimming lesson nor swum 800m in my life. It looked like lots of fun, apart from all the duck shit in Emmarentia Dam.

At the end of January I jogged the Benoni Marathon with Dowdeswell, Arnie Geerdts and Solomon Pongolo, a Xhosa friend of mine from East London. We ran at a steady 4min per km pace and finished in 2:46, which qualified me for my final Comrades Marathon.

In February I accompanied Vern to the Randburg Magistrates Court, where she testified as a witness to the assault of the black driver by a white thug two months earlier. The facts were presented. Every witness attested to the unprovoked assault without any retaliation from the black driver. Yet quite extraordinarily, the magistrate adjourned the case. Months later when we left for Australia we had still not been advised of the verdict, if any.

At the start of March we finally heard from the Australian Embassy in Pretoria. Just as well, because we had accepted an offer for our house and had to be out by the end of the month. The letter invited us for an interview on 24 March 1987 as part of their formal assessment. Their letter cautioned against interpreting this interview as an approval and warned against not making too many drastic plans.

The pace of change had picked up. At the time, I was running about 140km a week to prepare for my final Comrades, although as yet I had no idea which brand of shoe I would wear. I'd had a run-in with a journalist who felt I was being hypocritical in claiming to have a gentleman's agreement with Adidas while clearly receiving payment from the company. He had called Adidas to confirm that I was a contracted athlete and someone other than Lanham had said, yes, I was.

This annoyed me considerably because it was incorrect and I wanted to make the point by switching brands at a whim, just to show I was not bound by any commercial agreement. When Rohan Summers of Game, Set and Match called to reveal he had just secured the Asics franchise, I was interested. I remembered the demonstration of the extraordinary Asics gel at the 1986 Comrades Expo. He wondered if I would be interested in running in Asics so, at the start of March, I met him at his warehouse in Sandton.

His mother, Shelia Summers, had partnered Eric Sturgess to the Wimbledon mixed doubles title in 1949 and the French Open mixed doubles titles in 1947 and 1949. Similarly, Summers had a professional tennis background and was not a runner, so I had to explain both my aversion to having a commercial obligation to any supplier of equipment and my impending move to Australia. He accepted my position and we agreed that he would source a pair of size 48 shoes from Japan so that I could run in them to see if they suited my running style.

I also had to start swimming to avoid disappearing into the murky waters of Emmarentia Dam on 15 March, so I built up to 10 laps of a 50m pool. It was hard work and did not come naturally, but at least my woeful pace had an unexpected benefit. Checking in with another 550 novices, I noticed the absence of any bike racks. Equipment was scattered all over the car park and I was concerned about locating my gear, but when I finally emerged from the Emmarentia duck soup mine was easy to spot in an otherwise near-empty expanse of bitumen.

The 20km bike leg was great fun because it involved a very long, very steep climb to the top of Melville, and then a very fast descent down the other side. As novices, we had a complete lack of bike skills and a lot of skin was smeared in streaks on the road that morning. The 5km run was a blast but about 10km too short. I romped home in 25th position, only to discover that Plaatjes had cracked a top 10 finish. Who even knew that this guy could swim? My mind boggles at what he might have done in Ironman had he selected that as his specialty.

Finally, the biggest week of the year had arrived. We would attend our interview at the Australian Embassy in Pretoria on 24 March, the same day the international removers would pack our possessions before we moved into a nearby townhouse.

Our interview with a Mr Gugel was reassuring. He was pleasant and realistically positive. Once he had satisfied himself about our bona fides, I asked him whether a departure date of early July was realistic. He saw no reason why we should not receive approval within four weeks, subject to one final formality, our medical clearances. We left the embassy on a high and drove directly to the nominated radiologist in Sunnyside, Pretoria, for our chest X-rays.

The plates produced devastating news. Vern's revealed a large shadow at the bottom of her right lung. It appeared to be a tumour. Never mind the possibility of this disqualifying us from emigrating to Australia. This required urgent attention. On the way home, we called into the JG Strijdom hospital where my running partner, Dr Rob Dowdeswell, was the consulting physician. He was one of South Africa's top pulmonary experts and he felt the apparent tumour needed to be removed regardless of whether we were emigrating to Australia.

He arranged a consultation with thoracic surgeon, Dr Alan Conlan, and booked Vern for major lung surgery on 10 April. It was another of those moments in life when all seems to be moving ahead so positively, and suddenly you are reminded of your own mortality. I had a heightened sense of our vulnerability, never previously experienced.

Drs Conlan and Dowdeswell provided additional medical opinions that were attached to Vern's case. I delivered the completed medical reports, including Vern's chest X-ray, to the Australian embassy on 31 March.

There was one positive development during the week and that related to my running shoes. I had completed every second run in Asics and thus far, the shoes were brilliant. However, I was not even certain about my prospects of running Comrades. It would all hinge on the outcome ᶜ Vern's surgery. Regardless, my morning jogs always gave me some spective on life.

248

The day before Vern's operation we got a big break. The Australian officials had approved our migration application. The letter contained only a standard condition about no adverse change in respect of my health and character, or that of any member of my family, and concluded: I take this opportunity to wish you all the best for your future in Australia.

It was good news at the right time but, until the lump was removed and analysed, our lives were in the lap of the gods. Accessing the suspected tumour involved complex surgery. I sat in the hospital's waiting room for hours until Dr Conlan appeared to give me an update. He had removed a Schwannoma tumour the size of an orange from the base of Vern's lung, immediately alongside the spine. Miraculously, there had not been any spinal interference but had it remained undiagnosed, it may have resulted in some form of paralysis. Crucially, the preliminary pathology indicated it was benign and the outlook was positive.

During the first two weeks of April I had barely managed 100km per week between the house move, Vern's surgery and my work deadlines. When Vern was discharged on 15 April, two days before Good Friday and Nicole's nineth birthday, she and our daughters moved in with her parents for a couple of days. I was running very early in the mornings with Dowdeswell who was as solid as a rock. He could interpret Vern's Schwannoma tumour, her recovery and her health prospects for the future. He offered me an extraordinary level of friendship and support to my family and me at a crucial time. Running was my lifeline; it kept it all together for me. Luckily, the schools had broken up for holidays so there was no need for me to collect Nicole and Simone from Grandma and drive them to APPS in the mornings. At the office, I was consumed by the Premier Milling deadline and in the evenings after work I would enjoy dinner with my daughters and in-laws. I just had to keep it all ticking over one day at a time. All the hard lessons I had learned from Comrades were now assisting me in my personal life; one step at a time.

More good news arrived just before Easter. Following Vern's discharge after five days, the detailed pathology report confirmed the tumour was benign. We could once again look forward to our new life in Australia, and I was able to tell Len Verster at KPMG and Ross Norgard in Perth that we would be on our way in July.

I regained some of my mojo and suddenly looked forward to the Comrades. I was seriously distracted and under-trained but, on a more positive note, without any injury. Our family would travel to Ballito Bay, north of Durban, for the Comrades long weekend where we would join Vern's parents for some rest and recreation. In order to make the Comrades as enjoyable as possible, I would run it without any seconds, starting very conservatively and hopefully finishing in the top 10. I needed to savour it and soak up every molecule of the atmosphere because I knew I would never run Comrades again.

Rohan Summers generously kitted me out in Asics gear and Epirus model shoes, paid me R7,500 for lacing-up in Asics without any obligation whatsoever, and contributed R2,000 towards my Comrades out-of-pocket expenses. He offered me a series of incentive bonuses for finishing in the first three, but I warned him his money was safe. No papers were signed and none needed to be. It was a handshake agreement.

With Vern convalescing, I had to skip the Korkie and the Two Oceans. My longest training runs had been two standard marathons at four-minute pace and I desperately needed a longer run in my legs. Fortunately, the Jackie Mekler 56km ultra was to be run outside Pretoria on Easter Saturday. I started conservatively and then picked up my tempo in the second half, running the final 14km at 3.25 pace. My splits were 1:53.30 and 1:39.24 for fourth place in 3:32.55, four minutes behind winner Chris Pretorius. It had been an ideal long run.

The following weekend, I did another 56km run at a steady four-minute pace with RAC mates Day and Arnold. Leading into Comrades I planned long weekly runs of 50km, 32km, 30km and 30km.

At the end of April the media started doing the usual ring around about Comrades prospects. Hugh Eley penned an article in the 3 May edition of the *Sunday Star* that read:

De la Motte's going to take it easy and 'only' go for gold.

Two-time runner-up Bob de la Motte has re-evaluated his Comrades Marathon commitment and, in a surprising about-turn, has decided simply to go for gold on 1 June.

BOB de la MOTTE

He wanted to win last year very badly indeed, but settled for second when Bruce Fordyce proved to be the stronger man over the last 8km. This time he says his 'first prize' will be to help RAC retain the Gunga Din team trophy.

That's a statement which will be greeted with a certain degree of scepticism by some of his rivals although De la Motte insists that he has got what he describes as the 'hunger to win' out of his system.

"I haven't made the same sacrifices that I did in 1986," he said this week "and my mileage is 20% lower than it was last year."

Perhaps De la Motte has had enough of the Comrades merry-go-round. He admits that had he won in 1984, he would not have run Comrades again and he also concedes that he has other sporting diversions.

"On a bad day Bruce wins by five minutes – as he did in 1985," said De la Motte. "On a good day he can be as much as 15 minutes ahead of the field, so Bruce has got to feel comfortable on the up run."

If he does only go for gold, the race will have lost much of its needle because De la Motte is one of only a handful of athletes not overawed by Fordyce's great talent.

Let's hope De la Motte finds the urge to have one last crack at Fordyce too strong to resist. Then we will really have a race.

The journalists unanimously picked Fordyce to win, as did the total of 18 experts polled on their top 10. Eight felt I would finish second. I was healthy and running well, but none had any idea of the roller-coaster ride the De la Motte family had undertaken to get this far.

I would run Comrades without a team of helpers. Fortuitously, corn syrup and liquid carbohydrate had become commercially available in sachets for the first time. I had experimented successfully with a few on long training runs and I stitched a pocket on to the back of my running shorts that could hold five sachets. I also arranged three bottle pick-ups from spectators: my parents and sister Yvonne at the halfway mark at Drummond, Dowdeswell near the Lion Park around 63km, and RAC member Wendy Shaw at 67km in case I missed Dowdeswell.

On 29 May I drove over the Comrades course with RAC club mate Day. On reflection, I thought the course would suit me and I might do quite well, but I had absolutely no idea of what time I might run. My only experience of the up run was my 9:02 Comrades debut in 1981 when Fordyce had won in 5:37. I was under no illusion as to my condition and competitiveness. If it all went very well I would hopefully make the top 10, but I had no podium expectations. The weather forecast predicted a very hot race day of around 30°C. That evening I resolved to run behind Bruce, inconspicuously so.

On race day I was up at 5am. Apart from my usual cup of tea, I drank 250ml of liquid carbohydrate and another 250ml 10 minutes before the start. It was easy to get to the front of the race at the start line because, for the first time, the CMA had adopted a self-seeding system. That was one contentious issue out of the way.

After a few pensive minutes and the *Chariots of Fire* anthem followed by the Max Trimbourn cock crow, we were away. It was still dark at 6am so it would take a while for me to find out where I was relative to Fordyce. I did not want to be ahead of him. After 8km I started asking spectators whether Fordyce was ahead and the answer was consistently no. Soon afterwards, we ran under the freeway and took a sharp right turn. I pulled over and hid from the passing runners until the Fordyce group ran by. They were all talking and not paying much attention. They passed by as though it was a casual Sunday run. When they were 100m up the road, I re-joined the Comrades and this was where I planned to stay. I sat back and observed proceedings. I was determined to enjoy my final Comrades on my terms.

Not much later, I heard Fordyce calling to his seconds as to my whereabouts. They correctly replied they had not seen me. At about 20km, one of Fordyce's seconds shouted to him that I was behind. At the top of Fields Hill, around 24km, Fordyce was running with Halberstadt and Metcalfe. I lingered about 10 seconds adrift and just outside the top 20. At 30km, Fordyce stopped for a roadside pee. I pulled up beside him even though I did not need to pee. For that matter, nor did he – it was merely a game of cat and mouse. I waited for him to continue the race. The clock was ticking away, but I was determined not to set the pace for Fordyce one step of the way. Eventually he got going and I tagged him, letting him set the pace.

Tjale was pulling away and building a lead of nearly three minutes but I hung back, behind Fordyce. I had no idea what the top 10 looked like. We cruised through the halfway mark in a pedestrian 2:53.50, still well outside the top 10.

BOB de la MOTTE

At Cato Ridge, the roadside information was that Tjale had a lead of 3.22. I thought I had a good chance of a top 10, but there was still a long way to go. Despite the significant acceleration by Fordyce over the 13km since halfway, Tjale had raced 22 seconds faster than us. If Fordyce wanted to win he was going to have to chase with all his might, sooner rather than later. Next thing he took off like an escapee. My calculations favoured Tjale's chances. Fordyce had left it too late. For the next 10km Tjale matched Fordyce's 3.30 per km burst of speed. I was striding along at a steady 3.46 per km and passed Van Staden with 25km to go, to move into 3rd position.

Having already raced almost 70km, Fordyce ran the next 10km at a brutal pace of 3.24 per km and closed the gap on Tjale to 2.39 with 17km to go. It was still a very considerable gap and Fordyce had been racing absolutely flat out for 26km since halfway. To put this into context, I was running at about 3.50 per km and decisively running away from the entire Comrades field except Fordyce and Tjale. With 12km to go, after running another sizzling 5km at full throttle, Fordyce had Tjale in his sights. Fordyce scorched up Little Pollys. Most athletes in the world would have needed a breather at least but not Fordyce. He pulled alongside Tjale, delivered the patronising pat on the back and the handshake, and accelerated away up Polly Shorts to a 5:37.01 victory. His second half of an uphill Comrades took just 2:43, an astonishing ten and a half minutes faster than his first half. The supersonic Fordyce Finish had prevailed once again and in 1988 it would be even faster.

Further back, I was progressing as well as could be expected. It was very hot and I was soldiering up Polly Shorts. I ran until I lost momentum on this brutal climb, and so decided to walk for 50 paces. I needed three brief walks to get to the top but they gave me the most extraordinary respite. I felt really good when I got going again. I had to laugh when I watched a replay of the race and heard one of the expert commentators suggest I had blown it and my race had come to a tragic end. Nope, I was simply grinding up the climb as best I could. I celebrated the summit by dunking my head in a water-filled trough. It was heaven and, feeling remarkably well, I knew I was about to run the final 5km of my final

253

Comrades. It was all very personal and I was going to enjoy every stride. The moment was not lost on me.

Unlike the crowd-lined roads from Westville on the down run, the final 15km of the up race were comparatively sparsely populated in 1987. Eventually I got the message from spectators that I was closing in on Tjale. After passing the board indicating 3km to go, I got my first glimpse of Tjale. I had a good rhythm going and was not going to risk a change in tempo at this juncture. After all, I had third in the bag and that was fine by me. With 1.5km to go, Tjale was less than 10 seconds in front of me and I realised I'd be crazy not to give it a go. I was feeling okay, so I lifted my cadence and caught him. I neither patted him nor shook his hand; I respected Tjale enormously and had no idea what he was capable of if push came to shove over the final kilometre, so I simply ran as hard as I could.

As I crested the top of the embankment leading into Jan Smuts Stadium, I looked back for the first and last time in my five Comrades outings. He was not close. I could not contain my joy. It felt as though I had been given an extraordinary bonus by finishing second. Whereas in 1984 and 1986 I felt I had lost the race, this second position was something that I had won against all odds. I could not believe it. I threw my customised running hat into the crowd followed by my special sea sponge that I had tucked into my shorts.

The preceding 12 months had been the most challenging year of my life on several fronts, but my disciplined running had enabled me to maintain robust health, both physically and mentally. Against all odds, I had run, without seconds, through the Comrades field except for Fordyce. I ran around that oval like I was doing a track session on air. I have a picture taken 200m from the finish line showing great knee lift and my arms driving back into an almost horizontal position, and I am smiling. I felt wonderful finishing in 5:43.38, as the third athlete to run the up Comrades in under 5:45. Fordyce was sportingly waiting for me at the finish and was probably equally surprised and disappointed that it was not Tjale, who finished a minute behind me.

I ran the first half in 2:53.50 and, despite the television commentary about my condition on Polly Shorts, I ran the second half more than four minutes faster. Fordyce and I were the only athletes to run negative splits. Although Fordyce seemed capable of beating Tjale and myself at will, the gaps between the first three runners and the rest of the field were substantial.

Only once previously had Fordyce been able to run the second half faster in terms of relative speed. In 1984 on the down run, he ran the second half in 2:37 or 7.5% faster than the first half to catch me. Then again, just when we thought we had seen the best of Fordyce, he would run the second half of the 1988 up run in 2:35 or 10.1% faster than the first half, setting an astonishing record of 5:27.42. Never had any athlete dominated the Comrades to such an extent, and consistently run times that were beyond the reach of the best of the rest. He just never seemed to experience the law of diminishing returns. Such was the supersonic Fordyce Finish.

Unlike 1986, when the SAAAU official requested a urine sample for a drugs test, there were no officials in sight at the finish of the 1987 race. After greeting fourth placed Van Staden and fifth placed Lemos, I left the finish area with Fordyce and Tjale and headed for the showers with our iconic, freshly minted Coke towels. On the way out, Trevor Quirk of the SABC television requested me to wait a couple of minutes to be interviewed after he had chatted with Fordyce. I hung around and was feeling very well indeed, almost euphoric. I knew my wife, three daughters and in-laws were all watching on television at Ballito Bay. My mother, oldest sister Yvonne and Rob Dowdeswell were waiting for me outside the runners' enclosure. We were all smiling from ear to ear.

In my television interview, I praised the Fordyce performance as pure genius. Quirk then caught me off guard by mentioning that I was moving to Australia. It opened up an opportunity for me to express my heartfelt thanks to everyone involved with the Comrades, the CMA, the scores of volunteers, the clubs the spectators who gave us such extraordinary encouragement, sponsors, the media and our families. Comrades had been an extraordinarily rich South African experience for me, totally unexpected and way beyond anything I might have ever dreamt of, but it was time for me to move on. I was richer for the experience.

My feet were in amazingly good condition when I removed my Asics Epirus before the television interview. All my toenails were intact and I had one tiny blister under the little toe on my right foot. In Comrades terms, this was as close to a perfect score of 10 as you could ever achieve.

After my shower, I collected a can of Coke and needed a few minutes of solitude before I re-joined family. I wandered away from the race oval to the perimeter of the grounds where I found a quiet spot under the shade of a tree. I lay on my back and looked up at the blue African sky. A few minutes later, tears rolled down my cheeks. I was silently weeping for South Africa, my country of birth. I had just closed the door on the Comrades Marathon and one of the richest experiences of my life. Next, I would close the door on South Africa.

I stayed at Jan Smuts Stadium, savouring the atmosphere of the push for silvers, the bronze survivors and the emotional drama of the 11-hour gun rush. After the cut-off pistol had been fired at 5pm, I received my medals for both the individual race and as a member of the RAC quartet that had retained the Gunga Din. When I was presented with the magnificent silver medal for second place, I was asked whether it would ever be possible to beat Fordyce. My proposal: "Raise the height of the water troughs so they are out of his reach."

Bearing in mind that my car was parked in a hotel basement in Durban, I needed to hitch a lift back to Durban. Fordyce was getting a ride back to Durban with his business manager, Mike Gahagan, and I negotiated a ride with them. Gahagan's luxurious German sedan was parked some distance from the stadium and Fordyce was hobbling like a cripple. Beyond any doubt, he had run himself into the ground. He had used every muscle and every molecule of energy he could extract from his body. It was an eye-opener in commitment.

Anyway, the rivalry was over and I had no further role to play in the Comrades Marathon. After a friendly drive back to Durban, I retrieved my car and drove the 50km back to Ballito. I walked into the holiday house at about 9pm to the delight of my family. Three regal silver medals for my three runner-up finishes; one for each of my beautiful daughters. I was feeling pretty good. Unlike in previous years, my body was not distressed and I slept well.

The next morning I also felt pretty good. My calves were not tight as in previous years and when we walked to the tidal pool and back I realised I was not carrying any Comrades-related injuries. Vern was trying to regain some upper body movement and strength by swimming. She could just barely manage a sideways version of breaststroke. After breakfast, we packed and drove back to Johannesburg. The girls had school the following day. I bought all the papers and would have a look at them that evening. The headlines alone kept me occupied for some time.

Business Day, front-page lead: "Comrades runner-up De la Motte quitting SA."

The Citizen: "Triumphant Fordyce almost pulled out." The story revealed he had a throat infection and had been taking antibiotics.

The *Natal Mercury*: "Fordyce – greatest Comrade of them all."

And: "The Comrades should never have been run." Noakes suggested no marathon, let alone an ultra like the Comrades, should be run when temperatures exceed 28°C.

The Star: "'I'm going to run smaller races then I can live', says Tjale." He was legitimately lamenting the absence of prize money at Comrades, pointing out he could win between R200 and R500 in shorter races to supplement his meagre wages as a driver.

Overall, I thought the various papers from around the country had provided good coverage, well balanced and pretty accurate. It was a job well done.

A couple of days later, Kitt Katzin of the *Sunday Times* called. He wanted to chat to me about my decision to emigrate to Australia. Obviously, he had read the headline in *Business Day* and wanted to flesh out a story. I was intrigued as to why he wished to write about a personal family decision to quit the country. It had nothing to do with my career nor my Comrades running, so what was the point?

Katzin's response was pure journalist: "You've got a high profile in the country and you are newsworthy, so we are going to run an article whether you like it or not."

I told him I accepted his point of view, however, it was not a personal decision but a family one. Accordingly, he showed up at our rented townhouse with photographer David Sandison and spent about two hours with us. I had never met Katzin before, and we spoke from the heart. He had unrestricted access to the whole family as I felt it was important for him to understand just how tough and challenging the whole migration issue was. I had enjoyed an exceptionally rewarding and highly remunerative career with KPMG. My career opportunities were enormous. My daughters were being well schooled and educated at APPS. Our families all lived in South Africa. My running was a hobby but one that had accorded me media status and profile. Essentially, we loved South Africa but we could never defend its policy of racial discrimination and we were not prepared to live under a government that perpetrated such crimes against humanity through violence.

On Sunday 7 June, Katzin's article captured the headlines in the Sunday papers.

Comrades Bob on the Chicken Run

Call it what you like, I'm doing it for my kids
If fleeing racial conflict and ongoing violence in search of a just and secure environment means joining the 'chicken run' or being labelled the runaway comrade, then Robert Aristide Lenferna de la Motte is satisfied to have made that choice.

That's how Bob de la Motte, three times runner-up in the Comrades Marathon and winner of the Johannesburg Stock Exchange and Milo Korkie classics, feels about the dilemma of a country he has loved.

And he expresses his views as firmly as he has dominated the road running scene when he talks about his decision, at the height of his professional and running career, to quit South Africa for good.

Katzin quoted many other issues we had discussed, such as the total lack of dialogue between the Nationalist government and black leaders who legitimately controlled the black power base. Sadly, no one in South Africa really knew who these leaders were because most of them had been banned or imprisoned, like Mandela. At grass roots level, a friend of mine like Mark Plaatjes, physiotherapist and South Africa's marathon champion, could fix my sore muscles but could not live next door because of his race. I drew an analogy between running the Comrades and applying the political ground rules in South Africa.

> "Although the Comrades is a test of human endurance, at least you know how far it is, and therefore how to pace yourself. But in the political ball game, the rules are different – blacks have no idea of the distance in the contest in which they are involved. This is grossly unfair and if I were black I would not know how I would participate in that contest, or in the South African community.
>
> Anyone accusing me of being a quitter or joining the chicken run is free to endure the same hardships and setbacks my family had suffered in preparing to emigrate."
>
> For Bob de la Motte, a new course and a fresh challenge to adapt to a changing pace lies ahead.
>
> It could be the toughest run of his life.

Vern and I were both completely at ease with Katzin's article. He had taken the time and effort to engage with my family on a no-holds barred basis and he extracted all the information he needed. We were relieved that our situation and personal dilemma was accurately portrayed. At the time, I had no idea of just how prophetic his conclusion would be.

RAC held its post-Comrades aches and pains party in mid-June and I was presented with an RAC blazer as part of a warm send-off by the club, and then asked to say a few words. I suggested that Fordyce might think twice about relaxing now that I was headed to Australia because if Sibisi or Page should decide to race Comrades, he would have his work cut out for him. Page was at the party and admitted he was startled to hear my prognosis. It would prove to be accurate in the 1988 Comrades when Page pushed Fordyce to a new up record. A few days later, Tony Viljoen, Bob Norris and my East London friends flew Vern and me to East London for the Border Road Runners Association annual awards dinner.

The following week I received a letter from the CMA.

Dear Bob

On behalf of the Comrades Marathon and its Executive Committee I write to wish you and your family everything you wish yourselves and more in your new home in Australia.

For the past two years you have certainly added to the excitement of the race and you will be missed in the future. We also thank you for the times when you have put pen to paper and expressed your support for the Comrades Marathon Association.

> We all look forward to you coming back to run Comrades again, hopefully in the not too distant future. The really good news is that Coca Cola will be producing 'special' Comrades towels to be given to the top men, etc., so you will just have to come back to get yours!!
>
> Once again, our sincere good wishes to you.
>
> Sincerely
> Linda Barron
> Administrative Secretary
> Comrades Marathon Association

I read this totally unexpected letter with a lump in my throat.

On the final Friday in June the removers collected all our possessions and we moved in with my in-laws for our final few nights in South Africa. On Saturday night, we indulged in one of my father's famous Mauritian prawn dinners, with healthy doses of garlic and chilli. These family evenings were tough going. It's never easy to say goodbye, and we were hardly in a position to say "until next time" because we had no idea when the next time might be.

The following morning Brian Chamberlain picked me up and ferried me to the Boksburg Hypermarket 21.1km. It was his farewell gesture, our last run together and my last in South Africa. Another door had closed. Another great friendship abandoned.

My KPMG partners hosted a farewell lunch for me at the Rand Club on 29 June and that was the end of my business career in South Africa. Another door closed.

On 2 July we flew to Harare to connect with the late afternoon Qantas flight to Perth. It was the only way to reach Australia from South Africa. The final family farewells at Johannesburg airport were gut-wrenching. We were making this move for our three daughters but to witness their grief, together with the great sadness of four grandparents who were losing their granddaughters to Australia, was, at the time, the toughest pain I had ever experienced. The loss of family grief was exacerbated by my anguish about country. The wanton destruction, social and physical, inflicted on South Africa by the Nationalist government was beyond my comprehension. This was my moment of truth. I was walking away, shattered by what I had witnessed and deeply concerned about those I was leaving behind.

When we landed in Harare, we confronted a 22-hour delay because of a technical problem with the Qantas aircraft. It was just awful, despite spending the night in a very comfortable hotel with room service. We just did not wish to be there. Finally at 5pm the following day, our Qantas flight was called. An enormous white Qantas Boeing 747 gleamed in the late afternoon African light with the inscription *The Spirit of Australia*. As I stepped out of the airport terminal to walk across the concourse to the plane, a hand grabbed my left shoulder

"Mr de la Motte?"

"Yes."

"I am from the Australian Embassy in Pretoria."

My heart sank into my shoes and all I could think silently was, oh no, what now?

"Yes?"

"I just want to wish you every success with your new life in Australia. Good luck."

"Thank you, we will give it our best shot."

And with that we headed towards the boarding steps with daughters, teddy bears and all we could carry as hand luggage.

We flew eastwards over the Indian Ocean, only a matter of hours away from our new country, our new life and an uncertain future.

19

Unpacking in Perth

Sometimes even the softest of landings can go awry.

Perth, in July 1987, was an easy place to like. The central city was flanked by the magnificent Kings Park and the broad sweep of the Swan River and, in winter, it gleamed an emerald green. Its residents were friendly and generous and it offered a young family like ours a lifestyle unequalled to anywhere we had previously been, or could imagine.

In every respect, we had a comfortable touchdown initially. Perth had a sizeable South African community, and Peter and Jill Roberts, whom we had met through our daughters' school in Johannesburg, met us at the airport and hosted us in their riverside Dalkeith home for a couple of weeks. It struck me how remarkably adaptable and resilient kids are. While Vern and I were apprehensive about what awaited us, the girls and Michele Roberts had sorted out the adjustments they would have to make at school even before we were halfway through the drive from the airport.

Our hosts arranged a barbeque the following day to enable us to meet some South Africans who had done the hard yards in making the transition to Western Australia. We were surprised by the extent of the brain drain from South Africa. Australian companies had realised South Africa would be an increasingly fertile recruiting source, as professionals sought to escape the upheaval which seemed increasingly likely in the second half of the decade. In particular, experienced lawyers were approached and seasoned corporate practitioners like Ian Cochrane,

Rob Sceales, David Goodman, Peter Mansell, Robin Waters and Peter Jooste were soon looking down onto Perth city's main thoroughfare, St George's Terrace. The South African diaspora that spread across Australia included Johannesburg associates like Liberty Life chief executive Monty Hilkowitz, physiotherapist Clive Lipinski, and Ivan Glasenberg, who went to Melbourne to trade commodities for Mark Rich.

While Vern placed the girls in schools and excelled with her choice of a home in the suburb of Floreat, midway between the city centre and the Indian Ocean beaches, I set about re-establishing my career. I accepted it was not going to be easy, but I did not anticipate just how bumpy the road would be.

For a start, the Australian authorities did not recognise my chartered accountant status. I would need to complete university courses in Taxation and Corporations Law, plus a year of acceptable professional experience under the supervision of an Australian chartered accountant. If all went well, the Institute of Chartered Accountants would interview me and, if they felt I was suitable, would invite me to apply for membership. But no guarantees, irrespective of how one fared during the conversion process.

So, it was back to night school after my day job as business director for KMG Hungerfords. I had originally discussed joining the firm as head of audit leading into the proposed global KPMG merger but, in the space of a few weeks, found myself with a strange job title in a strange firm. Unbeknown to me, Norgard and his fellow equity partners had accepted an attractive offer from Arthur Andersen instead of being part of the KPMG merger. Professionally, it was like flying to Perth but touching down in Singapore. I had been looking forward to working within a KPMG culture and structure I knew well and had thrived in. Now I found myself working for a totally unfamiliar new owner. Deep breath time, Bob.

At the end of our first month in Perth, we moved into our new home, complete with the 15% interest rate for housing loans that was prevalent at the time. I was unsettled by the changes in the office, but life has a way of balancing out things. Four houses down the road lived Jim Langford and, from a running perspective, I could not have moved to a better street. Langford and his two brothers grew up on a chicken farm and they shared a trait: endurance. All three would go on to represent Australia at cross country. My biggest challenge running with Langford was that he went hard and fast right from the start, as is the wont in cross country races. I was an ultramarathon runner with an abundance of slow-twitch muscle fibre and always needed at least 10 minutes to warm up, especially at 6a.m. Inevitably he would hurt me on the way out, and I might push him a little on the way home.

There was never any slack when running with him. The great Ron Clarke discovered this in 1965 when, a month after becoming the first man to break 28 minutes for 10,000m, he was favoured to run away with the 1965 Australian cross country title. Instead, he found himself chasing home, by 150m, a bare-footed 19-year-old Langford from Western Australia. Langford and training regulars Keith Stewart and John Cresp ran on water alone. Very little of it. Their infrequent pauses for hydration were little more than bird sips. When Langford won the national marathon championship in Brisbane in 2:17 in 1978, he did so without interrupting his rhythm for a single drink. When I suggested midway through a 32km training run at Langford's relentless pace that we pause for a Coke and a chocolate bar, he and his compatriots were aghast. I was undeterred and spurned the proffered sip of water for something with more carbohydrates. I moved better on the way home but the disapproving silence made me feel like a drug cheat.

Langford had a Masters degree in science and worked in computers. He was as comfortable in the bush as he was at a keyboard and read *New Scientist*. He was not the most talkative person but, when he did speak, it was intelligent and meaningful. I was accustomed to the training runs in Johannesburg where banter was rated almost as highly as ability. There was as much competition for airtime as there was to set the pace. Langford, however, was a purist. I tried my best to engage him in conversation but he steadfastly let his feet do the talking – although I once got him to venture an on-the-move opinion of the Comrades Marathon.

"Novel," he uttered.

He and training partners took a lot of convincing that the times clocked by the likes of Sinqe, Plaatjes, Seleke, and Temane were legitimate and run on accurately measured courses. Because of the international sports boycott, they'd never heard of them so their scepticism was understandable.

Their eyes would roll when told that running 31 minutes at a decent 10km road race in Johannesburg, at high altitude, would not get you into the top 10, and seldom into the top 20. Temane and Sinqe had run a world best of 60.11 at the South African Half Marathon Championship and, when I ran against them over 32km at altitude, my time of 1:45 scraped me into 10th place, six minutes off the pace. What a shame they never got the chance to show the world what they were capable of.

In early August I received a call from Graeme Lindenberg, former Wits runner, physiotherapist and good friend of Fordyce. He was holidaying in Perth and wanted to catch up for a run. He joined the Langford group and we chatted about the next day's Perth Marathon. Lindenberg and I decided to jog it at a steady 4min. pace to check out the course, with a view to racing it at some time in the future.

The Perth running scene was miniscule compared with that in South Africa. Although this was the premier marathon in WA, the only refreshment on offer at the drinks stations was water. I should not have been surprised: Langford was on the committee of the organising WA Marathon Club. It was all very pleasant, running and reminiscing with Lindenberg, but at 28km our bodies started screaming for sugar. Luckily, we had some cash on us and persuaded a young lad on a bike to head for the nearest shop and buy us a couple of Cokes. I might have made the detour myself but had no idea where a store might be. When the boy returned we demolished the Cokes but the damage had been done. I was hypoglycemic. We ran 2:44, in even splits, but I felt so light-headed at the finish I thought I was going to faint. The final 10km of my social marathon outing was tougher than the final 10km of the 1987 Comrades. My body had virtually shut down.

On the last day of the month, Perth staged its biggest run of the year, the 12km City to Surf. I treated it as a fun run, an opportunity to experience something new. Vern and I attended a dinner party the night before and had a good meal and wine, worrying the hosts who thought I should be eating some scientific formula meal. I assured them that, in the life of an ultramarathon runner, 12km equated to a public holiday. A few hours later, I clocked 38.32 over a hilly course for sixth place.

265

The next day, I officially became an Arthur Andersen employee. A colleague let me know it was okay to miss the round of client cocktail parties in the evening because I was an elite athlete for finishing in the top 10 in a fun run. That was not the case at all; I was at university studying Australian tax law. Still, it was a novelty for my workmates to have someone in the office who ran competitively and it did my reputation no harm to win the South of the River 20km in September in a PB of 64.30.

At the end of November I sat exams in Taxation and Corporations Law, and then made my first visit to Rottnest Island as part of an Andersen executive planning retreat. The island was good; passing both subjects with good marks was great, because I earned a two-month break from night-time university study.

When I added up the distance column in my training diary at the end of the year, I found I had run a mere 1,782km in the seven months since Comrades. I'd have to get into a better routine if I was to have a crack at winning the only ultramarathon on the WA calendar, the Mundaring to York 40-miler (64.37km), in September 1988. The race was 10 weeks after my final conversion exam and I felt the need to do well for several reasons. I knew I would not be able to hold my residual ultramarathon conditioning beyond another year. I felt indebted to South African friends and clients who expected me to do something with my talent. And finally, I owed Australia a good effort in my specialty.

At the end of February 1988 I took delivery of a parcel from a business colleague of Dick Welch, chairman of my old running club, RAC. The accompanying note read: "Congratulations, the South African Road Runners Association has awarded you your colours for ultramarathon. Because they cannot award Springbok colours for this distance, they would like to have their colours regarded as the equivalent to the green and gold. So double congratulations. RAC, Vreni and Dick Welch."

Other recipients included Bruce Fordyce, Hoseah Tjale, Sonja Laxton, Titus Mamabolo, Matthews Temane, Zithulele Sinqe, Xolile Yawa and Thompson Magawana. The parcel contained a navy blazer with a handsomely embroidered pocket. I was speechless.

The first test of my fitness was the Fremantle Half Marathon at the end of March. I surprised myself by winning in 69.04 in very warm conditions, and followed up a week later with a 69.03 win in the Bunbury Half Marathon.

On 31 May I was still in the office at 8pm when I discovered Fordyce had won the up Comrades in a record of 5:27, an extraordinary 10 minutes faster than his time of 1987. Equally astounding was Frith van der Merwe's win in the women's race in 6:32. In only her second Comrades, she had managed to run 12 minutes faster than the seven-year-old record set by Isavel Roche-Kelly. A year earlier, she had run 7:22 in her debut Comrades. Fordyce and Van der Merwe had demolished Comrades records by miles not minutes. Big news in South Africa – no news in Australia. South Africa was on the boycott list and the Comrades results did not even make the sports summary. A week later, some South African expat friends managed to obtain a VHS recording of the race and I was thrilled to see my RAC mate Mark Page give Fordyce a real run for his money up to the point where the supersonic Fordyce Finish obliterated everyone else.

I was busy with exams during June so my training suffered, but I managed a 10-week block averaging 120km a week leading up to the Perth Marathon in August. Most thought I was there for the win; I just wanted to get a good hard training run for the 40-miler. I jogged 10km to the start and aimed to run at 3.45km pace.

Race favourite, Clive Hicks, set the pace for our little group as we ran along the banks of the Swan River. After 14km, Vern and my daughters were waiting with a pre-mixed drink, the same formulation I had used at Comrades and one I hoped to use in the 40-miler. An elite runner from the Australian Institute of Sport in Canberra, John Tuckey, suggested I should be disqualified.

"What?"

"Taking a drink from anyone roadside is a contravention of IAAF's rules. You are only permitted to take drinks from the official drinks tables."

I was dumbstruck. He must have thought I was a local yokel. I told him the race organiser was a private club and determined the rules. His attitude was nevertheless very smug until I noticed he had forgotten to pin on his race number.

I pointed out his lapse and indicated that, if there was a candidate for disqualification in our group, it was him. He became very thin-lipped and I decided there and then to beat him, never mind the training run. I tracked him to 34km when he encountered a headwind. He faltered; I surged and chased home Hicks by 30 seconds, clocking 2:25. I realised then that I was in decent shape for the upcoming ultramarathon.

A few weeks before the 40-miler, I took the family for a drive to review the contours between Mundaring and York. There were two decent climbs and a dream 7km downhill stretch to the finish which would suit my running style. Three days before the race, I was made partner at Arthur Andersen so I was in a good mood when I paid my $1 entry fee (yes one dollar) and lined up with the intention of running each five-mile (8km) split in under 30 minutes, and thus to dip under four hours.

After five minutes of running I was out on my own. Was there something I did not know or was I the only runner on sub-four pace? After passing five miles comfortably in 29.12 and getting feedback that I was two minutes ahead of previous winner, John West, I knew it was going to be a lonely morning. The distance markers were every five miles and organisers recorded my official splits at 28.05, 29.13, 28.38, 28.39, 29.45, 30.26 and 28.54. My seconds, Keith Stewart, Jim Langford and Peter Roberts took good care of me. I could never have run those splits without their support. It was the longest solo time trial I had ever run.

I won the race in 3:52.52, an Australian record and the fourth fastest time in the world over the distance, averaging 3.37 per km. I subsequently discovered that I had also run an Australian record for 30 miles of 2:53.31. While Vern drove us home, I reflected on my good fortune that my hardcore South African training had enabled me to eke out one last good long run, but that chapter in my life had now come to an end. I would not race another ultramarathon.

The *West Australian's* David Marsh reported:

A long, hard record for Bob

On a warm spring day, on the bitumen from Mundaring to York, Bob de la Motte yesterday produced one of the greatest endurance runs of all time.

His time of 3:52.52 for the 40-mile race was the fourth fastest in the world. It was also nearly eight minutes inside the national record, and 10 minutes better than the previous race record.

Briton, Don Ritchie holds the world record of 3.49.35 set in London on 16 October 1980.

De la Motte's time tumbled the 17-year old Australian record and 12-year-old race record.

It was my last competitive ultramarathon and I felt I had done it justice.

20

Striding out

If I thought I had left Bruce Fordyce behind when I emigrated to Australia I was wrong.

In September 1988 I got a call from Fordyce's manager Mike Gahagan, who asked if I'd be interested in taking on Bruce in a 100km race involving the world's best ultra-runners to be organised for the following February outside Cape Town. I struggled to comprehend the message for a couple of reasons. First, I was living in Australia and hoping to gain citizenship. I thought I had made that clear when leaving South Africa, so I was never going to break the international sports boycott and get myself offside with the authorities in my new country.

Second, the need for such an event puzzled me. Fordyce was Mr Comrades, unbeaten in the event for eight consecutive years. He'd won the 1988 race by more than 10 minutes and, on the 1989 down run, had a realistic shot at breaking 5:20. He had previously said it was within his reach. I did not understand why he'd push himself so hard in a 100km race. If he wanted to compete on the world scene, he had the option, through being born in Hong Kong and his British passport, of moving overseas and qualifying for Britain. Zola Budd had done that in 1984.

I declined with thanks. I did not know then that when I next ran against Fordyce, it would be on my Australian doorstep.

The 100km race, involving 20 South Africans and 10 internationals, went ahead in Stellenbosch on a hot day and Fordyce duly won the first prize of $30,000. Years later, I read an account of the race in John Cameron-Dow's biography of Fordyce and had a wry grin on my face after learning that pacesetter Holtzhausen had yelled at Bruce; "Don't touch me! Don't touch me!" when overtaken. It seemed I was not the only competitor who thought handshakes and congratulations were best left for the finish line, which Fordyce reached in a world best of 6:25.07, at an average pace of 3.51 per km.

To have competed in South Africa was unthinkable for someone aiming for a future in Perth. The mood in Australia in the late 1980s was distinctly anti-Pretoria. Three days after the event, on 7 February, the influential *Australian Financial Review*'s editorial was headlined:

Keeping the pressure on Pretoria

Fifty years ago, Australia's comradeship with South Africa, like that with Canada, came without a second thought. History, and similarities of ancestry and of economic geography, even to an extent of culture, bound the white dominions together, and World War II deepened that sentiment.

Today, Australia in certain respects leads South Africa's demonology. A traitor to that common heritage; worse, a hypocrite – how can a country which so cruelly treated its own blacks vilify South Africa for doing the same?

If South Africa cannot count on Australia as a friend, who can it count on? It would give pleasure to be able to report, no one.

Yet that is patently not the case. As economic sanctions, however piecemeal, self-contradictory and apparently ineffective, have gradually been imposed by the major Western powers – most importantly the United States – South Africa has been forced to redirect its trade. However, irritants have a way of getting under the skin. That is why sports bans, too, have their place.

Perhaps South Africa will have to await the advent of President Nelson Mandela – or his martyrdom through death in jail, and subsequent cataclysm – before it sees that day.

Every Australian of goodwill yearns for the opportunity again to embrace South Africa as a nation of friends across the Indian Ocean. But until then, the honesty of a true friend demands profound disagreement.

A few months later, when Sam Tshabalala became the first black South African to win the Comrades in 5:35.51, it was revealed that he had not been invited to participate in the lucrative 100km race. In my mind, it was the luckiest thing to have happened to Tshabalala because he clocked the slowest winning time for the down run in a decade. Only one of the competitors in the 100km race managed a decent position in the Comrades and that was Jean-Marc Bellocq of France, in third. Tragically, Tjale paid for his 100km effort when he ran 5:50 for 10th position, his worst position since his Comrades debut in 1979. From faraway Australia, it seemed the 100km run had adversely impacted Comrades performances in 1989.

Tjale had, in my view, missed a golden opportunity to make Comrades history as the first black winner. He had been such an extraordinary pioneer and so deserving of a win. I also remained mystified as to why Fordyce, who had won his eighth consecutive Comrades in 1988 by 10 minutes, the event that had underwritten his financial security as a professional athlete, would lure South Africa's top 20 male Comrades runners away from that very event. And not even contest the event himself? Surely the 100km event could have been scheduled for October and not taken precedence over Comrades. It appeared there were other forces in play.

Tshabalala, too, explained he was not one for congratulations on the run. Journalists asked him why he did not offer Shaun Meiklejohn and Willie Mtolo a friendly Fordyce-styled greeting when he scythed them down in the final stages.

"Because a marathon runner's maxim should be that dog eats dog," he replied. "It's certainly mine. I don't worry about things like that. But everybody who knows Bruce well says it is a tactical ploy in any case."

Back in Perth, my focus was on settling into work and the suburbs. I averaged only 70km a week during 1989. Apart from a win in the M35 category at the veterans' cross country nationals in Perth and several victories in low-key local road races in the first half of the year, I didn't achieve much competitively. The local wins came when I was building up for a full go at the Perth Marathon, but Arthur Andersen had other ideas: I would work in the Singapore office for a fortnight in early July, performing a peer group review of the firm's Singapore practice. The only running I could manage was on the hotel treadmill, and my Perth Marathon plans evaporated.

By September I realised I needed a career change and started talking to a placement agent. In the middle of this process, Andersen required me to undergo a medical examination as directed by its Chicago office.

The first part involved an appointment with a local physician because Andersen deemed my GP insufficient. The firm left no stone unturned when monitoring the health of its principals, and I had to answer a list of extensive questions about my medical history before being sent for a battery of tests including ECG and colonoscopy.

With the questionnaire completed, the specialist asked me to lie on his examination table to check my pulse and take my blood pressure. I knew I would enjoy this next bit. I knew I looked every bit the boring chartered accountant – and I knew my resting pulse rate would come in below 40. Sure enough, he did the arithmetic, shook his head and felt for my pulse again for another 15 seconds.

"Are you feeling okay?"

"No, doctor, I am pretty stressed at the moment."

"Please describe your symptoms."

"Well, doc, I am under an enormous amount of pressure at the office ..." and then I confessed and told him my pulse rate was normal for someone who had been running competitively for a decade. That put him at ease but I was still amused that the primary interview and medical history did not include a couple of questions about physical activity. Clearly, that did not fit into the health template devised by Arthur Andersen in Chicago. The following week I was subjected to stress tests, skinfold measurements, and more. That was the only area where I rewrote some records at Andersen. Within a month, I resigned.

A couple of weeks before my departure, I received a Blue Max marketing award from Andersen world headquarters in Chicago for being a member of the team that developed the successful bid for the Bond Corporation account. I had a good chuckle. The Australian managing partner of Andersen didn't see anything amusing about it: he was miffed with me for pulling the pin and told me so in writing.

My new position was with Challenge Bank. This was a regional financial institution with a blue-chip pedigree that started out as Perth Building Society in 1867 and, by 1989, boasted an impeccable board of directors and a controversy-free track record. That's not to say the future was all clear air. Challenge Bank de-mutualised in 1987 and listed on the Australian Stock Exchange. Two years later its market capitalisation was almost $1 billion and it was among the exchange's top-100 companies. It had expanded from Perth across Australia and doubled the size of its balance sheet. The consequence of this was corporate growth pains because it had outgrown many of its executives' level of competence, as well as its internal recording and financial reporting systems. Nothing was amiss, but a lot of compliance work needed to be done in a hurry.

During the next six years with Challenge Bank, I would learn an enormous amount about the Australian banking system and capital markets. My first move was to recruit six ambitious chartered accountants in their mid-20s who could add value to my team of about 40. We installed financial systems that enabled us to report dynamic results, weekly, across the entire organisation and product range. It made it easy to distinguish the real business generators, achieving good margins, from the loud-mouthed pretenders. We shortened the production time required for the annual report by two months. It was an enjoyable growth phase for the organisation and I enjoyed the mentorship of chief executive, Tony Howarth.

After a couple of years, the bank asked me to assume responsibility for the Treasury function, effectively financing the balance sheet of some $5 billion and managing all the proprietary trading and all balance sheet risks other than credit. I ran treasury offices in Adelaide, Melbourne, Sydney, Brisbane and Perth and we issued bonds domestically and internationally through the Euro bond market in Hong Kong, Singapore, Frankfurt and London. We dealt with all the international rating agencies and the Reserve Bank of Australia.

Throughout this period, the Australian economy was doing it tough with a recession "we had to have," according to Treasurer Paul Keating. His Labour government had floated the Australian dollar and deregulated many restrictive aspects of the Australian economy. Unemployment was edging towards 10% and interest rates occasionally climbed past 15%. Despite my increase in responsibility, I wasn't exactly raking it in because the bank had adopted an executive pay freeze. We rode a financial roller-coaster during the early 1990s, from break even in 1991 through a $62 million operating loss in 1992, to a profit of $60 million two years later. Of course, we were forever under pressure to reduce the overall cost base of the organisation and to lift productivity and profitability per employee. I worked for the bank for four years before I received a modest pay rise.

Still, you take the bad with the good. Our Australian citizenship came through in November 1989 and the De la Motte family represented five of 63 new Australians from 18 countries at the ceremony. The girls were doing well at school and were involved in surf-lifesaving and tennis. In fact, the local tennis club, Reabold, became our family's Saturday afternoon routine. The club reflected Australia's wonderfully egalitarian society. One afternoon, I partnered Supreme Court judge Des Heenan against federal Member of Parliament Alan Rocher and a club member of long standing, just released from a short prison term for a corporate misdemeanour.

Things in South Africa were also starting to level out. FW de Klerk had replaced the hardline PW Botha as head of the Nationalist government after the latter suffered a stroke. De Klerk could read the writing on the wall and immediately began to broker a transition towards a non-racial society. On 2 February 1990 De Klerk removed the ban on the ANC and Communist Party but that was just a precursor to the main event. Nine days later, at 10pm in Perth, I and thousands of others who had moved from South Africa sat spellbound in front of the television to watch Nelson Mandela walk out of the Victor Verster Prison and be driven to Cape Town's Grand Parade to address a huge crowd from the balcony of the City Hall.

"Friends, comrades and fellow South Africans, I greet you all in the name of peace, democracy and freedom for all. I stand here before you not as a prophet but as a humble servant of you, the people. Your tireless and heroic sacrifices have made it possible for me to be here today. I therefore place the remaining years of my life in your hands…"

I had never seen Mandela and I had never heard him speak. Tears rolled down my cheeks and I wished I could have been among the crowd in Cape Town celebrating the pivotal moment. I will never forget that night.

In 1991, I hit my stride in the Perth running scene. By the end of May I had won seven races between 8km and 21.1km. I was running shorter races and running faster. The Darlington Half Marathon indicated I was moving well. I ran the first half of a hilly course in 37.50 and raced home in 34.09. I also won an 8km in Carine in a PB of 24.11. After four years in Perth, I was finally confident I could balance my work with the training requirements for a full go at the Perth Marathon 10 weeks away.

I was able to average a good-quality 108km per week, with three more wins in races over 10km, 20km and 32km. The 32km was my main tester and I ran it hard. I had just managed to shake Ray Harris from my shoulder when a marshal misdirected me, converting a 150m lead into a 300m deficit. I chased hard to catch Harris and won by two minutes in 1:49.30. I even had enough breath to apologise to the marshal for my comments about his dodgy sense of direction, and we had a good laugh.

Four weeks before the marathon, I decided to run the South of Perth 20km without looking at my watch to monitor my speed. I ran intuitively and felt like I was floating. It was one of those special days when it felt easy throughout and I won in 62.58. Another PB.

The running gods smiled on me once again at the end of July. The weather for my first serious crack at the Perth marathon was a perfect 9°C at the start at McCallum Park on the banks of the Swan River, and it only got better from there. I led from start to finish for a 2:24.16 win and I still treasure the memory of my daughter Nicole, then 13, cycling alongside me for 5km between Canning Bridge and the Narrows. The win also provided me with an unassailable lead for the WA Marathon Club Founders Trophy, presented to the best performer each year. I had achieved all I had wished for on the Perth running scene. I accepted my competitive running days were behind me and my only future involvement would be for fun and good health. Oh, and to help look after a sport which had been so good to me, as honorary treasurer on the WA Marathon Club committee.

Mandela's release and the imminent lifting of South African economic and sporting sanctions created an opportunity for Australia to take a leadership role in dealing with the new South Africa. There was one important proviso: Mandela and the ANC first had to complete negotiations with the Nationalists about the transition of political power and the date for South Africa's first democratic elections.

Bilateral trade between Australia and South Africa had evaporated over the previous two decades, yet both economies had much in common. Cynics suggested sanctions against South Africa had more than a political goal; Australian industries like mining and wine benefited hugely from the absence of South African competition in markets, such as the US and Britain. The South African Grand Prix, held at Kyalami outside Johannesburg since 1967 as part of the Formula One world championship, was relocated to Adelaide as the Australian Grand Prix. However, the time for this manoeuvring was over and Australian equity markets now had the ability to invest in South Africa. Without jumping ahead of the political agenda being negotiated by Mandela, I became a founding member and honorary treasurer for the Australia Southern Africa Business Council. Our objective was to act as a conduit for bilateral trade and investment opportunities.

Our Perth strategy was to sign corporate members for a nominal annual fee and host lunches, breakfasts or evening drinks with invited speakers well qualified to talk about South Africa. This was like trying to understand what lay behind the Berlin Wall. We soon discovered in Perth – the closest Australian city to South Africa – a surprisingly large interest in listening to business leaders out of South Africa like Anglo-American's Michael Spicer and Clem Sunter, and Randgold's Peter Flack. We drew a big crowd for Nick Farr-Jones, who captained the Wallabies rugby team to victory over the Springboks at Newlands in August 1992 in the first Test match between the two nations in 21 years. We even managed to attract former Prime Minister Bob Hawke to the podium in Perth. Our functions attracted between 250 to 400 guests, figures not beaten by any other business forum in Western Australia at the time.

We were such an informative and well-supported interest group that Western Australian Premier Carmen Lawrence asked us to host an ANC delegation making its first visit to Australia in 1991. She made available the Premier's dining room at Parliament House, and the ASABC committee got to meet the faces attached to the names we had only read or heard about because they had been living either in exile or in captivity on Robben Island. ANC deputy-president Walter Sisulu, accompanied by wife Albertina, led the delegation. He was sentenced to life imprisonment with Mandela in 1964 and was visiting Australia for the first time since his release in October 1989, after 26 years' imprisonment.

Another first for a quarter of a century was South Africa's participation in the Olympic Games, in Barcelona in 1992. South Africa had last competed in the 1960 Games in Rome, represented by an all-white team. Given the prodigious depth of black male distance runners in South Africa in the late 1980s, expectations of medal performances were high. Sadly, Plaatjes was within a few months of qualifying for his US citizenship and was caught in Olympic no man's land.

The South African men disappointed in the track distance events and the marathon; Sinqe astonishingly did not finish the latter. Elana Meyer did all the front running in the 10,000m final for Ethiopia's Derartu Tulu who, after 24 laps, kicked with 400m to go and romped home for the gold. Meyer won the silver medal and the hearts of spectators and global viewers when she and Tulu embraced and ran a lap of honour, hand-in-hand with trailing flags. South Africa's only other medal was a silver in the men's doubles tennis. Sports officials in South Africa received a stark reminder of how much they had fallen off the pace. Barcelona was a reality check.

I found it hard to correlate the high-speed performances I had witnessed in South Africa with the Barcelona breakdown. My Australian friends like Langford knew just how tough it was to convert good form into Olympic medals, having watched as Ron Clarke, Rob de Castella and Steve Moneghetti achieved phenomenal success almost everywhere but the Olympics.

Fortunately, my faith in the talent of black South African runners was soon rewarded. David Tsebe won the Berlin Marathon in September 1992 in 2:08.07, the fastest time yet for the year. Two months later, Willie Mtolo won the New York Marathon in 2:09.29 for one of the most profound road running victories by a South African. But there was more in store.

On 14 August 1993 I turned on the television to watch the marathon at the World Athletic Championships in Stuttgart. I had missed the first part of the race and was pleased to see Luketz Swartbooi of Namibia setting the pace. The commentators were discussing just how tough the conditions were when Plaatjes came into view wearing US colours. He was third but I wasn't going to miss a second of his chase because I knew how well he went when the going was tough. Match him against the speed merchants on a fast, flat course in cool weather and he'd be outpaced, but confront him with a situation where grit counted for something and he'd prevail. I was desperately excited.

Sure enough, with two kilometres to go, he surged into second and then, outside the stadium, passed a fading Swartbooi to win in 2:13.57. Tears rolled down my cheeks as I sat in my lounge alone in the middle of the night. Mark Plaatjes: one of life's champions and now a world champion.

To my mind, the stunning performance of South Africa's distance runners was as symbolic as the release of Mandela from prison. Years and years of denial, accumulated frustration and discrimination was suddenly expunged.

South Africa's black marathon runners were finally free.

21

Seismic shift

Life as I had known it changed forever on 25 April 1993 when I separated from Vern and moved out of the family home for good. We had been married for 17 years.

Our daughters, Nicole (15), Simone (12) and Philippa (10), were distraught and our circle of acquaintances was shocked. They had no idea the marriage was in trouble because we gave none of the usual clues of quarrelling and friction. However, our families and close friends were less surprised than saddened that the inevitable had occurred.

When I stopped running at the end of 1991, and became more involved in domestic and community activities, I realised that I had an emotional void in my life. All my affection and emotional bonding was being channelled into my daughters. Vern and I had grown apart emotionally and we both felt stranded on opposite banks of the river of our lives. There were no external dalliances, just a growing sense of emptiness.

Throughout 1992, I wondered what on earth I was going to do once our three daughters had completed their education and left home. Vern and I would be empty nesters and there would be no escaping each other. I realised I was emotionally immature in that I had not worked out what I was seeking in life, other than a secure future for my daughters in Australia. I was a youthful 39-year-old who had been too busy achieving my ambitions to thoroughly consider life from the domestic perspective.

I realised, too, that Vern had had it tough. Nicole was born in London when we had no money and no family support. When Simone and Philippa came along, the situation had changed. I was earning more and we were back in South Africa, but that had brought new challenges as my work and running took up much of my time. When I started to challenge Fordyce for Comrades glory, I found myself in the fast lane. I was confident, outgoing, full of energy and constantly in the media or professional journals. Vern was quite the opposite: shy, reserved and cautious. She was a dedicated mother and always acted in the best interests of our daughters. The differences in our lives permeated our domestic environment and increasingly drove a wedge between us.

When we emigrated to Australia, we both hoped a new life in a new country would draw us closer as a couple, particularly as I would cease to be public property. But we hugely underestimated the hard work that was needed to re-establish ourselves, domestically and professionally.

Career-wise, I had also reached a crossroad. After converting my South African qualifications, I had achieved a partnership with Arthur Andersen and then moved to Challenge Bank, but I soon realised the banking establishment was too restrictive for me. I was not very good at playing the "Yes Minister" corporate politics, where incompetence is masked by padded job descriptions, and the salary scales were not to my liking. I wanted to make more money, enough for the security of my family, the education of my daughters and the adventure travel I was dreaming of.

I stopped keeping a daily running log when Vern and I separated. It was time to explore life outside the entrapment of daily recordings of kilometres, minutes and seconds on the face of the clock I had been racing since 1981. My running had been a rich passage of my life but in the same way I had to pluck up the courage to have a crack at the Comrades in 1981, it was time for me to take a deep breath and explore other commercial opportunities.

I was looking around for a role that would meet my needs when South Africans of all races voted for the first time for a government that would meet theirs. My father kept me up to date with the 1994 elections and we shared our delight at the elevation of Nelson Mandela to head of state. Four months later, my father died unexpectedly and I was on my way back to Johannesburg, reflecting on our relationship through the long night flight. I was battling to adjust to the finality of death and I drew consolation from a letter I had written to my parents a few months earlier, opening my heart to them about the importance of their contribution to my successes. As I have mentioned, I was at the crossroads domestically and professionally, and I sorely felt the distance from my parents, compounded by the reality they were growing older. I wanted to let them know I was indebted to them. I wasn't sure at the time if the letter was premature but, heading across the Indian Ocean that night, I realised it was one of the best things I had done in my life.

Although life in the tumultuous new South Africa held challenges for everyone, no matter their background, Mandela miraculously held the nation together. The country could so easily have torn itself apart with another of those post-colonial African civil wars fuelled by resentment and vengeance, but Mandela was up to the challenge. It was his greatest feat in a remarkable life. How I was to regret not competing in the 1996 Comrades. Mandela was guest of honour and I watched a webcast of the top 10 finishers receiving their gold medals and a handshake from the man they called Madiba. I would have swapped all my medals and race victories for a Madiba handshake. I was envious beyond belief.

A month after my father's death, I went hiking in Nepal, completing the Annapurna circuit. The high point of the hike was 5,200m which tested my endurance and fitness, and I even experimented by going for a jog at 4,000m. I felt like I was breathing through a drinking straw.

The opportunity to change jobs occurred a few months after my Annapurna adventure when the giant Westpac Bank bid $700 million to swallow Challenge. I did not want to be part of an organisation with more than 32,000 employees, so I made the move into the world of funds management, superannuation and investment banking.

I said goodbye to spectacles and contact lenses in 1999. I wanted to enter the new millennium with 20:20 vision and elected to undergo laser surgery to correct my short sightedness which was becoming a problem. I was so myopic that, if I emerged from the ocean after a swim, I would trip over someone without recognising him or her. Laser surgery has its risks but I was confident it would benefit me. It was the single biggest improvement to my health and wellbeing in my lifetime.

As we entered the new millennium, Nicole, Simone and Philippa were 21, 18 and 16 respectively, and I felt the best way to enjoy some quality time with them was to explore the parts of Australia we had not experienced yet. We flew to Cairns and spent five days aboard a 45-feet cutter at Thedford Reef, part of the magnificent Great Barrier Reef. It was beyond anything I had previously experienced and scuba diving has since been a part of our lives. We also trekked through rainforests and climbed Uluru (Ayers Rock) on the way home.

Although I had no running goals, I still jogged occasionally to keep fit and maintain my running club friendships. A couple of weeks after the 2000 Comrades had been run on 16 June, the WA Marathon Club staged a screening of the race video after a Sunday morning training run. I was curious about the way the Eastern Europeans had instantly dominated the Comrades, and hung around to watch the second half of the 2000 race.

Russian Vladimir Kotov, 40, switched on the afterburners over the final 10km of the Comrades and raced away from his rivals to set an astonishing new course record of 5:25.33 for the 87.6km up run. His unprecedented pace, on a course 300m longer, bettered the 1998 mark of 5:26.25 of compatriot, Dmitry Grishine. When Kotov had crested the 1.8km ascent of Polly Shorts, he knew he would win and went for the record and the associated prize of a 100-ounce bar of gold. Prize money had been introduced in 1995.

Three turbo-charged kilometres followed the 5km to go marker: 3.00, 3.06 and 3.08. Such speed was the equivalent of a 2:10 standard marathon pace: an astonishing athletic performance. According to statistician Hauman, it was as if the previous 80km had not affected his legs at all. He had run the final 8km of the 2000 up Comrades at a faster pace than he had ever run a standard marathon, including that at the 1980 Moscow Olympics when he was 20 years younger, and the dead-flat world titles at Stuttgart in 1993 when he was seven years younger – only, in this instance, he had already raced a gruelling 80km warm-up, almost a double-marathon.

The fastest pace I managed to hit during Comrades was on a 10km downhill stretch from Botha's Hill in 1984, when Fordyce and I were chasing Reynecke. We were running at 3.05 pace over the fastest section of the course, with about 50km behind us. It hurt us: our pace dropped to nearly four minutes per kilometre for the final 5km as we descended to sea level through Durban.

Then there was the 1986 downhill dice I had with Fordyce when he earned victory by averaging a 3.41 pace for the final 10km. Yet Kotov ran his final 5km, at Pietermaritzburg's 700m altitude, after an uphill 80km, at a pace 12% faster than Fordyce's furious final charge 14 years earlier – and showed no ill-effects afterwards. In fact, he boasted to the media: "I'm in good condition."

Following disqualifications among the top 10 in the 1999 Comrades because of drug cheating, the Comrades organisers decided before the 2000 race that no prize money would be awarded before all test results were received, and a thorough analysis of videos and chip mat readings was made. The day after the 2000 Comrades, Athletics South Africa announced all drug tests were negative.

This outcome was consistent with the Sydney Olympics only months later, declared to be the cleanest in the history of the Games by serving International Olympic Committee president Juan Antonio Samaranch. However, Sydney did not catch Marion Jones or Lance Armstrong – and probably dozens of lesser names. I doubt Athletics South Africa were better equipped than the Olympics to detect performance enhancers such as EPO, hormones, insulin and blood transfusions.

Dr Carmel Goodman, medical director of the Western Australian Institute of Sport and sports doctor to Australia's gold medal women's hockey team, told me that 20% of competitors at the Sydney Olympics were suspected of using beta agonist medication for alleged asthma. It was such an issue that the IOC insisted that competitors aiming for Athens in 2004 needed to provide documented proof of exercise asthma. Thousands of applications were submitted.

I returned to marathon running in 2001 because I was offered a performance stimulant I could not bring myself to reject: red wine The agent provocateur for my subsequent attempt at Ironman, Carolyn

Brinsdon, convinced a few members of our jogging group of the virtues of the Marathon du Médoc in France, where the seconding tables contain a tonic guaranteed to soothe the pain of the road: thousands of litres of the best reds of the Bordeaux region. I would need it because I had just 12 weeks to get into marathon shape from my weekly base of a gentle-paced 60km. My running body had gone into hibernation and I battled with assorted aches and pains whenever I ran more than 21km.

The Marathon du Médoc experience starts with a carbo-loading dinner the night before the 42.2km tour of the area's vineyards. This is no ordinary pasta party, but a five-course sit-down dinner with 29 Bordeaux vintages on offer from the premier producers. Little wonder the race enjoys a comparatively late 9am start. About 90% of the field of 7,000 wore some type of fancy dress and the party atmosphere was encouraged by the wine stops every 2km. To stop the alcohol going straight to your head, the organisers thoughtfully included another 21 gourmet stands, offering oysters, ham, steak, cheese and ice cream.

I had an awesome run to 28km but after that I was, well, in a spot of bother and my personal survival mission started. I dipped under three hours by a few seconds and was rewarded, not with a can of soft drink, but a gorgeous French model who sprayed my face with Eau de Cologne and wiped it with all the charm and seduction the French can turn on instantly. Another handed me my medal, a two-pack of Bordeaux wine and some local delicacies.

The run – it would be incorrect to call it a race – and the following week exploring the wineries bordering the Gironde estuary provided an idyllic break, cut short when we traipsed into the local baker for some of his freshly baked bread and were told about the September 11 attacks in New York.

A couple of days later, I headed for the Pyrenees with girlfriend Susan Vetten to visit Pau. My paternal grandmother Eva Berthier had been raised and educated in Pau. We then headed through Lourdes, horribly tacky and touristy, for the Pyrenees and San Sebastian in Spain. Unbeknown to me, we were tracking one of the most traditional mountain stages in the Tour de France.

A blanket of mist enveloped us as we climbed into the mountains. After one corner, the road kicked up into an almighty gradient and the bitumen surface was covered in graffiti. Hinault. Fignon. Indurain. Pantani. Lemond. Even I recognised these names. I parked the car and got out. We were above the treeline, at an altitude of about 2,000m. I had no appreciation of the Tour de France but I realised I was standing on one of the sacred, high-altitude battlefields. The names of the gladiators of the race were slowly fading like ancient Italian frescoes, yet I felt the souls of those who had raced up these mountains still resided here. It moved me so much I did not take any photographs. As we continued snaking our way up this dreadfully steep climb, the mist lifted at the crest of the pass and we spotted an enormous silver sculpture of an anguished cyclist with a plaque that read: Col du Tourmalet – altitude 2,115m.

We had, through sheer luck, just stumbled across one of the iconic stages of the Tour. The physical dimensions of the race mesmerized me. My mind was not able to process the physical effort required to race over this alpine road, but the Tourmalet ignited a tiny spark of fascination that was to lie dormant in my subconscious for a few years.

Meanwhile, I had built up some running fitness and wanted to incorporate it in my next adventure. Rottnest Island, or Rotto as it is popularly known in Perth, rises out of the Indian Ocean 18km off Fremantle. It was used for long periods of time as a prison, first for Aboriginals, then juvenile criminals, then during World War II to intern enemy aliens, mostly Italian immigrants. The 11km long island is also prison to tens of thousands of dugite snakes which, isolated from the mainland over the millennia, developed into a particularly venomous sub-species, only slightly less lethal than the black mamba of Africa. With motorised vehicles on the island restricted to essential services, the dugite has developed a habit of sunning itself on the side of the bitumen roads. What a great venue for a marathon.

The Rotto Marathon tee shirt is a snappy accessory I did not possess, so I decided to keep running with the 2002 event as my goal. Without the distraction of wine, and the footsteps of those in front of me clearing the roads of things with fangs, I ran a comfortable 2:44 over the undulating three-lap course. I accelerated over the final 20km to run into second, seven minutes behind chief snake sweeper and former RAC colleague, Mark Page. It was his fourth Rotto win since emigrating to Perth in 1999.

The following October I again took the ferry to Rotto for the 2003 race. Page was there to defend his title, as lean as always. Also there was Fordyce, who was in town for a corporate engagement, apparently a chain of funeral homes, and took the opportunity to run. I ran with my triathlon mate, Sandy Burt, and, nearing the finish, lapped a struggling Fordyce. Burt and I got home to share second in 2:46 to be met by Page whose face was split with an evil grin – and not only because he'd won again.

"Did you do it?" he demanded to know.

"No, just said g'day," I replied. "You?"

"I couldn't resist," laughed Page. "I tapped him on the shoulder and said 'Keep it up Bruce, you are running like a star.'"

When Fordyce finished an hour later, yes an hour later, we treated his aches with a few beers and had a good laugh about it. That karma wheel had gone full circle again.

While living in South Africa, I had been invited to run the Two Oceans 56km in 1986 and 1987 but, because of my work commitments, my Comrades build-up race was always limited to the Korkie. I knew the race had gone from strength to strength and decided to celebrate my 50th birthday in 2004 with a tour by foot of the Cape Peninsula. On top of a good base, I put in 12 solid weeks, including six runs of between 20km and 25km and another six of more than 30km. I felt I was in sufficiently good shape to go sub-4 hours and earn a silver medal.

It was a wet morning in Cape Town but the chills up my spine came from the chorus of *Shosholoza* (a traditional black miners' song, now used in sporting events to show solidarity). Thus inspired, I hit the standard marathon mark in 2:53 and survived the slog up Constantia Nek to finish in 3:55 for my first – and last – Two Oceans medal, a silver. All top 10 runners were black, indicative of the shift to professionalism in the ultra-distance races.

The following year, I decided to return to Africa to do something I had thought about since my teenage years but was precluded from doing as a South African passport holder.

Kilimanjaro!

The Tanzanian government did not allow white South Africans into their country during the apartheid era. But times change and I was ready for one of the iconic African experiences. Rearing 5,895m above sea level, Kilimanjaro is the highest free-standing mountain in the world. The main route itself is relatively easy, essentially a long, uphill walk. What makes it tough – so much so that an average of 10 people die on the mountain each year – is the altitude, particularly above 4,000m where atmospheric pressure is 40% lower than at sea level. At the summit, atmospheric pressure is 50% lower than at sea level and oxygen-carrying capacity of blood is reduced by 40%, explaining why only four of 10 attempting Kilimanjaro get to the summit.

Susan Vetten was easily up to the challenge and joined me on the Lomosho route for a two-day acclimatisation hike up to the Branco Hut at 3,900m, where the difficulties began in earnest. The following day, we slogged up to the Barafu camp at 4,600m for a few hours' sleep before a midnight start for the summit. Susan wasn't feeling good. She had a headache, a sign of mild altitude sickness, but felt she could go on. It was freezing when we set off in the middle of the night, and the wind penetrated our multiple layers of clothing. We were all feeling the lack of oxygen and needed a five-minute break every 30 minutes as we slogged up the shale slope in the darkness, our head torches just two pinpricks in a long line of lights snaking upwards into the heavens.

I really struggled those last few hundred metres to the crater rim. I now understand how even a superb physical specimen like tennis champion, Martina Navratilova, had to turn back on the upper slopes. If the altitude gets you, it gets you, and you become one of the 60% who don't make it up. Simple as that.

I was encouraged to reach the rim at Stella Point and the gradient eased considerably as we approached the highest point and the sign which is the backdrop for all summit photographs:

Uhuru Peak Tanzania 5,895m.
Africa's highest point.
World's highest free-standing mountain.

I was freezing, but euphoric. That moment completed my African chapter, with Johnny Clegg's music rolling through my head: *I'm sitting on top of Kilimanjaro, where I can see a new tomorrow.*

Witnessing the African sunrise from the top of Kilimanjaro, I was swamped by a sense of huge optimism for South Africa and a newfound joy in my heart.

Call back the past 5

The world learned about the full range of Nazi atrocities at the Nuremberg trials of 1945 and 1946. Adolph Hitler, Heinrich Himmler and Joseph Goebbels committed suicide before they could be arrested, but the likes of Herman Göring, Rudolph Hess, Albert Speer and Ernst Kaltenbrunner faced the court and were sentenced to death or long terms of imprisonment for their crimes against humanity.

Fifty years on, South Africa had its own version of Nuremberg. The world looked on and listened in horror as those Nationalists tasked with defending the apartheid system confessed to a litany of murder, execution, poisoning, torture and bombings in a bid to save their skins, seeking a privilege they had not offered to their victims: amnesty.

The new South African ANC government opted for a Truth and Reconciliation Commission (TRC) in preference to an amnesty law to deal with the crimes of apartheid. Justice Minister Dullah Omar suggested that an amnesty law would have ignored the victims of apartheid violence. In his view, the ANC government could not forgive perpetrators unless it attempted to restore the honour and dignity of the victims, and to give effect to reparation. The TRC was to transcend the divisions and strife of the past. Amnesty was to be granted in respect of acts, omissions and offences associated with political objectives and committed in the course of the conflicts of the past. In order for amnesty to be granted, the incident must have occurred between 1 March 1960 (the month in which the Sharpeville massacre took place) and 10 May 1994 (the date of Mandela's inauguration as president), and the amnesty would only be granted if perpetrators were completely truthful.

Between 1996 and 1998, Archbishop Desmond Tutu chaired the TRC hearings which rammed home the sheer evil of apartheid and the increasing desperation of the Nationalists as they sought to stave off the inevitable transition to democracy. I suspected bad things were happening behind the scenes while I lived in South Africa until my 1987 departure; a decade later I was staggered to learn just how bad they were. A Gestapo-like murder squad operating from a base near Pretoria? Licences to kill? Dr Death? Even I, one of the white liberals who could not live under apartheid, was stunned at what emerged at the hearings. A decade of living in out-of-the-way, peaceful Perth had thinned my political skin from the tough hide that even I had developed living in South Africa. The revelations that were reported by victims seeking acknowledgement, and perpetrators seeking amnesty, were horrific beyond belief.

Not satisfied that the army and the police could deal with the internal uprising that gained momentum after the 1976 Soweto uprising, it was revealed that the Nationalist government had created a third force to enforce its security measures. This included unofficial units such as the Eastern Cape's Hammer Force and the Civilian Cooperation Bureau (CCB), hit squads whose job it was to permanently disrupt opposition, whether ANC or otherwise.

In absolute disbelief, I read in *The Australian* newspaper of the notorious secret police death squad at Vlakplaas outside Pretoria, established by Brigadier Jack Cronje and commanded for eight years by Colonel Eugene de Kock, which undertook a series of kidnappings, tortures, bombings and executions. Brigadier Cronje gave the TRC an example of his unit's work that resulted in the disappearance of 10 teenagers from Mamelodi township, outside Pretoria. In 1986, an agent provocateur – or askari – called Joe Mamasela posed as an ANC recruiter and arranged for 10 teenagers to sneak out of South Africa to join the ANC in Botswana. Mamasela drove them westwards in a minivan and plied them with beer to get them drunk.

Brigadier Cronje and others followed at a distance. At a deserted spot near Nietverdient, close to the Botswana border, Mamasela stopped and the hit squad dragged the intoxicated youths from their vehicle. They injected them with poison and dragged them back into the minibus, which was doused with petrol, packed with explosives and pushed down a nearby incline. It blew up and 10 potential ANC recruits vanished. Just like that.

One of the boys was Jeremiah Ntuli, 16, whose mother Maria confronted Brigadier Cronje at the commission. He told her he believed he was doing his duty in committing preventive assassination. "I thought I was doing the right thing," he said as he tried to justify his claim for amnesty. Cronje and cohorts, Warrant Officer Paul van Vuuren, Colonel Roelf Venter, Captain Wouter Mentz and Captain Jacques Hechter, confessed under Commission questioning to a total of 41 murders during the 1980s.

The TRC had uncovered a previously hidden reservoir of pure evil.

In Port Elizabeth, a former CCB sergeant brought to an end 25 years of uncertainty for the families of the Cradock Four when he revealed details of their execution. Matthew Goniwe, Fort Calata, Sparrow Mkonto and Sicelo Mhlauli were driving from the small Eastern Cape town of Cradock to Port Elizabeth in June 1985 when police intercepted Goniwe's beige Honda and took the four to a deserted Indian Ocean beach. Sergeant Gerhardus Lotz claimed he had been told to deal with the four to prevent a communist uprising. He revealed he smashed Goniwe's skull with a steel spring he had brought from home, and then the rest of his group stabbed Goniwe and the others to death, to make it appear they were victims of black faction fighting. The corpses were doused in petrol and immolated.

When the bodies were found, the Nationalist government denied involvement, attributing the slaughter to black vigilantes. The families felt otherwise but had to wait 13 years for their suspicions to be confirmed when Lotz and six others – Nic van Rensburg, Herman du Plessis, Sakkie van Zyl, Eric Taylor, Harold Snynman and former Vlakplaas boss De Kock –applied for amnesty on the grounds that they were trying to quell unrest on the order of Nationalist government ministers. As amnesty was only granted if the complete truth was told, more horrifying details continued to leak out. More than most South Africans could ever have imagined.

Church on Sunday, murder on Monday? Most of the security forces were regulars at the NGK, or Dutch Reformed Church, but their principles deserted them when they went back to work. Dirk Coetzee commanded the counter-insurgency unit at Vlakplaas. He told the Commission he had ordered the deaths of many ANC members, including Griffiths Mxenge, a human rights lawyer, who was stabbed 40 times at Umlazi Stadium in Durban, and Sizwe Kondile, a young law graduate from the Eastern Cape, who was interrogated and tortured before being passed on to Coetzee, who had him shot and his body burned. When an operation he commanded went bad in Swaziland, he was demoted and had an attack of conscience, moving overseas and even joining the ANC in London. That made him a target, and the man who commanded Vlakplaas for eight years tried unsuccessfully to have him killed. That man, Colonel Eugene de Kock, was nicknamed Prime Evil by his colleagues because he created such mayhem. He was involved in most of the atrocities carried out by the Vlakplaas unit in the 1980s, including the assassinations of ANC members in Swaziland and Lesotho, as well as South Africa, plus the Johannesburg bombings of Cosatu trade union headquarters in 1987, and church council offices Khotso House in 1988. Despite testifying at the TRC, De Kock was sentenced to 212 years in prison.

Nationalist defence minister Magnus Malan pulled away the CCB's shroud of secrecy in his 1997 submission to the TRC. He said the CCB was a component of the Special Forces, fronted by private companies, with the role of infiltrating and disrupting the enemy around the world. Records were probably destroyed when apartheid fell but it is estimated the CCB was involved in about 100 operations, including the assassinations of the Cradock Four, Namibian activist Anton Lubowski in Windhoek in 1989, ANC member Dulcie September in Paris in 1988 and Wits University academic David Webster, shot by hitman Ferdi Barnard outside his home in the Johannesburg suburb of Troyeville in 1989.

The CCB masterminded the bombing which claimed the life of Zimbabwean woman Tsitsi Chiliza, although the target of the booby-trapped television set was the future president of South Africa, Jacob Zuma. The CCB was also behind the explosions which killed ANC members Ruth First in Maputo and Jeanette Schoon and daughter Katryn, 6, in Luanda, plus those which cost ANC activist Albie Sachs an arm and an eye, and anti-apartheid priest Michael Lapsley both hands and an eye.

The bombs which killed First and the Schoons were assembled by CCB explosives expert Roger 'Jerry' Raven, and dispatched by security police major Craig Williamson. Both received amnesty, to the outrage of many South Africans, who felt they were less than forthcoming with the truth. Raven, for instance, claimed he did not know the intended targets.

Although more rotund than robust, Williamson was South Africa's James Bond, complete with licence to kill, for the final 15 years of apartheid. He was mentioned in court as being involved in the 1986 assassination of Swedish Prime Minister Olaf Palme, although this has never been proved; drew up plans to kidnap the entire London leadership of the ANC, although this was never carried out; and penetrated the anti-apartheid National Union of South African Students, rising to vice-president of the organisation in 1975, and subsequently deputy-director of the International University Exchange Fund in Geneva, from which he gained insight into left-wing cause funding and access to money for covert operations.

When London newspaper *The Guardian* exposed Williamson as a South African spy in 1980, he returned to the Republic to plot against the ANC, resulting in the bombing of the ANC's North London office in 1982 with a device built by Raven. The deaths of First and the Schoons followed, again the work of this pernicious duo.

Williamson ostensibly left the security police to go into business in 1985, but was involved in the establishment of organisations such as Longreach and the International Freedom Foundation (IFF), purportedly conservative think-tanks, but in reality an elaborate South African military intelligence operation, codenamed Operation Babushka, to undermine the ANC. Henry Kissinger and Senator Jesse Helms were among those who spoke at IFF functions.

Perhaps the most chilling testimony to emerge from the TRC involved the man nicknamed Dr Death. When South African agents learned the Soviet forces in Angola had access to chemical weapons, President PW Botha appointed his personal cardiologist, Dr Wouter Basson, to create and head a chemical and biological warfare (CBW) programme, codenamed Project Coast.

Basson was just 30 in 1981 when he was hired by the Defence Force to travel to Europe, Libya and Iraq to collect information about other countries' CBW programmes. He reported the programmes were more offensive than defensive in nature, and recommended South Africa quickly get up to date. He was appointed project officer with the aim of developing both offensive and defensive CBW weapons. Much of the dirty work was done at the Roodeplaat Research Laboratory near Pretoria where, in Basson's words, he oversaw an extensive and advanced biological and chemical warfare programme "on the frontline against the spread of communism and godlessness in Africa".

At the TRC and a subsequent criminal trial for drug possession and embezzling state funds, it emerged the research at Basson's laboratory included the following aims:

- Assassination by poisoning of opponents of the Nationalist government
- The development of devices to surreptitiously deliver the poison
- Mass sterilisation of blacks through genetic engineering
- The use of 'love drug' Ecstasy to pacify mobs
- Pathogens such as cholera, botulism and anthrax, to create epidemics
- Protective clothing to withstand chemical attacks.

Much of what Basson did is still secret. Some suggest he is on the ANC government's protected list because he knows too much, and that pressure has been applied to keep him in South Africa to prevent him selling his considerable CBW knowledge to other nations. Whatever the truth, the facts that emerged at his trial shocked me.

Former Special Forces officer, Johann Theron, testified that he was involved in the deaths of more than 200 political prisoners at Basson's behest. He said muscle relaxants developed at Roodeplaat were administered to more than 200 captured SWAPO guerrillas in Namibia, then still South West Africa. The relaxant caused the prisoners to suffocate from collapsed lungs, and their bodies were then dumped into the Atlantic Ocean from thousands of metres in the air. The court dismissed Theron's claim on the grounds that, since independence, Namibia was beyond South Africa's jurisdiction.

Theron also claimed that Basson ordered him to tie three political prisoners to a tree at a secret camp in KwaZulu-Natal and smear them at dusk with a gel-like substance containing lethal toxins. The men were not dead by morning, so Theron killed them with the muscle relaxant and dumped their bodies in the sea.

Jan Lourens, an engineer in Basson's employ, told the court he had designed and made devices to deliver the poison, such as walking sticks and umbrellas, while others testified to working on poison envelope flaps, poisoned tee-shirts and anthrax-infused cigarettes.

Basson's dirty-tricks team came close to killing anti-apartheid spokesman and secretary for the South African Council of Churches, the Reverend Frank Chikane. He collapsed during a 1989 trip to the US and the FBI discovered his clothes had been infused with phosphates designed to trigger a heart attack.

Basson's organisation was responsible for manufacturing Ecstasy on an industrial scale, apparently for use in a tear gas. After President FW de Klerk closed down his operations while negotiating with Nelson Mandela for a peaceful transition to democracy, Dr Death was caught in a 1997 sting trying to sell 100,000 tablets of the drug.

I, and millions of others across Australia, felt we were reading the script of a Bruce Willis shoot-and-burn movie. Sadly, it was not so.

These atrocities had happened in the country of my birth and were committed by some of the most evil human beings on planet Earth.

22

Adding iron to my diet

The murk of Johannesburg's duck-filled Emmarentia Dam or the azure clarity and visibility of the Indian Ocean off Perth? No choice.

If road running is the bigger sport in Jo'burg, triathlon wins that particular race in Perth. I had enjoyed my first go at the swim-bike-run trilogy shortly before emigrating to Australia and, with our house in Perth just a few minutes from the beautiful white-sand beaches, I was destined to get involved.

Heading into our first Christmas in our new city, I entered a novice triathlon and finished seventh out of 300 competitors. Aussies grow up in the water and move through it like fish, compared to my splashing and thrashing, but I was happy to jump into the ocean and have some fun. It was a lifestyle bonus of living in Perth.

Unlike South Africa, the Western Australian running calendar does not boast several races every weekend. The heat does not lend itself to summer running and, without an obsession like Comrades to focus on, the competitor numbers don't justify a heavily populated fixture list. Conversely, triathlon – particularly the shorter forms – is particularly suited to Perth's summer climate. A swim in the coolness of the Indian Ocean, an hour or so on a bike in a self-created breeze, before a run of 10km or so to build up a sweat – what was there not to like?

Perth's prevailing wind in summer is a southwester which puffs a cooling breeze off the ocean, hence its nickname of the Fremantle Doctor.

297

Occasionally, an east wind fan-forces heat from the desert to bake the city in 40°C plus temperatures during the day, and not much below 25°C at night.

I quickly learned the allure of weekend triathlons in the sea was far more appealing than running in such heat. I subsequently entered five Olympic distance triathlons – 1.5km swim, 40km cycle, and 10km run – and enjoyed diving straight back into the Indian Ocean after crossing the finish line. The depth and quality of competition was an eye-opener. Swimming is a major sport in Australia and these guys and girls also ride bikes fast. Although I managed a few podium finishes in my age group in the novice category, I was no threat to any Perth triathlete. I loved the fun of the cross training including the swimming. It was like a seaside holiday.

I continued to flirt with triathlons, even pencilling a notation in my diary at the beginning of 1990, of a fantasy to complete an Ironman when I turned 40, although this was as unrealistic at the time as my ambition to run the Comrades in 1976. Yet, just as it took the Comrades seed years to germinate, the idea nibbled at me until 2003, when it started to gnaw and I decided to give the Half Ironman a crack.

I made the commitment because I had realised my exercise regime almost resembled that of a triathlete. I cycled twice a week, swam twice a week and ran three or four times a week. It was all done at recreational pace, just to keep fit. Sure, I had lots to learn about cycling and I'd have to fix my inefficient swimming technique, but it was bound to be another fun experiment with a few like-minded friends.

I started the build-up with my first 2km open water ocean swimming event. I was thrilled with my relatively slow time of 49.20 because that was all I needed for the Half Ironman four months later in May.

My cycling went well until March, when a university student and I collided at a roundabout. She had not seen me, but I took sufficient evasive action to collide with the side of her car rather than the front. Even so, the impact somersaulted me through the air and I landed on my side, fortunately not my face. I took an almighty knock but survived with sore wrists, heavy bruising and a bursa the size of a golf ball on my right hip. So close to disaster!

Business commitments also did their best to knock over my aspirations. The Half Ironman event was to start at 9am on the Saturday, but I was in the final stages of negotiating the sale of one of Australia's largest forestry plantations to a European sustainability group. The lawyers from both sides engaged in one of those one-upmanship contests prevalent in the profession, a complete aside from the commercial aspects of the deal. We were in the law offices until 11pm on the Thursday before the race, and again from 7am to 8pm on the Friday. There were times I feared the legal eagles would never reach agreement and their contest would stretch into race day.

When all the signatures were where they needed to be I phoned Sue Vetten and she picked me up, still in pin-striped suit, from my city centre office at 9pm and drove south for 270km to Busselton.

I felt I was capable of a time of 5:15, possibly 10 minutes faster if all my stars were aligned, and I delivered three PBs. After a short but sound sleep, I joined 400 others for the progression of 1.9km ocean swim, 90km cycle and 21.1km run, and completed my first Busselton Half Ironman in 5:08.12, finishing fifth in my age group. I thoroughly enjoyed the event, particularly the run which I knocked off in 89.01. Sue also did pretty well, placing second in her age group in 6:20, and a feeling of satisfaction filled the car for the return trip to Perth. The camaraderie on the day helped stimulate the explosive growth of the event, with more than 1,800 individual entries and a further 1,500 team entries completing the 2014 Busselton Half Ironman, making it the largest event of its type in the southern hemisphere. Its popularity and atmosphere, not dissimilar to that of Comrades, has necessitated a restriction on competitor numbers.

When you run your first half marathon, experienced marathoners will try to sell you on the full marathon experience. Likewise, after the Half Ironman, we listened to many stories about how it was possible to step up to the full Ironman. It sounded plausible but it was not on my agenda, not least because the only Ironman race in Australia at the time was on the other side of the continent, north of Sydney.

Back in Perth, a few weeks after my silver medal in the April edition of the Two Oceans 56km in Cape Town in 2004, my right knee had started playing up. Dr Carmel Goodman found a minor medial meniscus tear on my scans and told me to lay off running for six weeks. I didn't want to lose my hard-gained fitness and asked her if I could swim and cycle instead, and got the all clear.

In a happy coincidence, some of my running mates had started cycling and swimming a few months earlier because the Asian financial crisis had resulted in the Malaysian Ironman losing its main sponsor. Event organiser International Management Group, with the underwriting support of the Western Australian government, chose to warehouse the event in Busselton for a few years, with no guarantee of a long-term slot on the international calendar. I had been so focused on the Two Oceans that any Ironman talk went over my head but, when I got back in the saddle to ride with my social training group, I was persuaded to join them in their bid to finish the Busselton Ironman in November 2004.

Leader of the pack was Kiwi Carolyn Brinsdon. Pips Woodhouse and Mike Hodgson were her willing lieutenants and the group included Di Ball, Steve Schalit, Sue Vetten, Colin McCrory and Sandy Burt. Hanging out with them took me back to my days with Varsity Kudus and my first Comrades Marathon in 1981.

I had been riding with this group on Sundays since the beginning of June for a break from running. They were a fun, interesting group. Their sense of enjoyment and enthusiasm proved infectious. In for a penny, in for a pound of hurt in November. Hodgson was the main instigator. He pointed out he had arrived in Perth from England as an adult not knowing how to swim at all, but he was going to give Ironman a go, all four kilometres of the swim, 180km of the bike ride, and the 42.2km marathon. How could I decline?

Burt and McCrory were the only dinkum Aussies in the group. The rest were migrants, mostly former South Africans – and our number soon increased by one: Nicky Ivory. She really knew how to ride. She had raced in South Africa and Europe, and showed us how it was done properly. Never mind her partnership status with Deloitte and her academic gold medal earned at South Africa's notoriously difficult FQE. She kept us on our toes.

Saying yes is one thing. Doing it is another, and before I would be in a position to submit my entry by the 30 September cut-off, I had two obstacles to overcome: my knee and my swimming. I would not be able to run properly before mid-September and, even if it held up, I had scant time to build up marathon fitness. Mentally I was confident I could soldier through 42.2km, but I wasn't willing to damage my knee permanently.

The swim leg would be tricky. I had never swum 3.8km and knew I would have to spend a lot of time in a pool. Hodgson had done all this before; he referred me to his swimming coach Paul Newsome, who relieved me of $50 for my first and last swimming lesson at Challenge Stadium, site of the 1991 world titles. I asked him to come up with some quick fixes. I was not interested in drills, squad training or racing tumble turns. All I wanted was to get through the 3.8km swim leg in the time limit.

He videoed me swimming a lap or two and told me he would not live long enough to turn me into a decent swimmer. However, some obvious mistakes in my technique were easily correctable: don't let your bum sink so readily, use bilateral breathing, and reach as far forward as you can with a straight arm and pull all the way back to your thigh.

By the time entries were due, I had run for three weeks without any issues. I was up to 2km of swimming after nine weeks of watching the black line at the bottom of the pool, and our weekend bike rides had pushed out to 140km. All in all, sufficient for me to log on to the Ironman Western Australia website and pay my entry fee of $565 to IMG. My calculations indicated a finishing time of about 13 hours but, with PBs in each discipline, I could go close to 11 hours. Either way, it was going to be a long day at the office.

When I registered at Busselton on 27 November and checked in my bike, I weighed 76kg. Over the previous 18 weeks I had averaged 5.1km a week in the pool, 207km in the saddle and 47km in running shoes. Borderline in every Ironman sense, but in reasonable shape for a 50-year-old.

On race morning, our training pod, decked out in tri-suits, caps and goggles, had a friendly huddle on Busselton's pristine beach. I confessed to having a beer with the final pasta meal the previous evening, only because I was so nervous. It wasn't enough to settle the nerves. Down went a glass of red wine. Then another. I still went to bed with my eyes wide open.

As we entered the ocean for the 6am start of the 3.8km swim leg, the energy was crackling. I was one of 876 competitors from 30 countries and, because I started at the back of the pack in the slowest group wearing yellow caps, it was like being tossed into a washing machine. I knew my biggest challenge would be to swim straight, avoiding the pitfall of going off course. When I headed in to the beach in the final 200m of the swim, I felt like a swimmer for the first time in my life. I was breathing smoothly and rhythmically with good buoyancy and clear water around me. I had caught a number of blue cap swimmers from the faster group ahead. I hit the beach with my stopwatch reading 1:09. I was amazed.

My transition was efficient and it went like clockwork. In no time at all, I was out of the bike pound and about to jump onto my bike on the course when I checked the overhead clock at 1:24. What? Impossible! The clock must be wrong. But when I checked my stopwatch, it was flashing. Then it went blank. It had failed and my swim time was not as swanky as I had thought. I found out later my time in the water was 1:19.40, still well ahead of my expectations yet back in 647th position, or the slowest quarter of the field.

The bike leg got off to a wonderful, wind-assisted start. Although it takes a while to get comfortable on the bike, I was able to spin downwind for 10km before heading into sheltered forested areas. I had hoped to ride at an average of 30kmph but I found myself comfortably cruising at 35kmph.

I was acutely aware of the drafting rule and I ended up cycling in the middle of the road because the stream of cyclists ahead was going way slower than me. No one overtook me for three laps. With less than three kilometres to go to the end of the 180km bike leg, I was averaging more than 35kmph. I was delighted: good time, no mechanicals, no punctures. I was out of my saddle, standing on my pedals trying to stretch my hamstrings for the approaching run, when I spotted Joanna Milward, a handy Perth age group competitor. I pulled alongside her and mentioned we had a great chance of finishing in a decent time, when an official on a motorbike pulled up and flashed a yellow card.

"Go to the sin bin for five minutes," he yelled.

"What for? I am not drafting, I have been riding virtually in the middle of the road and have overtaken at least 500 cyclists."

"You're blocking."

I was astounded. I had never heard of this. I looked over my shoulder and the next cyclist was 200m behind.

"Blocking who?"

"It does not matter. You are blocking."

"Look, it is not illegal to ride two-abreast. I am not drafting," I shouted.

"If you had attended the race briefing yesterday you would have understood what the blocking rule is. Any more argument from you will result in a red card."

I could not believe it. With less than a kilometre to go, I had to sit in the sin bin for five minutes. Never in my life had I experienced this level of power wielding from an over-officious marshal. My enjoyment of Ironman WA hit rock bottom. The cyclist who was trailing me stopped at the sin bin and offered me his support as witness if I wished to appeal the time penalty. Unbelievable! Adrian Pearce from Wishart, Queensland, under no obligation whatsoever, took time out of his race to do the right thing. It emphasised the spirit of the ultra-distance athlete and I decided then and there not to appeal. The official was clueless; my closest competitor understood instinctively.

Even so, I was seriously pissed off when I exited the sin bin. My transition into running kit was smooth and I was off running, without a stopwatch but with plenty of adrenalin. We had to complete a three-lap course in the middle of the day under clear skies and a temperature of 22°C. It was hot and I steeled myself for a grind, attaching myself to strapping 25-year-old Kiwi James Sheather.

An-out-and-back section of the course near Busselton Hospital was the only part of the route which was well shaded and thus attracted a lot of spectators who had laid out chairs and picnic baskets. As we passed by at a 4.30km pace, a group of Perth spectators, some of them South Africans who were aware of my Comrades background gave me a chorus of loud encouragement. Ten minutes later, on the return leg, the same thing happened.

RUNAWAY COMRADE

Sheather turned to me and asked: "What's going on? Are you a local politician or something?"

I was too tired to explain that, when he was still in primary school, I had been a half-decent runner on another continent. Two decades later, I couldn't hold his young-leg pace; he beat me by four minutes.

Cloud cover provided some respite on the second lap but the third lap was pure survival. I resisted the urge to walk for as long as possible. With 7km to go, the route cruelly takes you right past the finishing area, with 3.5km to go to the final U-turn. I reached this point in a state of utter exhaustion, jealously watching those turning in to the finishing chute. I decided I would run the 3.5km leg to the U-turn, collect the biggest drink on offer, and adopt the Comrades Marathon strategy offered to novices of walking one lamppost and then running the next 10. That was how I would haul myself to the line.

Based on stopwatches worn by fellow competitors, I calculated I could still make it home in less than 11 hours. During my third lamppost walking interlude, a young South African guy who had flown to Perth for the event, Quinton Walker, jogged past and offered a personal compliment about Comrades. He would barely have been a teenager in the mid-1980s. How on earth did he recognise me? It was like magic dust and restored my dignity and spirits. I ran the final two kilometres to complete the marathon in 3:46 and clock 10:30.13 for the event in position 152. My mate Burt was waiting for me, having finished in 9:39 in 43rd position with a 3:08 marathon. He was 1:33 behind winner, Jason Shortis of Queensland, who reeled off a 2:45 marathon. Both represented the ideal of the true Ironman.

As soon as I emerged from the finishers' area, my three daughters mobbed me. They were as relieved as me that I had survived the Ironman ordeal. I was as exhausted as after my 4:25 bruising in the 1976 Vaal Marathon. Over the next few hours, every member of the Brinsdon group finished Ironman with beaming smiles. Englishman and non-swimmer, Hodgson, had swum 10 minutes faster than me for an overall time of 12:15. It was a rapturous day for us.

At the next day's awards ceremony, I was astonished to discover I had finished second in the men's 50–54 age group. Peter Bennett of New South Wales had won the category in 10:15, meaning my penalty had no effect on the outcome. I had earned a place to compete at the Ironman world championship at Kona, Hawaii, in 2005 but I was not interested. My Ironman itch had been well and truly scratched.

I still wanted to complete the Half Ironman in less than five hours, though. I decided to give it a go at the next year's edition in Busselton, thinking I would have little trouble lifting my race tempo slightly. After all, I was far more experienced than my 2003 debut when I had managed 5:08.13 as an utter novice with minimal swimming training.

In May 2005 I started the Half Ironman in pretty good condition and emerged from the water with a properly functioning stopwatch that indicated I had taken 48.27 for the swim. This was almost 25% slower than my Ironman swim of double the distance. The swim was clearly longer than the required 1.9km. The bike leg was more of the same. My computer clocked it at 93km. I ran the 21.1km in 87 minutes with even splits, my only acceptable leg, for a combined time of 5:05.59 and third in my age group. This constituted unfinished business, even if it was meant to be fun.

I immediately thought ahead to 2006. I would need to train harder in the pool to minimise my time loss in the swim leg. I would have to cycle with much faster groups to improve my cadence and raw speed, and I had to maintain my running fitness to repeat an 87-minute run for 21.1km.

A year later, I was back in Busselton. I had trained well, even though I was still the most awkward of swimmers. I tried to buy some insurance in the form of equipment: expensive Zipp 404 carbon wheels. My training was directed to achieve a 4:50 finish, allowing for a 44-minute swim, three-minute transition, 2:35 bike leg and 87-minute half marathon.

Instead, I emerged from the water in 44.07 and took 4.29 in transition. Not a great start. My bike leg of 2:26.25 recouped my lost time, possibly because my computer recorded it as 1.5km short. My transition was much better, about 90 seconds in and out. The run was an out-and-back, three-lap course on a bike path, about 2m wide. When we picked up the slower competitors on our second lap, it was like a fun run with the faster runners having to start at the back. We had to pick our way through two-way human traffic, not the finest logistical planning by the organisers.

Even so, I felt good and crossed the line in 4:42.51, slightly peeved that I had just failed to catch Bill Whalley, winner of my age group. Running was his weakest leg and I needed another mere 200m to catch him. I was confident I would have got him over a regulation course had I not been impeded by the masses in my strongest leg. Still, finishing second to a guy who had previously won the Australian national title in the men's 50-plus age group gave me a bit of a buzz.

Just like my tilt at the Comrades Marathon, I was not going to die wondering. I had given it my best shot and finally bettered five hours for the Half Ironman. The thought of spending hours each week following a black line, lap after lap, blowing bubbles in a chlorinated swimming pool to improve my swimming enough to better 4:30 held no appeal whatsoever. My thoroughly enjoyable dalliance with triathlon was over with a totally unexpected bonus, cycling.

Before my triathlon adventures, I had no idea of the thriving cycling sub-culture that existed in Perth. It turned out cycling was far more popular than running and my introduction to the chain gang reminded me of my introduction to Comrades in 1981: great company, interesting conversation, plenty of exercise.

I experienced Ironman cycling as a sterile 180km time trial, akin to running on a treadmill, with none of the high-adrenaline, high-risk thrill of racing flat out in a peloton over a snaking route. I was hooked when I started riding with a few of the hundreds of informal bike groups in Perth. In 2004, I cycled a total of 5,000km. Five years later, my annual total was past 17,000km – and that represents only 40% of the training distances covered by professionals like Cadel Evans.

It took me a few years to learn to ride a bike properly in terms of kit, cadence, gearing, bike set-up and crucial handling skills. The last really is crucial. The sense of speed is similar to that on a windsurfer, but that of falling off is a lot less pleasant. Most of my running outings were meditative and creative thinking opportunities but cycling demanded absolute concentration, particularly when you are in the middle of a group, sucking a wheel in order to avoid getting dropped. You need to be able to avoid panic and hold your line.

You know your fellow riders trust you when they invite you to join them on a European cycling trip. I joined Vince Ulgiati and his group for a tour of Italy in September 2006. We spent a few days in the rolling hills of Tuscany before heading north to the Dolomites for the serious stuff. On successive days, we cycled Bormio 2000 (yes 2,000m), Gavia (2,621m) and then a double ascent and descent of Passo Stelvio (2,757m) one of Europe's highest sealed roads. The Stelvio ride was awesome. We set out from our hotel base in Bormio at 1,225m and climbed solidly for 24km, including 38 switchbacks, until we reached the tundra snows of the top. We descended the eastern side of Stelvio via 48 switchbacks, had a pause for a Coke and panino at the bottom, and then did the climb in reverse. The descent to Bormio heightened our survival senses. One mistake and you would be over the edge or shedding skin and breaking bone against bitumen. I restrained my bike at 70kmph clenching both brakes with the bike snaking down the mountain pass but screaming to descend without resistance, much, much faster. The pros race the Giro d'Italia over this circuit descend at 100kmph with ease.

We finished the tour with some easy riding along the Adriatic coastline. I was already planning my next trip when Yvonne, my sister in Cape Town, sent an SMS with the horrible news that Lindsay Weight – winner of the Comrades in 1983 and 1984 – had died suddenly at her home in Cape Town at the age of 44 from a heart attack. I had become good friends with Lindsay and her husband Ian, visiting them on my trips to Cape Town and corresponding regularly by email. That unpredictable fine line between life and death galvanized my resolve to stick to my 2009 retirement plans in pursuit of a rapturous life.

In 2007 I had improved to the point I was able to enter real bike races. I also joined 2,000 other riders for the Bicycle Tour of Colorado, a six-day, 665km ride during which we crossed the continental divide six times, climbing a total of 10,800m. It wasn't long before I joined a group of Perth riders aiming to test themselves in the Pyrenees. We landed in Nice, and could not avoid the lure of nearby Mont Ventoux, the iconic Tour de France climb notorious for the 1967 death on its slopes of Englishman, Tom Simpson. The morning was hot and dry and, after a 30km warm-up, we tackled the 22km, 1,610m ascent with a gradient that hits 11% in parts. When we cleared the treeline at Chalet Reynard and entered the barren moonscape with the summit still 6km away, I felt as though I was melting. Arriving at the summit 30 minutes later, I immediately rated it as my least favourite climbing experience ever. That evening, my legs cramped badly, reinforcing Ventoux's bad karma which lingered from the Marco Pantani–Lance Armstrong duel in 2003. Their ferocious battle to the summit pitted two remarkable pharmaceutical creations against one another. Armstrong's aura and credibility is now destroyed; Pantani is dead, killed by a cocaine overdose while he still retained some €11-million in bank accounts at the time of his death.

In the Pyrenees we climbed Col de Marie-Blanque (1,035m), Col du Abisque (1,709m) Col du Soulor (1,474m) and finally Col du Tourmalet (2,115m), which I had inadvertently stumbled upon after the Marathon du Médoc 6 years earlier. We also climbed the Col de Peyresourde (1,563m) and the Col de Portet d'Aspet (1,069m) where, on the descent, we came across the memorial to Italian Olympic gold medallist, Fabio Casartelli. On this seemingly innocuous descent a rider fell in the 1995 Tour de France, bringing down those immediately behind. Casartelli was one of them. As he slid along the road his head hit a concrete bollard, killing him. Other riders who went over the edge tumbled into the alpine vegetation and survived. You need a bit of luck in cycling.

Having experienced many of the famous passes that feature in the Tour de France and the Giro d'Italia, I could understand what race speeds meant. In running, once I had achieved a sub-2.30 marathon and continued improving, I could calibrate the effort needed to run a sub-2.20, and fully appreciate a sub-2.10. Similarly, I was able to comprehend the performances in the Tour de France, and my reaction was disillusionment. Armstrong was king of the Tour and his dominance was the market catalyst for the sport in the US, and then globally. But his performances were too good to be true. Many turned a blind eye, preferring to concentrate on the feel-good story of a cancer survivor achieving miracles. He and millions of others pointed to the fact he had not publicly failed a drug test. As someone who had competed at the top level, I was sceptical. Very sceptical.

I tested my hypothesis towards the end of 2006 at a fundraising dinner to assist promising young Perth cyclists. The guest speaker was Robbie McEwen, who had won the sprinter's green jersey at the Tour de France in 2002, 2004 and 2006. The last few Tours had not been without controversy. Armstrong had retired in 2005 after seven consecutive Tour wins. In 2006, Floyd Landis rode one of the most decisive mountain stage wins yet to claim the yellow jersey, only to be disqualified for doping a couple of days after the Tour had ended. The following year, Dane Michael Rasmussen dominated the final mountain stage finishing atop Col d'Aubisque, only to be withdrawn from the race by Team Rabobank for, ahem, "administrative reasons."

McEwen invited questions from the floor after his excellent presentation. I plucked up the courage to ask Robbie how Tour de France riders could quarantine themselves from disgraced riders like Rasmussen and Landis, yet simultaneously remain competitive against them. Before I had finished my question, the majority of attendees were jeering and telling me to shut up. I also heard the word "dickhead" directed at me. McEwen said he didn't understand the question, so I clarified: "Doping or drugs like EPO, human growth hormone, steroids, blood transfusions and more."

McEwen replied like a true politician: "Well, in all walks of life we have to deal with individuals who might break the law and cycling is no different. There may be some unsavoury individuals who shun the law. Next question."

To give McEwen his due, he chatted to me at the end of the evening and listened politely to my point of view without committing himself one way or the other. I wonder how those who had jeered me felt in January 2013 when Rasmussen confessed to doping between 1998 until 2010, using EPO, growth hormones, testosterone, DHEA, insulin, IGF-1 and cortisone. Like Armstrong, he never tested positive yet ended up disgraced.

In 2008, I rode in the Tour de Corse, a 1,000km circumnavigation of Corsica, followed by a few of the Granfondo (GF) one-day races in Italy. The GF Sportful Dolimiti, raced over 216km in the Dolomites with a net elevation gain of 5,400m, went well until we hit snow on the climb to the crest of the fifth mountain pass at 1,970m, Passo di Rolle. My hands were so cold I could barely feel my brake levers. The descent was the scariest thing I'd done, with the road surface covered in sleet and decorated with a few bodies of crashed riders who wouldn't or couldn't hit their brakes quickly enough. I finished in 9:18 but my right thumb was numb for three days from the cold. I subsequently discussed the cold weather experience with Rabobank professional bike rider and dual Australian Olympic gold medallist, Graham Brown, who revealed competitors in the freezing Tour of Poland rode with thick dishwashing gloves under their snow mitts. I have always enjoyed receiving great practical tips like this.

Things went better in the 249km GF Fausto Coppi out of Cuneo, with a net elevation gain of 3,710m. Conditions were good and I felt great, despite five mountain passes. Much to my surprise, I finished in 9:09 and won my M50+ age group and collected my prize pack which included an 8kg prosciutto crudo. This I had to return to the bemused Italian organisers who could not comprehend how Australian quarantine laws would preclude the importation of their world-beating prosciutto.

I also tried mountain biking, in the inaugural four-day Cape to Cape race at Margaret River in Western Australia. I tended to go over the handlebars every time I hit a patch of soft sand, but some South African riders from the Loots family and their mate Dewet Marais managed to convince my Perth cycling mate, Ian Sandover, and me how our lives would be enriched if we had a crack at the Cape Epic. The following week I raised the topic with Sandover.

"Well, the equity markets are down 40% this year," he pointed out in his Aussie twang. "What the hell else will we do next year? Sounds like a good idea Dalai Mottee."

It certainly was an epic – 700km over eight days including 14,663m of climbing, equivalent to climbing Everest twice. My chain snapped during the prologue on Table Mountain and I ended up in the medical tent after stage one at Villiersdorp with severe dehydration. I required an intravenous drip for the first time in my entire life. Sandover was perfectly understanding: "For goodness sake Dalai Mottee, sit down and have a beer. No need to look so bloody miserable, mate, we are in Africa on holiday." The following day I was back in the medical tent, having a cut to my left knee dealt with after a somersault over the handlebars into rocks. Doctors joked about me buying a season ticket to their medical tent when I showed up the next day, too, to have a gash in my calf closed. Gee, Comrades was never like this.

I stayed upright thereafter but Sandover came down hard on the final day. No matter: he got going again and we finished in the top half of the field overall, not bad for one of the oldest teams in the event.

The Cape Epic numbed me in a way that no other physical challenge had. It was the toughest sporting event I had ever undertaken. It took me a while to recover and rediscover my zest for these multi-day mountain bike treks. In January 2010 I invited my partner that I had started dating in 2009, Zelinda Bafile, to Tasmania for a holiday. She knew she'd be doing some driving; what she didn't realise was that I'd be travelling the hard way, on a mountain bike in the Wildside four-day race. It was a great event through the rainforests, with a superb Tasmanian pinot noir to sooth the aches every night. I noticed another rider who performed a bit like me: good on endurance, less so on technical skills. He headed me by a few seconds on the first two days, but then fell and broke his arm. I spotted him in a sling and introduced myself. His name was Andrew Lloyd and he mentioned he had been a professional runner in his younger days.

The penny dropped. Lloyd had been involved in one of the closest finishes in Commonwealth Games history in the 1990 5,000m final. In a memorable sprint finish, he caught and passed Kenya's John Ngugi on the line. Ngugi was the Olympic champion two years previously in Seoul, and four times world cross country champion. Lloyd was the Australian counterpart of South Africa's Mr Versatile, Johnny Halberstadt, with bests of 3:56 for the mile, 62.54 for the half marathon and 2:14 for the marathon. I tried to interest Lloyd in the Comrades but he shrugged it off as too long, opting instead for trail running. He had a high regard for Charles Coville and the Sydney Striders. The magic of the sporting network.

In August 2010, aged 56, I won the M50+ age group in the Dwellingup 100km MTB event, but life soon demonstrated to me the fragile distinction between pleasure and pain in cycling. I was riding home from my midday Pilates session when a car turned in front of me and hit me head on. It was fortunate I was wearing the best helmet money could buy because I flew over the bonnet and landed head first on the concrete verge. The impact was huge and I feared I had lost my teeth. I was in agony from head to foot. It was the worst accident I have been involved in and it took me a long time for wrists, legs and neck to recover. The only visible sign I carry today is a scar below my left eye, but mentally I know I came close to paralysis or death.

There was still one challenge to conquer in mountain biking, however. Whenever a European rider in the Cape Epic learned I was from Australia, the question was always whether I had done the Crocodile Trophy. This race is a badge of honour in mountain biking, harder even than the Cape Epic because of the furnace-like climate, and longer, too – 933km over nine days, including 12,900m of climbing. How could I ignore it?

I struggled through it in November 2012 with only one minor fall, but what made it so hard was the heat, ranging from 43°C to 45°C. It was so extreme that I resorted to jumping into irrigation canals and creeks in full gear, including shoes, just to get some respite. I would get through about 10 litres of water daily and ate more food than my eyes could believe. At 58, I was the second oldest finisher but, believe me, I felt a whole lot older at the time.

Zelinda, to whom I had got engaged in Lisbon, Portugal, in 2011, met me for a recuperation holiday in Noosa, Queensland. I rested. I ate fresh food and I reflected. I realised I had learned as much in the previous four years about mountain biking as I had about the Comrades Marathon between 1982 and 1986. Both experiences were profound. The Comrades had given me the confidence and strength to sustain my career and pursue all my subsequent adventures.

Gazing across the Pacific Ocean, I realised that my dalliance with multi-day mountain bike races was over. I yearned for Italy where my love affair with cycling began. Riding at my own cadence through Tuscany, climbing the Dolomites at my own tempo, and descending with the angels through some of the most beautiful valleys and villages on earth.

I no longer needed a race number.

23

Goodbye to work

"No matter what you do in the rat race, success is not certain but if you do nothing, failure is."

– Paul Ulasien, author of *The Corporate Rat Race: The Rats are Winning*

The politically correct term in Australia is an accompanying person. The impolite term is a handbag, popularised by tabloid journalists to describe Tim Mathieson, partner of former Prime Minister Julia Gillard. Pick your preference: on 8 August 2011 I played the part when I partnered my fiancée Zelinda, Pro Vice-Chancellor of Perth's Curtin University, to a dinner in honour of US ambassador Jeffrey Bleich and former Australian Prime Minister Paul Keating. Earlier in the day, Bleich had delivered the annual John Curtin memorial lecture, and Keating was there as patron of the university library.

My father's interest in politics had rubbed off on to me so this was one of those once-in-a-lifetime dinners, particularly with only 10 around the table. Ambassador Bleich was very close to President Obama, with whom he had studied law before moving into Democratic politics. Keating remains to this day the most insightful Australian leader about the strategic relevance of South East Asia to Australia and for that matter the US.

The conversation was tantalisingly stimulating and honest but unfortunately, I cannot reveal what was said because it was off the record. However, when host, Professor Jeanette Hackett formally closed the dinner, I took the chance to thank Keating privately for an action he took which, nearly two decades later, had yielded a huge positive change to my life.

"Mr Keating," I ventured, "I am Robert de la Motte, an immigrant in 1987 and I wish to thank you for your vision in introducing compulsory superannuation in 1992."

I explained to him I had not always been a fan of his policies because, as a supporter of free markets, I did not like the idea of the government forcing me to make fixed contributions to my retirement fund. I felt I was best placed to decide that on my own.

He admitted that, as a politician, he spent all the political capital he had at his disposal to pursue his policies and therefore re-election. He considered compulsory superannuation contributions to be a vote winner as well as a sensible long-term strategy

"Well, I'm delighted you pushed it through," I admitted. "The system and the concessions generated by your policy made it possible for me to retire two years ago aged 55."

We both left smiling.

Keating had great vision and an extraordinary understanding of the economy despite the fact he did not go to university. Through the introduction of compulsory superannuation, Australia now enjoys one of the highest savings rates in the developed world. Between 2006 and 2010, Australia's gross national savings rate of 24% of GDP matched that of Germany, and was almost 20% ahead of both the OECD average and the G7 average. By 30 June 2013 the assets or savings accumulated within Australia's superannuation system amounted to a staggering $1.6 trillion, having increased by $35 billion in the quarter to 30 June 2013 alone. That is the Keating legacy.

Thus it came to pass that at lunchtime on 30 June 2009 I drove out of my parking bay in the basement of a building in the centre of Perth for the final time. Aged 55, I was voluntarily retiring from full-time work. Pulling the pin on the pinstripes. Heading for the sidelines or, rather, the beach.

My days of chasing deals and raising millions of dollars of equity for new investors and wealthy vendors had come to an end.

Every equity transaction over the preceding decade had required a matador-style performance, loaded with risk, adrenalin and hopefully, the thrill of successful execution. When the dust had settled, the reward lay in an acknowledgement from happy clients and a meaningful success fee for surviving another round of raising new equity without getting gouged. In reality, at least 80% of my effort every year was without reward, like fishing for marlin. You don't catch one every day and you may not even catch one for a year.

The mantra that resonated with many testosterone-fuelled investment bankers was you only eat what you kill. It is not for the faint-hearted. I was still fit, healthy, commercially astute, and well-connected in the Australian economy. I had a solid record of good deal origination and execution. There were many more deals to be done but I was happy to drive away into retirement.

In earlier years, I had stumbled across a passage from American author Joseph Campbell's *The Power of Myth*:

> People say that what we're all seeking is a meaning for life. I don't think that's what we're really seeking. I think what we're seeking is an experience of being alive, so that our life experiences on the purely physical plane will have some resonance within our own innermost being and reality, so that we actually feel the rapture of being alive. That's what it's finally all about.

I thought he was right on the money. As I emerged into sunshine and blue sky on an almost breathless mid-winter's day, I opted to drive home through Kings Park, my morning spiritual running territory of the past decade. I opened the sunroof, removed my tie, unfastened my top button and turned the volume up on the car stereo system. Grace Jones serenaded me up St Georges Terrace and through the great park on the hill above Perth into retirement with *La vie en rose*. Those passionate French lyrics rekindled great memories of my father, Frenchy.

Ten minutes later, I pulled up outside my home and reflected on my mother's constant reminder to count my blessings. In the greater scheme of life I was extraordinarily fortunate. Yes, I could make more money, a lot more, but how much do you need? When is enough ever enough?

When do you take charge of the rest of your life and shape it to your own desire, rather than let career and corporate status define who you are? I considered myself wealthy, way beyond financial independence. I harboured the energy and enthusiasm to explore the world, enjoy my family and regularly visit my ageing mother in Cape Town.

Financial independence had always been a desire of mine. After 22 years of full-time work in Perth and 13 years before that, mostly in South Africa, plus another six years of part-time work as student, I felt I had made enough of a contribution to my goal. I don't think I could have worked harder, but I didn't want to hang around and slowly rust. It is always better to leave the party when you are still having fun.

On reflection, my career successes mirrored my amateur sporting experiences in an uncanny way. When I expected to get a career break or convert a lucrative transaction, disappointment inevitably resulted through unexpected circumstances beyond my control. Yet I often made money and enjoyed career breaks when I least expected. Similarly, I had some big disappointments during my running when I felt I was heading for glory, interspersed with a few equally good surprises against red-hot competition. Without ambition you cannot succeed, and sometimes to succeed you need a little bit of luck. If you don't try, you will never know.

Following my separation from Vern and marriage break-up in 1993, I had experienced a relationship that was an unmitigated disaster. Occasionally, my daughters remind me of this. My luck changed. In 2000, I accompanied running mate Jim Langford and five other adventure seekers on a two-week trek through the immense and complex Kimberley wilderness, in the remote north-western Australian outback. I met Susan Vetten on this trek and shortly afterwards we started a relationship that continued for five years. Towards the end of 2000, as we were getting to know each other, Susan asked me an unexpected question: "Bob, do you really know what makes you happy in life, outside of your adrenalin-fuelled corporate career, and do you have any idea how much money you would need to sustain it?"

My answer was 'no', but my curiosity had been suitably stimulated; a timely wake-up call.

I was preoccupied for weeks afterwards trying to figure out the answer. Eventually, I started to develop a clearer picture of my ideal future and what was important, truly important, to me: my daughters; family and friends; my health and fitness; my enjoyment of outdoor adventure; my curiosity to see the world; artistic creativity through photography and writing; intellectual curiosity through reading and discussion; my interest in genealogy; and yes, a level of financial independence to fulfil these desires.

My life-plan had been reshaped. Now I needed to fund it. I engaged in some disciplined financial planning and investment over the next nine years that ultimately yielded the luxury of choice: the ability to design each day, week and month to my own taste and values. I had earned one of life's richest prizes, freedom. Admittedly, my freedom was not entirely consistent with German philosopher Immanuel Kant's view on happiness. He postulated three criteria: something to do, someone to love, and something to hope for. But in 2009, according to my mother, I had nothing to do as I no longer had an office job. I was also undeniably single (again) but, hey, I had much to hope for.

As I took off the sober suit that was my uniform in the corporate army, I reflected on the previous three decades I had spent in similar attire. I acknowledged that my decision to qualify as a chartered accountant was a good one, maybe my best, because it provided me with an internationally recognised status that enabled me to work on four continents before embarking on a corporate career. Getting a job with KPMG in Johannesburg was a stroke of luck that paid off with a partnership at the age of 28, and a dream run that lasted until I emigrated to Perth in 1987.

Man, those first two years in Australia were tough. The position I ended up in at Arthur Andersen was not the one on which I had based my decision to move to Perth, and I had to learn a new system of taxation and corporate law. The steep learning curve tested me but ultimately gave me the skills and knowledge that enabled me to transition from a major international accounting firm into a finance and treasury role at Challenge Bank; it absorbed me for six years. This passage of my career was like a stint at business school: I learned a lot about the banking sector and capital markets.

Shortly before the giant Westpac Bank swallowed Challenge, I made the move to Sealcorp Holdings in 1995. Sealcorp chief Graham Morgan had taken advantage of the burgeoning superannuation industry to deliver a financial product and advice service called Asgard. My banking experience paid off when I had a 'eureka' moment in the first year of my new position that quadrupled the value of the Sealcorp business to its shareholders. I shared my realisation with Morgan and other executives at a meeting in Sydney, that significant value would be unlocked if the business was owned by a bank. I felt that shares coughing along at $3 would be worth a minimum of $13. Morgan subsequently put the business up for sale. Good for them; mediocre for me, because I had no equity in the company. I decided then and there that my days of salaried employment were almost at an end and that in future I would back my own financial acumen to make a living. Like they say, no risk, no reward. I resigned and joined Hartleys Ltd in Perth as Director of Investment Banking, to be paid on what I delivered.

My exasperation at uncovering the golden nugget for Sealcorp, but not sharing in the reward, grew when St George Bank acquired the business for $272 million, equating to more than $20 per share. Morgan walked away with a huge slice of the spoils but his fellow shareholders weren't happy, and the matter was before the Supreme Court of Western Australia when an out-of-court settlement was reached. When serious wealth manifests itself, relationships are tested, often in the courts. I was to witness a lot more of this behaviour over the next decade in equity capital markets.

Investment banking has one focus: money. It permeates everything. It is an adrenalin-fuelled life with punishing hours when a transaction is underway, and uninhibited manoeuvring leading up to annual bonus time. Stand back and you get nothing. No matter how much you feel you are entitled to, you have to fight to get it. There are no guarantees in this particular game.

More often than not your hardest efforts go unrewarded. I recall our efforts as part of a consortium bidding for Perth Airport, when the government was privatising Australia's federal airports. I was based in Sydney, working around the clock for six months. I hardly had time to go for a jog during the process and was absolutely shredded by the time we finalised our bid. We came second and had nothing to show for our efforts. Zip. Zilch. Zero. I returned to Perth empty-handed.

Still, my 13-year stint in the Australian equity capital markets until my retirement in 2009 paid off for me. It was an interesting and turbulent period: the commercial evolution of the internet; the dotcom boom and bust; the World Trade Centre attack and subsequent global upheaval; China's economic emergence; and two Gulf wars. The Australian financial climate was influenced by the election of the Liberal (in reality, conservative) government of John Howard which presided over falling interest rates and a huge rise in domestic savings from superannuation, plus all the economic activity stimulated by the Sydney Olympics of 2000.

I experienced more letdowns like the Perth Airport bid, but also some successes like iiNet, an initial public offering, or IPO, that I listed on the Australian Stock Exchange. The founders of the fledgling company were two university mathematics students, Michael Malone and Michael O'Reilly. They started the business in 1993 in the garage of Malone's parents in Perth, like Steve Jobs of Apple, exploiting an opportunity presented by the internet before all but a few were connected. There were no barriers to entry in the early days and they sold internet connectivity to domestic customers in Perth via monthly subscription plans.

They had a foothold before dozens of internet service providers sprang up; iiNet's niche was to be more nimble than the monolithic Telstra which dominated the Australian telecommunications market. They steadily built their base among computer aficionados and reinvested their cash flow into iiNet. This is where I came onto the scene. They needed money to expand, but the banks would not lend them any because, frankly, banks did not yet understand internet companies.

The two Michaels were smart but had no capital behind them, and had derived little benefit from their strong cash flow and growing customer base. It had all been ploughed back into the business. The word among financial institutions was that the internet would ultimately be free and potential investors had no way to value a business such as iiNet. No one really knew what its life span would be.

319

In late 1997 O'Reilly wanted to cash in his shareholding because the stakes were being raised even higher without much tangible reward. Optus offered to buy iiNet for $5 million. Only a couple of years out of university, O'Reilly opted to sell. The person who bought him out was Malone, who believed he was onto a winner and was prepared to back his intuition.

I listed iiNet on the Australian Stock Exchange in 1999 as a junior internet service provider domiciled in Perth. Junior, because of the abundance of competition which had arisen around the world, such as Worldcom, the largest provider in the United States. On the day iiNet listed, it had a market capitalisation of about $30 million and the shares traded at $1.12. Advance the clock another 15 years and iiNet has prospered. Sure, shares hit a low of 20 cents during the dotcom bust, but it is now Australia's second-biggest provider, behind Telstra and ahead of Optus, with 1.7 million customers. It was trading above $7 in 2014, boasted a market capitalisation in excess of $1 billion, and had consistently made a profit and paid a dividend. Worldcom filed for bankruptcy in 2002, the magnitude of which eclipsed Enron as the biggest on record.

In 2012 the *Australian Financial Review* rated Malone as Australia's fourth most influential tech head, noting he embodied the garage geek who turned a good idea into megawealth. His reputation only grew when iiNet vanquished the collective muscle of Hollywood's biggest studios in a landmark piracy case against internet service providers. iiNet now employs about 2,000 creative thinkers in the tech industry. Not bad for a guy without a rich relative to sponsor his initial business foray. Malone's father was an Irish immigrant who worked as a fencing contractor in Perth and roped in Michael for labouring jobs during his school and university years. In March 2014 Malone voluntarily resigned from iiNet and handed over the reins to his successor in order to pursue his other passions in life. You have to respect the man.

I regarded my investment banking role as similar to that of a sports agent. Spot the talent ahead of the competition, fund it, and watch it develop and perform. Most of my ASX successes were Malone-type personalities who had the ambition and courage to pursue an opportunity, in the end making serious money personally, and also creating employment and wealth for others. That was the beauty of equity markets: a good idea coupled with a good business model had a chance of succeeding as long as the founder was not overcome by arrogance or the illusion of wealth that was not theirs.

I watched my fair share of companies that had a good fundamental product go bust through bad management. Consider the cases of Kodak and Anglo-American. Less than 20 years ago, Kodak was the fourth most valuable brand in the world behind Disney, Coca-Cola and Microsoft. It only recently emerged from bankruptcy. Sure, you argue, digital technology made photographic film redundant. Goodbye, Kodak. But it need not have come to this: Kodak invented the digital camera as far back as 1976 and a decade later, invented the first handheld digital camera. The problem was that management didn't know what to do with the new technology. They opted to stick with their core products and got trampled in the stampede to digital photography.

When I was growing up in South Africa, Anglo-American was the Goliath of mining companies, the world's biggest producer of gold and platinum. These days the Goliath is Glencore; it has a market capitalisation in the order of $80 billion, more than double that of Anglo. Glencore's major shareholder, Ivan Glasenberg, had a very modest net worth in the mid-1980s when we ran together most Saturday mornings, yet today he operates as the world's number one commodity trader, and one of the world's largest diversified mining corporations. His challenge is to remain relevant, profitable and smarter than his competitors; and to make the right calls on the relevant commodities at the right time. It's much, much harder than it appears.

I have also lived through some spectacular failures. When I was treasurer of Challenge Bank in 1993, I accompanied chief executive, Tony Howarth, on an international EuroBond road show. We had a meeting with Banca Monte dei Paschi, the world's oldest bank founded in Tuscany in 1472, to seek their participation in our $200-million EuroBond bond raising exercise. The meeting went well. The Italians were interested as we were forced to pay a higher yield than the AAA-rated banks because of our relatively weak credit rating. Over lunch, an impeccably polite executive chose to offer us some sage advice about prudent bank management, in the manner his company had operated for centuries. He subtly inferred we had much to learn.

I wonder if he was still a mover and shaker when Banca Monte dei Paschi subsequently decided to forego prudence and embarked on an acquisition orgy just in time to get clobbered by the global financial crisis. It took successive Italian government loans of $1.9 billion and $2 billion to Banca Monte dei Paschi to stave off a debt crisis. After 540 years in business, even the Banca Monte dei Paschi was not immune to hubris.

All the ups, downs and upside downs ensured I was seldom bored during my working years. I learned a lot. I loved recruiting and working with ambitious twenty-somethings who had energy and a challenging perspective, just as much as I valued the advice of the older generation who had seen it all before and were no longer playing politics in corporate structures. I may not have earned my Comrades green number or a Two Oceans blue number for 10 completions but I did manage to achieve Fellowship status with both the Institute of Chartered Accountants in Australia and the Australian Institute of Company Directors.

After 22 years of hard work in Australia (including 20 years as an Australian citizen), I attained financial independence and managed to retire at 55. I had worked darn hard and played equally hard. I would not have had it any other way. En route I met hundreds of individuals who offered me wisdom, support, advice, competition and friendship.

That was the reward of the day job.

But what about my family?

We all acquired Australian citizenship in 1989 and have never regretted that decision.

After our marriage breakup in 1993, Vern returned to university to study languages, majoring in Indonesian. She also completed a post-graduate diploma in education and, after a sabbatical in Indonesia, started teaching in Perth. She has been an attentive mother and active participant at all our extended family gatherings and celebrations. She has visited South Africa frequently since 1993, as have our daughters.

Nicole is a qualified architect and has spent her professional years designing major public buildings in Perth. She married her long-term partner, Jason Hick, and they have a daughter. They continue to travel extensively in pursuit of outdoor adventure. They live in Perth.

Simone graduated in Fine Art and did a post-graduate diploma in education before launching her teaching career in Perth. Her extensive international travels have encompassed everything from summer camp work in New York to community volunteer work in remote Fiji. After living and teaching in Brighton, UK, she returned to teaching in regional Western Australia where her partner, Balazs Markus, works as a pilot. They intend to relocate to Perth.

Philippa graduated in Science before commencing her career in the health sector, working for state government on health policy issues. She is married to Ashley Gifford, with two sons, and they live in Perth.

The consensus is that they left South Africa as proud young girls who had experienced a rich depth of affection and emotional support from their extended South African family. In addition, they had only experienced kindness from all South Africans. Theirs was a proud family history in South Africa and the loss of this emotional support structure was traumatic, especially after Vern and I divorced. The initial years in Perth were very tough years for our daughters.

Today South Africa is less relevant because they were so young when they left – only one grandparent is still alive. Although they arrived without any family heritage in Australia, they gradually assimilated and today Australia is their home; it's where they grew up. It's where we live, by choice. We are still an immigrant family, but we have all established a modest footprint in our community through personal effort and shared experiences.

Back in Perth, we currently enjoy watching the first Australian-born generation grow up. I have asked the grandkids to call me *oupa* because one of the kindest men I have ever known in my life was my grandfather, Johannes Liebenberg, my *oupa*.

We relish our freedom, a healthy democracy, an independent judiciary, a secure future, a great health system and a well-endowed education system, available to all. The next generation has untold opportunity to pursue whatever talent or passion it is that may excite them in their lives. Hopefully, we will continue to enjoy family rituals, milestones, birthdays and celebrations as an extended, and growing, Australian family – occasionally dancing to the beat of some cool African jazz.

That was the reward of emigrating to Australia.

24

Comrades crystal ball

Here is an awkward question for the Comrades Marathon organisers: how fair is it to exclude a runner who took 12 hours and two seconds to reach the finish line, after needing 10 minutes after the official 5.30am start to cross the starting line?

Admittedly, there is no greater sporting drama, no more riveting spectacle, than the final minute's 'gun rush' to beat the cut-off time. It is compelling viewing, on television or at the stadium. But it is still inherently unfair, and that's not what the Comrades is all about.

Tradition is one thing; common sense another. The time has come for the organisers to rethink their procedures and move into line with other major marathons around the world.

The rules in 2014 limited the number of participants to 18,000. In a mass start, the tail-enders surrender about 10 minutes before they cross the starting line, at which point the front-runners are steaming towards the 3km mark. So when the final gun is fired on the finish line at 5.30pm, exactly 12 hours after the start, hundreds of runners miss out on that elusive Comrades finisher's medal they should reasonably have achieved.

Most of the major marathons such as London, New York and Boston have split starts and separate groups who set off in waves behind the elite, seeded runners. This improves the efficiency of the start and assists with course congestion and aid station management. Times are also calculated using mat times as opposed to gun times.

Here's another difficult question for the organisers: why let the leading women benefit from male pacemakers? Again, most big-city marathons send off the elite women in advance of the men to eliminate arranged or inadvertent pacemaking. Without a doubt, men have assisted women in the Comrades, even if the leading women finish around the six-hour mark. There is significant prize money on offer, equal to the men, plus the added financial incentive and prestige in breaking a record. So why not make it a fairer competition and start the elite women 45 minutes ahead of their male counterparts?

It stands to reason an equitable contest should also be facilitated for the elite men, who need a clean start without the 'stampede of the anonymous', seeking a few moments of exposure on television by sprinting away at suicidal pace and creating unnecessary risks for the contenders. Seed the top 100, or even 200, men and release them 15 minutes ahead of the general field, which would start exactly one hour after the elite women.

And, hey, while we're on a roll, let's arrange a split start for the masses, to give everyone a fairer opportunity of making the time limit. Why should the Jardine blind runners have to start so far back? It simply isn't necessary for a huge horde to start simultaneously in the same street. And don't throw the tradition argument at me because the finishing points of both the up and down runs have been changed over the years to meet changing needs. In Durban alone, the race has finished outside the Town Hall, at Lords Ground, the Track Ground, Hoy Park, Kings Park, the Beach Pavillion, the Drill Hall, University of Natal, and Kingsmead.

The organisers put expedience ahead of tradition in extending the time limit from 11 to 12 hours to grow the race. Staggering the start is a logical progression.

The tradition that should be maintained ahead of all else is the course. There should be an over-riding commitment to sticking to the old Durban road for as much of the route as possible. Boston has done this most successfully. The up run would not be the same without Field's Hill, Botha's Hill, Inchanga, Little Pollys and Polly Shorts. All despised, cursed and rued on the day by every competitor, but essential elements of the Comrades menu.

Likewise, the down run means the dawn descent of Polly Shorts, the ululating Zulus at Inchanga Mission, the festival atmosphere of the halfway mark at Drummond, the run under the tree-lined, schoolboy-lined road outside Kearsney College, the crowds of Hillcrest and Pinetown before the final indignity to the thighs of the ascents of Cowies Hill, 45th Cutting and Tollgate.

The traffic authorities and the hordes of volunteers make this happen remarkably well, but it is the intangible electricity that spectators bring to Comrades that makes it special. The event needs to remain relevant and accessible to the hundreds of thousands, if not a million-plus, energetic, eccentric spectators who provide that extra bit of magic. Any loss of spectator support would be the death knell of Comrades.

Young South Africans are no different to their peers internationally. They are adventure seekers and they want variety; well-organised variety. At any moment a dozen fit young people – for the past 50 years the prime Comrades demographic – could be cruising the internet and asking themselves: "Should I run Paris, Boston or London … or New York? Should I do the Half Iron Man in Zurich or in Pucon, Chile? Should I cycle the Pyrenees or the Dolomites? Should I climb Kilimanjaro, Mont Blanc or hike Everest Base Camp?"

To continue to lasso this group, the Comrades organisers should consider co-branding with other events, domestically or internationally. For example, a major African ultra series comprising Comrades, the 56km Two Oceans in Cape Town and the 50km City2City event in Johannesburg, along similar lines to the World Marathon Majors. This series was launched in 2006 by the Boston, London, Berlin, Chicago and New York City Marathons, offering a $1 million prize purse to be split equally between the top male and female marathoners in the world.

In creating the World Marathon Majors, the organisers of the five races recognised an opportunity to advance the sport, raise awareness of athletes and increase the level of interest in elite racing among running enthusiasts. Tokyo joined as the sixth city marathon in 2013. Collectively, the group annually attracts more than five million on-course spectators, more than 250 million television viewers, 300,000 applicants and 150,000 participants. It also raises more than $80 million for charity worldwide and, according to its website, generates an economic impact of more than $400 million.

A local series, or a link to international ultras like the Marathon des Sables, would help forestall a threat to television coverage in this era of variety. Comrades would suffer badly if television coverage was reduced or deemed to have lost commercial value.

A special medal could be struck for runners completing all three ultras within a 12-month cycle, and a ranking system introduced, similar to that of tennis and golf. And, borrowing from Wimbledon, a Podium Club could be initiated, admitting the top three men and women finishers into a legacy group that remains connected to the events.

Another special medal ought to be struck in honour of the Comrades equivalent of Roger Bannister. Alan Robb was the first runner to complete the Comrades in less than five and a half hours in 1978. Yes, it ranks up there with a sub-4 minute mile and even more astonishingly, Robb achieved this as an amateur. It is still a remarkable Comrades benchmark and why shouldn't the Comrades recognise those few runners in the same fashion that the Wally Hayward medal acknowledges runners who finish outside of the top ten but still finish in less than six hours?

There is ample scope for the Comrades Marathon tradition to be further enriched through ongoing association with as many of the great characters and legends of the event as possible. Comrades and the South African nation are still indebted to the amazing black runners who were the first to participate, doing so with extraordinary dignity in the face of oppression. They need to be remembered beyond a mere museum photograph and an amusing anecdote. They played their part in uplifting the Comrades into all South African homes, yet most are no better off than if they had boycotted Comrades and stayed at home until Mandela was released. The pioneering Vincent Gabashane Rakabaele, for example, died a pauper in the mountains of Lesotho in 2003 from an unknown illness. Tragically and quite inexplicably, Rakabaele had simply vanished from the running fraternity and it was not until 2009 that his death was confirmed through the forensic efforts of journalist Duane Heath.

During the apartheid years of the 1970s and 80s, and the rainbow nation period that followed, the Comrades Marathon provided the nation with a dignified public event to display its true character. In years ahead, the issues are likely to again be political, this time directed at corruption and wealth inequalities.

Finally, there is the vexing issue of drugs. Until the 1990s, the drug-testing procedures adopted at Comrades were rudimentary if, and when, they happened to be applied. I know from personal experience. In my four competitive runs in which I finished 16th and runner-up on three occasions, I was tested once. Yes, once, in 1986 when I pushed Fordyce to a record 5:24. My time of 5:26 also dipped under the previous record. A urine sample was taken and that was it. No blood tests – and there was certainly no out-of-competition testing.

Historically, event organisers have used the façade of strict doping controls to reassure fans and sponsors that cheats would be caught. During the Sydney Olympics in 2000, we were assured that EPO was being tested for, and that significantly more tests were being conducted than at previous Games. IOC president, Juan Antonio Samaranch, declared Sydney the cleanest Games in the history of the Olympics. We now know that wasn't true. The fact is the public utterances on the subject are designed to create a reassuring illusion.

The Comrades' organisers are doing their best with limited resources. In recent years, the prizes were not distributed until the results of the dope tests were known, but the sad truth is that the chemists will stay a step ahead of the testers, as they always have done.

I would like to see biological passports for all Comrades runners who wish to claim a record, or a prize or significant position in any category, with extensive out-of-competition testing. Samples should be retained beyond a decade, to be retested in line with enhanced analytical testing procedures. Prize monies, likewise, should be paid into trust funds and distributed to athletes via an annuity stream in the years following the big win. Prizes have been so large in recent times as to encourage athletes to adopt a rob-the-bank approach to sport.

This gives rise to the obvious question: has Comrades been subject to cheating as deceptively successful over time as, say, that undertaken by Lance Armstrong? No one will know for sure, other than the possible perpetrators, but we can at least examine the statistics for anomalies.

True, conditions vary between events but a 20-year period should provide a meaningful set of data. The world best for the standard marathon offers similar confirming trends, enabling predictions of when and by how much the next record is likely to be broken.

I have taken a starting point of 1985, when South Africa was isolated from international competition, but when domestic standards were regarded as being internationally competitive. Benchmarking the improvements in Comrades performance against the world record progression in the standard marathon produces the following observations:

The world standard marathon record for men was bettered five times, improving by 1.8% over 20 years. By comparison, the Comrades up record improved by a modest 1.41% and the down record by just 0.97% over the same period.

The women's standard marathon mark record was bettered seven times, and improved 6.24%. This is understandable because women were late starters in the world of marathon running and improving relatively faster than men who had been racing for the best part of a century.

The Comrades women's race is far more fascinating. The up record was lowered twice and improved by 7.96%, not entirely out of line with the standard marathon benchmark. The down record was improved once only, in 1989 by Frith van der Merwe, but it was a 12.76% improvement, more than twice the international benchmark. Over a quarter of a century later, this still stands as the down record.

Another interesting angle is the longevity of records and dominant runners around this era.

The longest standing women's records are:

1. +25 years Van der Merwe – 1989 – 5.54.43* – down
2. 10 years Trason – 1996 – 6.12.23 – up
3. 8 years Van der Merwe – 1988 – 6.32.56 – up
4. +8 years E Nurgalieva – 2006 – 6.09.24* – up
5. 7 years Roche-Kelly – 1981 – 6.44.35 – up
6. The dominant men's records are:
7. 21 years Fordyce – 1986 – 5.24.07 – down
8. 10 years Fordyce – 1988 – 5.27.42 – up
9. 8 years Kotov – 2000 – 5.25.32 – up

10. +7 years Shvetsov – 2007 – 5.20.41* – down
11. +6 years Shvetsov – 2008 – 5.24.47* – up
12. 6 years Robb – 1978 – 5.29.14 – down
* denotes record holder at time of publication

In a country that has been rocked by racial segregation, enduring civil unrest, two world wars, the imprisonment and release of Nelson Mandela, and the faith in a fresh democratic ANC government followed by disenchantment with a corrupt ANC government, the Comrades Marathon remains a beacon of hope. South Africans today are as tough, resilient and robust as always, to the point that many outsiders view the country as a hardened society still littered with social inequality.

Be that as it may. On Comrades day, the nation cheers as one. It is a friendly cheer, an emotional cheer, a spiritual cheer and a hopeful cheer. It does not matter that the last white South African won in 1997 or that foreign runners have made their mark: the interest and participation in Comrades continues to be stratospheric in the republic. Race day remains the one day of the year when all South Africans take time out to reveal their true dignity and to applaud and support every single participant who has plucked up the courage to take on the almighty challenge of the Comrades Marathon.

I will never forget my first Comrades experience on 31 May 1981.

It changed my life.

Call back the past 6

No democracy can survive or flourish if the mass of our people remain in poverty, without land, without tangible prospects for a better life.

– South Africa's Reconstruction and Development Programme (RDP) 1994

In November 1993 I visited South Africa for the first time since emigrating to Australia. A lot had happened during those six years. Not quite knowing what to expect added to the in-flight adrenalin about travelling to Africa, in anticipation of some unknown excitement and a palpable beat of life.

When I left Johannesburg for Perth with my family in 1987, sanctions had severely restricted air travel for South Africans, forcing us to travel first to Harare in Zimbabwe to catch a Qantas flight because the Australian airline refused to land at what was then Jan Smuts Airport in Johannesburg. Yet, six years on, I was winging my way directly to Johannesburg with daughter Nicole, 15, to visit a new South Africa just five months away from its first democratic elections. Although apartheid-era FW de Klerk was still the elected President, the majority of South Africans and the world looked to Nelson Mandela as the de facto leader. His legitimacy would be confirmed at the general election scheduled for 27 April 1994. Already a nationwide competition was underway for the design of a new national flag. Overnight, South Africa had become the Rainbow Nation.

We felt the energy of an excited African nation as soon as we disembarked our aircraft. The display boards for arrivals and departures reflected destinations all over Africa, Asia, Europe and America. South

Africa was no longer the untouchable pariah – the place was buzzing and exuded a newfound optimism. It had everything to look forward to.

I felt like the Prodigal Son returning after being in exile for six years. It was a joyous reunion. In every direction, there was a sea of smiling black faces that would ululate and break into dance at the mere hint of a rhythm. There was a genuine joy in the black faces that welcomed me in 1993 as opposed to the repressed, resentful, angry scowls I had left behind six years previously.

The media was free of the draconian censorship imposed by the Nationalist regime and there was an enormous amount of good news in the pipeline. Massive housing and education projects, and improved employment prospects prevailed in an optimistic environment in which all South Africans enjoyed freedom of movement for the first time. Foreign governments and global investment banks were lining up for the billion-dollar deals anticipated following Mandela's inauguration. The global economy wanted to deal with Mandela to secure some of the action and participate in the rehabilitation of a nation.

Former US President Bill Clinton once said: "It's a terrible burden oppressing someone else; it's like being in chains yourself." The new South Africa that I experienced in November 1993 was an unchained nation, filled with hope, pride and a dignified respect for Mandela.

Sports crazy South Africa was also smiling, having returned to the Olympic family in Barcelona in 1992, albeit under the neutral flag of the International Olympics Committee, and had resumed playing Test rugby and cricket. Although the Springbok rugby team was battling to regain its competitiveness after years of isolation, progress was rapid and the nation had earned the privilege of hosting the 1995 Rugby World Cup. The cricket team, renamed the Proteas, re-joined world cricket at a one-day international against India at Calcutta in November 1991. The team many South Africans followed with passion, the predominantly black Bafana Bafana national football team, had designs on qualifying for the World Cup. Good things were happening quickly and a sense of optimism pervaded sports officials and competitors alike.

Indeed, optimism and opportunism flared across the nation like a bush fire. Just two months before my visit, Mandela had addressed the

United Nations to call for all sanctions against South Africa to be lifted and a month later was awarded the Nobel peace prize together with FW de Klerk. Embassies opened in Pretoria, reflecting the nations who had opposed the old white regime and supported the ANC. When I was living in South Africa, it would have been unthinkable for countries like Russia, China and Libya to have an official presence in South Africa. Their diplomatic arrival happened in a blink.

All in all, my encounter with the new South Africa in that extraordinary spring of 1993 was eye popping. The changes that had occurred since my 1987 chicken run to Australia were hard to comprehend. Over the next few days, my father's deep interest and insight into politics, plus the easing of media censorship, gave me some understanding of the extraordinary forces that had been at play during my absence.

The cost of apartheid was a major contributor to its ultimate demise. Trade sanctions had devastated the economy and the cost of circumventing the international trade boycott had increased South Africa's price of crude oil by $2 billion annually for more than a decade. There was minimal foreign investment and no access to foreign capital or debt. South Africa's export markets had increasingly been shut down. The Nationalists had simply run out of both money and international customers – by 1990 South Africa was broke, its coffers had been depleted by propping up apartheid.

Only five years earlier, (then) President PW Botha and his *bittereinders* (bitter-enders) were armed to the teeth and preparing for a fight. They thought that if the Afrikaner nation was going down, they would take everyone and everything else down as well. That's why the Nationalists had developed, with Israel, the ultimate deterrent to those who would topple their regime: a nuclear bomb.

The extent and intent of South Africa's nuclear programme was confirmed in a parliamentary speech by President FW de Klerk in 1993. He revealed that the Nationalist government's fear of isolation and communism led to the start of a weapons programme in 1974, which yielded six crude nuclear bombs. Work was progressing on a seventh at the Pelindaba nuclear facility west of Pretoria when De Klerk came to power in 1989 and dismantled the arsenal.

Each of the completed bombs was 1.8m long, 65cm in diameter and weighed about a ton, of which 55kg comprised weapons-grade uranium with a calculated yield of between 10 and 18 kilotons. The weapons were originally designed to be dropped by the ageing Buccaneer bomber, but were adapted for use on the RSA-3 missile, based on Israel's Jericho intercontinental ballistic missile.

Whether South Africa detonated a nuclear bomb in testing has never been officially confirmed. Two shafts were sunk in the Kalahari desert, north of the town of Upington, for a test in late 1977. An overflight by a Lockheed SR-71 Blackbird spy plane confirmed to US intelligence analysts that the site was being prepared for a preliminary, or cold, test, and international pressure was brought to bear to call it off. However, mystery surrounds the detection by a US Vela satellite of a double flash over a remote part of the South Atlantic in September 1979. A double flash is a signature of a nuclear blast and evidence, albeit unsubstantiated, points to a joint South African–Israeli test.

What is known is that the South African navy was conducting unspecified manoeuvres in the area of Prince Edward Island at the time and the Simon's Town Naval Dockyard was closed to the public from 17–23 September 1979. Key reports from US intelligence and the South African Navy which would shed light on the matter remain classified more than three decades later. It seems we are destined never to know.

Nuclear bombs aside, the apartheid hardliners cared little about collateral damage. In 1987 the Johannesburg high-rise headquarters of South Africa's main trade union organisation, COSATU, were inexplicably destroyed by an almighty powerful bomb. A year later, the South African Council of Churches offices at Khotso (Peace) House and the headquarters of the South African Catholic Bishops Conference, Khanya House, were virtually destroyed. It subsequently emerged PW Botha was involved in the first and FW de Klerk had knowledge of the second of these attacks against these religious groups.

Nationalist terrorism was demonically evil. In 1989, the Indicator Project of South Africa released a report on political unrest over the four years between 1984 and 1988 that indicated more than 3,500 dead and 55,000 injured or imprisoned. The Johannesburg-based Human Rights

Commission listed 113 attacks on anti-apartheid groups and individuals. At the end of 1989, the number of arrests of the perpetrators of these atrocities stood at ... nil.

Despite the political repression, labour solidarity prevailed and was devastatingly effective. More than a million black workers had participated in a nationwide stay-away from 6 to 8 June 1988 to protest against apartheid, and again on 16 June to mark the 12th anniversary of the Soweto uprising. And that was just one month's worth of labour movement muscle-flexing. South Africa's economy was being choked from inside and outside.

The beginning of the end for one of the most reviled political regimes of the second half of the 20th century was initiated by something so tiny it can be measured in microns. A brain blood vessel ruptured, inflicting a stroke on the irascible, bellicose PW Botha, allowing the more moderate FW de Klerk to accede to the leadership in September 1989. De Klerk had reluctantly accepted that his fellow conservatives could not cling to power indefinitely. He read the writing on the wall and heard the clamour for change beyond it.

Not all were as pragmatic. Bitter-enders had deserted the Nationalist reformers in such numbers that the ultra-right wing Conservative Party had become the official opposition, replacing the liberal groups which had merged into the Democratic Party. Even though De Klerk collected a share of the Nobel peace prize, his government remained duplicitous. My father outlined how, at first, they covertly engaged with Mandela and the ANC, releasing political detainees and openly participating in conciliation talks. Simultaneously, sinister government-sponsored para-militaries, like the CCB, were inciting factional violence to try to destabilise the situation. My father was convinced that De Klerk's clandestine support of Chief Buthelezi's Inkatha party was purely to weaken and discredit the ANC in the eyes of white South Africans.

The black-on-black bloodletting that followed was unprecedented. In 1992 the Black Sash estimated 11,000 deaths had occurred through political violence since 1986. On 17 June 1992 armed attackers shot and hacked their way through the black township of Boipatong outside Vereeniging, leaving more than 40 dead. Witnesses stated the atrocity was the work of workers from a nearby migrant-worker hostel. Four days later, Mandela announced he was suspending talks with the Nationalist government. He and the ANC leadership were not going to be bludgeoned into negotiations.

Six weeks later, the ANC and its allies led millions of workers on a nation-wide general strike to demand a multi-racial interim government by the end of 1992, and effective steps to halt violence. Mandela personally led more than 50,000 supporters to the seat of government at the Union Buildings on a hill above Pretoria. He emphasised that the aim of the protest was not insurrection but the peaceful removal of President FW de Klerk from power.

De Klerk also had challenges from within the white South African community. On 10 April 1993 Chris Hani was assassinated in broad daylight outside his Boksburg home. Hani was general secretary of the South African Communist Party and one of the most popular black political leaders since his return from exile. As the news spread, South Africa exploded into rage. My father described how the panic amongst whites was as palpable as the anger amongst blacks. The nation was on the brink.

It took an astounding display of leadership from Mandela, and a lucky break with a witness to the crime, to stop a blood bath. Mandela, on his own initiative, rushed some 600km from his home village of Qunu in the Eastern Cape to Johannesburg to broadcast a message on national television that same evening. Mandela effectively stepped into the spotlight as the embodiment of South Africa's future leader. Had the witness, Margarita Harmse, not assiduously noted the assassin's motor vehicle registration, South Africa would be a very different and less peaceful place today.

Three members of the Conservative Party were subsequently charged with Hani's murder: Clive Derby-Lewis, a former Member of Parliament and the Presidential Advisory Council, his Australian-born wife Gaye, and Polish immigrant, Janusz Walus. There was still no relenting on the part of the crazy ultra-conservatives. Days later, former South African military and police commanders met to form a Committee of Generals to resist Pretoria's anticipated handover to majority black rule. The deluded diehards had not yet given up on a military coup.

During my November 1993 visit, South Africa's destiny lay in the hands of Mandela's political nous and brinkmanship. Both Mandela and South Africa were in uncharted territory. The election date had been set, and the nation awaited the transition to majority rule.

As good a job as the ANC leadership was doing to keep the volcano from erupting, decades in exile or prison had not prepared them fully for the realities of power. Politically they may have been astutely aware of their clout; yet economically it subsequently transpired they were extremely naïve and allowed the Nationalists to engineer the most brazen financial deal of the apartheid era.

Firstly, the ANC government-in-waiting agreed to do the right thing morally – it assumed the $30 billion debt accumulated by the apartheid regime even though the black population had received minimal benefit, if any, from the Nationalist's apartheid spending. Unwisely, the ANC did not seek or request any debt forgiveness, domestically or internationally. If ever the ANC government had an opportunity to request the support of global debt markets it should have been right up front at the time of assuming government, before reputations were tarnished.

But the most astonishing financial ANC concession was to agree to alter the Nationalist government's pension fund from a pay-as-you-earn-type fund to a fully funded scheme. Instantly, this guaranteed the payment of pensions (and double retirement benefits) to white Nationalist politicians and civil servants who, to my mind, should not have received any benefit beyond their own personal savings for retirement. This subtle concession had devastating financial consequences that the public would never really comprehend. The assets of the white government pension fund increased from $3 billion in 1989 to $13.6 billion in 1996. The retiring Nationalist politicians left office on the back of a $10 billion golden calf. A financially naïve ANC government was saddled with $30 billion worth of debt and an extra $10 billion in pension costs.

Those few days in South Africa in November 1993 were an eye-opener for me. I had only been away from South Africa for six years, having left at a time when 82% of whites who voted in 1987 had consciously voted in favour of maintaining the apartheid status quo. Wow! My family and friends had given me a good insight into the developments, and it took me back to my days as a full-time student at Wits University where we would sprawl on the lawn outside the Old Library and discuss anti-apartheid and anti-government politics. I was spellbound. The sheer magnitude and speed of political shifts that had happened in South Africa during my short absence seemed absolutely unbelievable. Despite the blue Highveld skies, wood-fuelled *braais* and cold Castle Lagers, I had returned to a birthplace I could barely recognise. The political climate in South Africa simply oozed optimism and mutual respect. It seemed like everyone had something to look forward to as the nation anticipated its first democratic general election on 27 April 1994.

After this vibrant and highly informative four-day family reunion, I was filled with hope, a hope I did not possess six years earlier. It was a genuine hope, something I always thought South Africa was capable of achieving. I had learnt a lot. I flew home to Perth with my eyes wide open. I was still in disbelief about the miraculous advances in South Africa. The country had extraordinary resilience and capacity for change.

I was back in South Africa sooner than I expected. On 2 September 1994 my mother phoned to tell me my father had passed away at home, suddenly and unexpectedly. Within 24 hours I was airborne, en route to Johannesburg, experiencing the grief that any son might experience at the death of his father. There was so much I still wished to discuss with my father about his youth and wartime experiences, but that would never happen. I could only imagine how he must have enjoyed the election – witnessing the displacement of Nationalist politicians by members of Mandela's ANC government. For the first time since 1948, when DF Malan and his pro-Nazi cronies had won government, South Africa was finally a free, democratic nation.

Despite the sadness around my father's death, the stories about the election were simply ethereal with not a single reported incident of violence. Black South Africans had been accorded their vote and they voted with dignity. Only a few months earlier, African melodies had spontaneously erupted in Parliament when South Africa's new constitution had been adopted. Long-suffering black South Africans appeared to embrace the dreams of Mandela's life and his values.

The successful ANC election campaign slogan had been: "Vote for jobs, peace and freedom." The party committed to a Reconstruction and Development Programme (RDP) to improve the nation's quality of life. Friendly nations and global investment banks had billions of dollars in the South African pipeline and everyone wanted some part of the action. The ANC had received 62.6 % of votes and Mandela had been inaugurated with an overwhelming majority. South Africa was open for business.

I still retained a broad cross-section of friends and contacts in South Africa; all shared a healthy sense of optimism and confidence. Mandela's compassion and leadership had earned him an aura of respect amongst the vast majority of South Africans I encountered. The nation had come to realise that Madiba was a global statesman and could deal with any world leader from a position of dignity and strength that made all South Africans mightily proud for the first time in decades. His stature had assisted South Africa in gaining the right to host the Rugby World Cup in 1995, and that was just one of many exciting items on the Rainbow Nation's agenda. South Africa would also bid for the Olympics and capture the biggest prize of the lot, the FIFA World Cup in 2010. The emergence of black political leaders and entrepreneurs, including many who had been living in exile for decades, added to the buzz. They were unknown faces and personalities.

After laying Frenchy to rest and spending a week with my family, I flew back to Perth with a growing sense of optimism about South Africa. There were so many deserving causes and so much opportunity, a part of me wished I could return and assist with the rebuilding of South Africa. Another part of me, however, acknowledged my paternal obligations and responsibilities to three daughters in Australia, and to my business career. For the first time since my anger-filled departure from South Africa in 1987, I anticipated returning to South Africa in future years as an ex-pat visitor.

Indeed, I happily took the chance to stop over in South Africa on the way back to Perth from a business trip to London in late 1994. My mother was in the process of moving to Cape Town and it was a timely family catch-up. The glowing, growing nation I had experienced months earlier had seemingly gone from strength to strength. Many whites felt 'life as it was' had not changed under the ANC government – it may have even improved without the Nationalists. Many black South Africans believed their lot would soon change for the better in terms of jobs, education, housing and health. It was a brief visit but it conveyed a sense of contentment amongst the majority of South Africans.

The nation was hard at work.

25

Boomerang Bob

I regularly returned to South Africa over the ensuing years, for business, family reunions and holidays. In 1995, Mandela announced that he would not stand for re-election in 1999 but that hardly altered the political landscape. After polling 62.6 % in the 1994 election, the ANC polled 66.4 % in 1999 and 69.7 % in 2004. New president Thabo Mbeki had done as well as Mandela. The ANC was running South Africa with a resounding majority. From my visits and perspective on the other side of the Indian Ocean in Western Australia it all seemed good. South African associates, friends and family would bemoan the largesse of the indulgent ANC parliamentarians, and how they were only hiring ANC insiders to the civil service. It seemed the ANC had learned the technique from the Nationalists who had done exactly that for 45 years.

My faith in the ANC was first tested after media reports in 2000 and 2001 detailed corruption in awarding contracts around a 1999 defence contract worth $5 billion. Jacob Zuma, Thabo Mbeki and the late Joe Modise were all mentioned. I was bewildered as to how the ANC government could prioritise such a monumental defence spend above critical housing, jobs, health and education requirements in impoverished black communities. Why on earth would the ANC wish to purchase 28 Gripen fighter aircraft from Sweden, as well as state-of-the-art corvettes and submarines? Who was the newfound enemy of the state? Andrew Feinstein, former ANC leader of parliamentary public accounts watchdog

Scopa, resigned when the government moved to curtail investigations into the arms deal. He wrote a book *After the Party,* giving an insider's view of the process. British and German investigators suspected that bribes of more than $500 million had been paid to facilitate the deal. Unbelievably, the ANC had commenced replicating the crooked deals of the Nationalist government with unproductive military expenditures. Those notorious intermediaries, or arms dealers, must have presented the naïve ANC government with compelling proposals of instant personal fortunes at a time when, for the first time in its history, South Africa did not have an enemy on the surface of the earth.

Meanwhile, I continued to boomerang between Australia and South Africa, taking a keen interest in business and political developments. In February 2001 I visited South Africa in a commercial capacity, seeking out opportunities for cross-border investment and trade. This was a natural extension of the work I had been involved with in setting up the Australia Southern Africa Business Council following the release of Mandela in 1990. Bilateral trade between South Africa and Australia was virtually nil in 1990 because of trade sanctions. By 2012, two-way trade between South Africa and Australia was worth $2.4 billion. In the space of a week, I attended 16 one-on-one meetings with some of South Africa's most senior business leaders. The business community was bullish about South Africa's opportunity to emerge as the strong economic hub of Africa, facilitating trade in South Africa and with as many other African states as possible.

Business leaders were also positive about the ANC government and firmly committed to the Black Economic Empowerment (BEE) requirement to continue doing business in South Africa. The ANC advocated that BEE policy was aimed at levelling the economic playing field that had been distorted by decades of apartheid economics that favoured whites. Black South Africans soon saw the upside of participating in BEE opportunities, a crude approach to the redistribution of wealth that favoured but a few. Oligarchs would soon emerge in South Africa in much the same way they had surfaced in China and Russia.

Former black trade unionist turned ANC parliamentarian Cyril Ramaphosa elected to leave Parliament in 1996 in pursuit of legitimate commercial opportunities. He had been the only real challenger to Thabo Mbeki to succeed Nelson Mandela as president. Ramaphosa would soon emerge as one of South Africa's new oligarchs, a black billionaire. In the general election of 2014 he was appointed deputy president of South Africa.

I was enjoying my dialogue with the new South Africa and ventured a little further in 2002 as one of 5,200 starters in the Two Oceans 21.1km support event. Lining up on Main Road in Cape Town's Rondebosch, on the slopes of Table Mountain, with thousands of proud black South Africans around me singing *Shosholoza* in those final pre-dawn minutes before the starter's gun was fired sent a tingle down my spine. I had not competed in South Africa for 15 years – it was impossible to feel happier about what I was witnessing. It was an indescribable experience.

My personal and commercial involvement continued with South Africa but the news out of my former country was increasingly bittersweet. Great accomplishments like securing the FIFA World Cup for 2010 were always countered by the steady stream of revelations from the Truth and Reconciliation Commission relating to the atrocities of the grotesque apartheid regime, and the creeping accusations of corruption and incompetence against the ANC government. Many within the ANC fobbed off such speculation as vitriolic jealousy and racist attitudes going back to the apartheid era.

In 2004 I enjoyed an Easter holiday in South Africa and, as a 50-year-old, competed in my first (and last) Two Oceans ultramarathon. A few days later, I hiked up majestic Table Mountain and gazed at Robben Island, visited the vineyards of Franschhoek, spent a few days in Plettenberg Bay, and visited family in Johannesburg. I was overwhelmingly impressed by what I had seen and experienced, despite the visible growth in squatter camps and informal settlements around Khayelitsha, near Cape Town airport and those on the outskirts of Plettenberg Bay, Johannesburg and Germiston. Khayelitsha was reputedly the largest, fastest growing shantytown in South Africa. Understandably, the ANC government was dealing with a 45-year housing backlog and it would not be redressed overnight. On the positive side, there was no evidence of the factional violence that the Nationalist regime's CCB had sponsored so demonically in its final years of apartheid rule. The old National Party that had morphed into the New National Party (NNP), post democracy, did something totally inconceivable despite the party's track record, for decades, of sanctioning behaviour no fair minded human being could ever contemplate. In August 2004 the NNP announced its dissolution and simultaneous merger with the ruling ANC by individual NNP members. Whoever said pigs can't fly?

In 2005 I returned to South Africa for another round of business meetings, soliciting cross-border investment. I had secured meetings with a number of senior business leaders including former South African ambassador to Australia Zolile Magugu who had quit politics in pursuit of a commercial career alongside Cyril Ramaphosa. My South African business education continued as I learned how deals could be secured with new order mineral rights, as opposed to apartheid mineral rights as they existed under the Nationalists. Considerable cross-border business was being done in coal, diamonds, platinum and nickel. Shortly after my trip, South African mining boss Brett Kebble was assassinated. The subsequent prosecution of his assassins, who claimed the murder was "assisted suicide", revealed South Africa's new underworld of organised criminals, corrupt cops, power, money and greed.

Back in Australia, I followed South Africa's presidential snakes and ladders game which had, as its prize, the right to rule the biggest economy in sub-Saharan Africa and the continent's only member of the G20 group of influential countries.

In June 2005 President Mbeki removed Zuma from his post as deputy president following the conviction of Zuma's financial adviser, Schabir Shaik, for corruption and fraud related to the $5 billion arms deal by the ANC government in 1999. The Durban High Court had found Shaik guilty of corruption for paying Zuma $250,000 to further their relationship and for soliciting a bribe from French arms company Thomson-CSF. In addition, he was found guilty of fraud for writing off more than $200,000 of Zuma's unpaid debts. KPMG acted as the State's forensic auditors in Shaik's trial. Judge Hilary Squires sentenced Shaik to two terms of 15 years for corruption. Shaik appealed, unsuccessfully. Judge Squires also alluded to the risks of systemic corruption within government.

Zuma was charged with corruption as a result of Shaik's conviction and subsequently resigned as a member of parliament but remained deputy-president of the ANC. In December 2005 he was also charged with rape in the Johannesburg High Court. The accuser was known by Zuma to be HIV-positive at the time of the alleged rape. Throughout the trial, Zuma joined his crowd of supporters in singing *Awuleyhu mshini wani* (Bring my machine gun). Both the ANC Youth League and Communist Party Youth League spoke in support of him. The trial generated political controversy when he admitted he had not used a condom despite knowing his accuser was HIV-positive. He stated in court he took a shower to try to reduce the risk of infection. At the time he headed South Africa's National AIDS Council.

In May 2006 the court found Zuma not guilty of the charge of rape, which increased his standing among the rank and file. Six months later, Mbeki lost the ANC presidential contest to Zuma, who was in pole position to take over the South African leadership when his rival's term expired. That is, until the National Prosecuting Authority served Zuma with an indictment to stand trial in the High Court on various counts of racketeering, money laundering, corruption and fraud. A conviction and a sentence to a term of imprisonment of more than a year would have rendered Zuma ineligible for the 2009 general election and squashed his hopes of serving as president of South Africa.

Zuma appeared in court in August 2008. A month later, Judge Chris Nicholson ruled Zuma's corruption charges were unlawful on procedural grounds. In this context, Mbeki's position was untenable and he resigned. New ANC president Zuma, who was not a member of parliament at the time, appointed his deputy, Kgalema Motlanthe, as acting president until the 2009 general elections. Mbeki tried his best to regain lost ground and appealed Judge Nicholson's ruling. In January 2009 Judge Harms of the Supreme Court of Appeal ruled that Judge Nicholson's ruling on procedural grounds was incorrect and that he had overstepped his authority with inferences of political meddling by Mbeki.

Too late. Zuma was now entrenched in power as the new South African president. The ANC had polled 65.9% of votes cast. In April 2009 all charges against Zuma were dropped on procedural grounds. Significantly, this was not an acquittal.

Mbeki was history.

Not that Mbeki's term in the presidency was unflawed. In September 2007 a warrant was issued for the arrest of Jackie Selebi. The police commissioner and head of Interpol was accused of corruption, fraud, racketeering and defeating the ends of justice, and Mbeki sent him on indefinite leave. During Selebi's trial, convicted drug smuggler Glenn Agliotti told the court he had bribed Selebi and acted as an intermediary between Selebi and mining tycoon Kebble, who wanted Selebi to stop an investigation into his company, JCI. Kebble was assassinated in 2005.

On 2 July 2010, the day South Africa was joyfully hosting the quarter-finals of the FIFA World Cup, Selebi was found guilty of corruption. After a lifetime of service devoted to the ANC, as leader of the ANC Youth League, as a member of the ANC's national executive, and after serving as South Africa's ambassador to the United Nations, he received 15 years' imprisonment. He appealed but this was rejected.

There were ramifications within the ANC. Zuma suspended Vusi Pikoli, the head of the National Prosecuting Authority, for his relentless pursuit of Selebi. General Bheki Cele, who played a key role in Zuma's hard-fought 2009 election campaign, was appointed police commissioner but he, too, tried to cash in on his position and was fired in 2012 for committing the government to multi-million dollar leasing deals of city buildings in Pretoria and Johannesburg at highly inflated prices. Cele's sacking followed the dismissals of public works minister Gwen Mahlangu-Nkabinde, also involved in the leasing scandal, and cooperative governance minister Sicelo Shiceka for unauthorised expenditure including trips to visit a girlfriend jailed in Switzerland for drug smuggling.

Then, tragically, South Africa witnessed a replica of the 1960 Sharpeville massacre at the Marikana platinum mine near Rustenburg in 2012, this time with black policemen firing the guns. Mineworkers had called a wildcat strike to protest poor wages and, on 16 August, police opened fire, killing 34 who were later found to have been mostly shot in the back. At the time of the tragedy, Ramaphosa was a non-executive director of Lonmin Plc, owner of the Marikana platinum mine. A wave of strikes followed across the mining sector, undercutting investor confidence in South Africa. This led to the nation's credit rating being downgraded for the first time since the 1994 elections by all big three global agencies: Moody's, Fitch Ratings and Standard & Poor's.

The slide continued in 2013 when all three downgraded South Africa further still. The government tried to blame that latest downgrade on the Eurozone crisis but the agencies indicated they felt South Africa's problems extended well beyond its exposure to Europe. In their view, fractious labour disputes, rising corruption and a growing inability to deal with economic and social problems were contributing to a loss in investor confidence.

In 2011 South Africa's elder statesman, archbishop emeritus and Nobel laureate Desmond Tutu accused the ANC government of "kowtowing" to China, after the government delayed issuing a visa for the Dalai Lama, who had been invited to attend the archbishop's 80th birthday celebrations.

On 10 May 2013 Tutu said he would no longer vote for the ruling ANC. "I would very sadly not be able to vote for them after the way things have gone," he wrote in South Africa's *Mail&Guardian* newspaper. Inequality, violence and corruption were among the reasons costing the ANC his support, he added.

"The ANC was very good at leading us in the struggle to be free from oppression, but it doesn't seem to me now that a freedom-fighting unit can easily make the transition to becoming a political party," he continued.

Describing South Africa as "the most unequal society in the world", he highlighted corruption, unaccountability and weaknesses in the constitution as key issues that needed to be addressed.

In July 2013 former Democratic Alliance parliamentary leader Lindiwe Mazibuko asked the Public Protector Thuli Madonsela to investigate the $21 million (R246 million) upgrade of Zuma's private Nkandla Estate in KwaZulu-Natal. In March 2014 the Public Protector presented her report which said that President Zuma had benefited improperly from the upgrade to his private residence at "unconscionable" state expense; he had failed to act as "any reasonable person" would to stop excessive expenditure of taxpayers' money; and that high-ranking members of his government acted "unlawfully" and were guilty of maladministration for their handling of the project.

Calls were also growing for a phasing out of the policy of black economic empowerment, designed during Mandela's leadership to deliver a hefty slab of the economy into black hands. Many financial players, even in Australia, consider it to only benefit a coterie of ANC acolytes rather than the poor masses.

In the May 2014 general election, the ANC was returned to government, having polled 62.2% of votes cast. The Democratic Alliance (DA) increased its percentage to 22.2%, securing its position as the official opposition, but it was newcomers, the Economic Freedom Fighters (EFF), led by firebrand and ANC outcast Julius Malema, who surprised all with a poll of 6.4%.

On a positive note, in 2013, for the first time, the spending power of the black middle class exceeded that of their white counterparts. My old university, Wits, is a visible affirmation of this trend. During my student days in the 1970s, the campus represented a sea of white faces with a sprinkling of blacks. During a 2012 visit, my wanderings around the university confirmed a sea of black faces with a sprinkling of whites. Wits had delivered its social promise to South Africa. I felt proud walking around my old campus with my family. When I asked about the missing white students, I was told that many had elected to attend former conservative Afrikaans universities like Pretoria University (Tukkies) and Stellenbosch University (Maties). Further discussion also intimated that many of those former white conservative universities, including Pretoria and University of Johannesburg (formerly RAU) had principals, rectors and vice-chancellors who were not only black, but women. During my Wits student days in the mid-1970s, this would have sounded like science fiction, except that a few years earlier I had learnt to expect the unexpected in South Africa.

During 2012 and 2013, I toured South Africa with my daughters, a grandson and two Australian sons-in-law who had never previously visited Africa. We enjoyed every vignette of South African beauty including Cape Town, the game parks, the Drakensberg and memorable visits to the Hector Pietersen Museum in Soweto followed by a sombre

Castle Lager in Vilakazi Street. The Soweto experiences of 2012–13 were radically different to my Soweto visits during the 1980s.

In our travels we drove through Alexandra, an apartheid-era township that has now been engulfed by the sprawl of greater Johannesburg. Our hired family mini-bus was almost identical to the taxi fleets of over-crowded Toyota mini-buses. It was bumper to bumper in 5.30pm rush hour. We were the only white faces in the whole of congested Alex and were stationary for much of the time when traffic was in gridlock as pedestrians and hawkers swarmed on either side. Did we feel threatened? Not at all. There was no hostility directed towards us. We were ignored.

However, we could not ignore. Here we sat, a few kilometres away from Johannesburg's most affluent area of Sandton, and Alex looked exactly as Alex did in the 1980s, squalid, impoverished and littered with squatter shacks. Alex was where Mandela had lived when he first moved from the Eastern Cape to Johannesburg in 1940. Mandela lived in a corrugated iron shack tacked on to the back of a little brick house. The floor was dirt, there was no running water, and he had studied by candlelight. Apart from a few newly tarred roads and some street lighting, nothing much seemed to have changed on the housing front in Alex. It anguished me to witness how the political system seemed to have failed these people once again. They could understandably be disappointed at their government's lack of delivery on the promise of freedom, jobs and prosperity.

Against this backdrop of social and political volatility and upheaval, South Africa has reached some extraordinary high points, partially diluted by ill-deserved disappointments, in its infancy as a democratic nation.

A snapshot of South Africa's euphoric post-apartheid triumphs could feasibly include the release of Mandela in 1990; a free press; Elana Meyer embracing Ethiopian Derartu Tulu after the 10,000m at the 1992 Barcelona Olympics and the duo doing a victory lap hand in hand (Derartu had just become the first African woman to win an Olympic gold while Meyer's silver gave the entire nation cause for celebration. Meyer was draped in the neutral Olympic flag as the new South African flag had not yet emerged); the first general election in 1994 with its snaking queues of voters, all South Africans; Mandela's inauguration attended by world leaders; an independent judiciary; the new South African flag; Mandela's attendance at the 1995 Rugby World Cup final at Ellis Park; Josiah Thugwane winning the men's marathon at the 1996 Olympics in Atlanta and becoming the first black South African to win an Olympic gold; Penny Heyns winning gold for both the 100m and 200m women's breaststroke swimming at the same event, and remaining the only woman to have won both races; Bafana Bafana opening the 2010 FIFA World Cup against Mexico at South Africa's Soccer City, outside Soweto, amidst the deafening blasts from 84,000 fans blowing *vuvuzelas* (plastic horns); the Proteas cricket team rising to the top slot in the world test cricket boasting both the world's best batsman (AB de Villiers) and the world's best bowler (Dale Steyn); the lightweight Men's Fours who rowed South Africa to gold at the 2012 London Olympics with Sizwe Ndlovu on board, becoming South Africa's second black Olympic gold medallist; Chad Le Clos's gold medal victory over Michael Phelps in the pool; and many more. The nation has had much to celebrate.

Some of the post-apartheid tragedies and challenges South Africans have had to endure include the heinous crimes of apartheid divulged to Archbishop Desmond Tutu at the Truth and Reconciliation Commission; the involvement of South Africa's cricket captain, Hansie Cronje, in cricket's global betting scandal; the $5 billion arms deal; Mbeki's approach to HIV and Aids; the Marikana massacre; the booing of President Zuma at Mandela's funeral; evidence of systemic corruption and maladministration at the highest levels of government, including the upgrade of Zuma's private residence, Nkandla; the 240 rhinos illegally poached in the first three months of 2014, and more.

As Kipling's poem 'If' goes:

If you can meet with triumph and disaster
And treat those two imposters just the same ...

South Africa is one of the youngest or newest democracies in the world. Most democracies have taken decades to govern effectively with the appropriate checks and balances in place. For two centuries, the United Kingdom and the United States have functioned as representative democracies (although women were not represented until well into the 20th century). These mature democracies have not been without their challenges and controversies. South Africa got off to a miraculous start in 1994 under the presidency of Mandela and then lost its way. Dr Alex Boraine, deputy chairperson of the TRC from 1996 to 1998, has recently written a book *What's Gone Wrong? South Africa on the brink of failed statehood*, that reflects on how the ANC government correctly identified South Africa's priority (attacking poverty and deprivation) but then ignored it. South Africa's democracy is still in its infancy and initial expectations were, possibly, unrealistically high.

So, are the challenges facing South Africa, governed by the ANC, any different to South Africa's challenges of 1987, governed by the Nationalists, at the time of my chicken run to Australia?

I need to revisit those pockets of South Africa that I understood best at the time.

In my professional career I qualified as a CA in 1977, the same year South Africa's first black CA, Wiseman Nkuhlu, qualified. Concurrently, the South African Institute of Chartered Accountants was dominated (98%) by white males. Between 1977 and 2014, a further 3,000 black South Africans had qualified as CAs on an almost equal gender split. White CAs represented about 78% of total CA membership with the proportion of white males having decreased to 55%. Females now represent 33% of total membership and the current ratio of trainees eligible to write the final qualifying exam is 50:50 between whites and other South Africans, compared to 1% a decade earlier. In the context of significant barriers to entry, including a five- or six-year tertiary academic requirement, the progress is simply extraordinary. There are now 3,000 young black South Africans well qualified to manage South Africa's most complex businesses and financial issues. Back at my old firm, KPMG, 56% of the executive policy board positions, including that of chairman, are held by black South Africans.

On the CA front, the country is doing a commendable job, especially given the very substantial barriers to entry. There is still much work ahead, but their educational and professional infrastructure is in place and appears to be working well.

On the running front, my last running club in South Africa, RAC, is still run by Dick and Vreni Welch. With around 2,300 members, RAC is one of South Africa's largest clubs and remains the single biggest participant in Comrades (600 runners) and Two Oceans (400 runners). Dick, Vreni and the RAC committee have tirelessly continued to assist economically disadvantaged members. In the 1980s, assistance included club kit and transport to races. In 2014, this form of assistance has continued with the added complication of entering races online. Historically, most road races collected entries on the day via a cash payment from all the runners. But after cashboxes were targeted by armed robbers a couple of times, race organisers reverted to online entries. Many of the black runners do not possess the internet technology to enter and once again clubs like RAC continue to assist.

The entry numbers at South Africa's prestigious road races are impressive. Comrades 2014 was capped at 18,000 runners; Two Oceans 56km capped at 11,000 runners; but the Two Oceans 21.1km support event that had been capped at 25,000 runners in 2011 has since been scaled back to 16,000 runners (for logistical reasons), with the number of female runners in the field exceeding 50%. The number of applicants is at least twice the 16,000 field size. The best ultramarathon athletes in the world have been drawn to compete in South Africa, including former marathon world record holder Alberto Salazar of the US, who won the Comrades in 1994. Road running continues to serve South Africa well, not only in a health sense but also in a capacity that continues to transcend social, racial and gender challenges. The running health of the nation looks fabulous.

Also on the sports front, new events like the annual Cape Epic mountain bike race have flourished in the new South Africa. This gruelling eight-day event has capped participation at 1,200 riders despite receiving applications from some 10,000 prospective participants, globally. It sells out instantly each year and attracts the best mountain bikers from across the world, plus celebrities like Frenchman Alain Prost, three-time Formula One world champion. These athletes all voluntarily return to South Africa because this exotic event is as well managed and executed as any mountain biking event in the world, greatly enhanced by the breathtaking beauty of the 700km course in the Western Cape.

Despite all the doom and gloom stories one reads in the international media about South Africa, I always enjoy doing anecdotal research whenever I visit the country. Most visitors to South Africa tend to see black faces as homogeneous whereas, having grown up in Africa, I like to think I can identify the different ethnic identities of my former African countrypeople. So whenever I engage with a black person who to me appears to belong to an ethnic group outside South Africa, I will respectfully enquire about their country of origin. It astounds me to this day that Africans from countries thousands of miles away continue to seek employment and some economic advantage from the South African economy. In restaurants, I have been served by qualified high school teachers who have fled Zimbabwe. At petrol pumps and service stations, I have been assisted by attendants from the Central African Republic who may be university educated. In Greenmarket Square, Cape Town, I have been served by West Africans who are equally adept at speaking French and English and monitoring informal security at car parks. My family in Cape Town employ a highly enterprising Malawian handyman who can fix anything. There are many other African nationalities working within the South African economy. These hardworking migrants make me believe that South Africa still offers tangible prospects for a better life. They can see it where others cannot.

In March 2014 the Public Protector Thuli Madonsela went to Wits to talk about her Nkandla report. About 350 students packed out the Senate Hall and a few hundred others listened in a hastily arranged overflow venue. Her well-educated audience of predominantly black students listened to her metaphorical use of George Orwell's *Animal Farm* to describe the unconscionable upgrade of Zuma's private residence at taxpayers' expense. In my view the political wheel had turned full circle. During my years at Wits in the 1970s, the *Animal Farm* analogy was used equally effectively against the despised Nationalist government.

Despite the sheer enormity of South Africa's challenges under the ANC government, it is my simple assessment that they are far more capable of being addressed than the unsustainable predicament South Africa faced under Nationalist rule when I opted for the chicken run to Australia.

One of apartheid's legacies is poor black literacy amongst more than 40 million South Africans who are engaged in a daily struggle for survival and have slim prospects of a better life without an education. For them life is tough, really tough. As Mandela said, "Education is the most powerful weapon which you can use to change the world."

Optimistically, South Africa post 1994 enjoys free speech, an independent judiciary, a democratically-elected government, and peace. The Nationalists were at war with fellow South Africans and the world. Today, South Africans enjoy freedom of movement and anti-discrimination legislation. Despite the scandalous arms deal, South Africa is not involved in any military conflict and is not under threat from its neighbours or a third force.

There are also 11 million middle-class South Africans, the majority of whom are black. This educated, affluent group has much to protect and lots to look forward to. This elite group represents the engine room of the South African economy and pays its way. Fewer than six million individuals pay 95% of total income taxes, and 90% of all company tax is extracted from only 2000 companies. They are the South Africans who understand and realise that active participation in the economy by increasing numbers of South Africans, via education and employment, will uplift millions of others. The threat emanating from the enormous imbalance between the haves and the have-nots is well understood by this exclusive group and the ANC government. Fortunately they are well endowed with *ubuntu* and *chutzpah*, the former an African reference to helping those less fortunate than us and the latter a Yiddish term connoting courage or confidence.

There are glints of diamonds in the rough.

Postscript:
Boston Marathon, 21 April 2014

2.30pm Boston time

I am smiling like a winner after completing my debut Boston, aged 60, in 3:06.52. The added bonus was finishing in the top 10% of the field of some 36,000 and ninth in my age category.

A little background as to why Boston represented unfinished business at the age of 60. When I was living in the US in 1980, I watched the live broadcast of the Boston Marathon won by Bill Rogers and an unknown runner, Rosie Ruiz, in a new US record time of 2:31. Rosie had cheated by jumping into the race less than a mile from the finish and beat the best female athletes in the world. The sport was wonderfully simple in 1980. Boston Marathon, like all other marathons, simply had one mass start for all competitors and the only piece of technology available at the time was a stopwatch. No timing mats with electronic chips and no video surveillance of the race. Rodgers won fair and square but it took days to default and disqualify Rosie despite her inability to answer any running related questions in her television interview shortly after finishing. So the bug bit me in 1980 but I doubted I would ever run fast enough to qualify for the world's oldest and most prestigious marathon.

Fast forward to the start of my running days in South Africa in the early 1980s when I had the good fortune to meet Mark Plaatjes, a Wits University physiotherapy student and one of South Africa's hottest running prospects. Entirely at his own initiative, Mark took my social running level up to the elite standard within 18 months. That was the generosity of the guy. He was a multiple South African champ over cross country and the marathon, yet his efforts to test himself against the best in the world were thwarted by apartheid as detailed in Chapter 5.

The night before Boston Marathon I had dinner with Mark and his wife Shirley – we last saw each other in 1987 when I emigrated to Australia. I had resolved many years ago to run Boston with "Plaatjes '85" boldly displayed on the front of my singlet. I did that today and ran with great pride, especially when encouraging supporters yelled "go Plaatjes."

No matter how high the hurdles placed in front of Mark, his personal resolve and positive attitude to life always prevailed. He has subsequently enjoyed a successful career as a physiotherapist specialising in the treatment of high performance athletes (In Motion Rehabilitation) and as a business partner in the Boulder Running Company, Colorado, all built from scratch.

Plaatjes and fellow ex-pat Halberstadt opened BRC in Pearl Street, Boulder, in 1996. This was the first store in the US to implement free video gait analysis to help runners select the right shoe model. BRC was soon ranked as the best running store in Denver and Colorado and in 2006 attained the No.1 spot in the US. In June 2013 BRC was acquired by Denver-based Running Speciality Group.

Now for Boston, which was simply an indescribable experience. Take 10,000 volunteers, 3,500 cops, 36,000 runners, 588 buses that delivered us to the start, a million insanely enthusiastic supporters lining the route, including the shrieking and kissing Wellesley College girls, perfect weather and another spectacular day to be alive. I have participated in many well-organised events in many beautiful parts of the world – running, cycling, mountain biking and Ironman – but Boston 2014 takes first place in my experience, hard on the heels of two demonic brothers who detonated their bombs at the Boylston Street finish line last year. The motto for this year was "BOSTON STRONG" and the wider Boston community certainly triumphed over the tragedy of 2013.

Then again, I did not run Boston entirely on my own. A number of medical specialists led by Dr Goodman helped me overcome an unexpected setback six months before Boston when I was diagnosed with peripheral neuropathy plus vitamin B6 toxicity and thought Boston was lost to me.

I was aided and abetted by family and all my friends who have shared a love of the outdoors and especially Zelinda who managed Boston logistics and ground control in our CBD hotel as I snaked my way back to the finish on Boylston Street with 36,000 other joyful Boston runners.

It was hard work but worth every step.

Acknowledgements

- Philippa's curiosity in probing my childhood in South Africa
- Duane Heath for encouraging me to write
- My four siblings Yvonne, Michele, Jean-Paul and Dominique for being just who they are
- Wits University for my education
- Charles Coville for guiding Vincent Gabashane Rakabaele to, and through, the 1974 Comrades unofficially, stimulating the hopes of millions of black and white South Africans
- Barry Bauer for offering me a job at KPMG, Johannesburg, in 1974
- Smooch Hodgskiss of Varsity Kudus for deconstructing the 1981 Comrades for novices as "no effort at all, so long as you are not too fat"
- Every sports club, event official, volunteer, organiser, sponsor, spectator and supporter – it has been a rich journey
- Gordon Howie (New Balance), Johnny Halberstadt and Nick Lanham (Adidas) and Rowan Summers (Asics), for a supply of shoes, kit and confidence that made me feel like a pro
- Mark Plaatjes, Brian Chamberlain and Dr Rob Dowdeswell for running lessons, friendship and invaluable wisdom
- The Comrades Marathon Association for hosting a world-class ultramarathon that helped emancipate black South Africans and heal a nation severely fractured by apartheid
- Bob Norris and the late Kevin Flint for their socio-political leadership in the running community in the Eastern Cape in 1982
- Tony Dearling for encouraging me to follow his 1983 Comrades top 10 finish by joining the Wednesday evening Sweat Shop run

- Weston Dickson for casually suggesting, over a beer in March 1984, that I could win the Comrades
- Hoseah Tjale and Bruce Fordyce for those scorching Korkie and Comrades races in 1984, 1986 and 1987
- Riël Hauman, South Africa's leading road running statistician, for his invaluable treasure trove of statistics and anecdotes
- Australia for offering my family a fresh opportunity in a free, democratic society in 1987
- Jim Langford for inducting me into the Western Australian distance running scene and guiding me through Australia's ancient Outback
- Vincenzo Ulgiati and Marc Sherriff for introducing me to the heavenly world of alpine cycling in Italy in 2006
- Ian Sandover for tolerating Dalai Mottee in the 2009 gruelling eight day Cape Epic mountain bike race
- The business community and my workplace colleagues who facilitated my career on four continents
- The generosity, support and compassion of all my Perth friends
- Fellow adventurous souls I may have met running, riding, sailing, hiking, camping, climbing, swimming, travelling, playing tennis, squash, hockey or in conversation and debate – your companionship has enriched my personal enjoyment
- My parents for never having any expectations of their five children other than for us to use our talent, to behave with dignity, to count our blessings and never expect a second serving at mealtimes
- South Africa for the opportunity to roam the highveld as a young boy and learn from all those around me
- The media for exposing governments' misdeeds, business crooks and sports cheats
- Zelinda Bafile for helping me unlock the text that had been accumulating over the years. Grazie mille bella!
- Everyone I know who may not be mentioned in this manuscript – please excuse the oversight
- My daughters Nicole, Simone and Philippa for being my greatest trifecta

- Finally, Dave Hughes, my patient editor for deleting more than half of my original manuscript, invigorating the political vignettes and reordering my remaining text. 'Hughesie,' this would not have been possible without you. Thanks mate!

Photo acknowledgements

P179 – Gavin Stapleton

P180 – Two Oceans Marathon Association

P181 – Mick Winn / Comrades Marathon Association

P182+183 – Two Oceans Marathon Association

P184 (bottom) – Dave Hughes

P185 (bottom) – Portrait Place

P186 (top) – Daily News

P186 (bottom) – Portrait Place

P187 – Daily News

P188 (bottom) – Sportograf

P189 (top and bottom) – Fotoeventi

P190 – Gray Mortimore/Allsport

P191 – Boston Marathon

P192 – David Sandison

BOB de la MOTTE

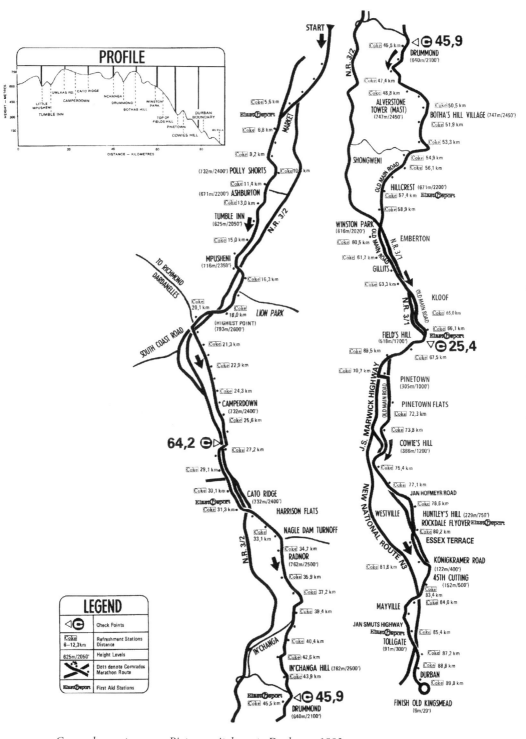

Comrades route map – Pietermaritzburg to Durban – 1982

The author

Bob de la Motte is an experienced ultramarathon runner, cyclist, mountain-biker and Ironman competitor. He was born in South Africa where he attended Wits University and worked for KPMG. His career as a chartered accountant and investment banker has taken him to London, the USA and ultimately to Australia where he has lived since 1987. Retired at 55 in 2009, Bob continues to pursue his sporting interests all over the world and has been a frequent visitor to South Africa since the release of Nelson Mandela in 1990. He is a Fellow of the Australian Institute of Company Directors and a Fellow of the Institute of Chartered Accountants in Australia.

The editor

Dave Hughes, former sports journalist of Johannesburg's *The Star* newspaper, was one of South Africa's leading sports journalists and athletics writers up to his emigration to Australia in 1985. He is a former contributor to *SA Runner* magazine. Between 1985 and 2009, Dave was a senior sportswriter for the *West Australian* newspaper. He has attended four Olympics Games, three Commonwealth Games, and also covered a diversity of events such as the Rugby World Cup, F1 Grand Prix, several heavyweight world title bouts and two swimming world championships.

Printed in Germany
by Amazon Distribution
GmbH, Leipzig